...EELEY

Printer, Editor, Crusader

By Henry Luther Stoddard

In two delightful books, AS I KNEW THEM: Presidents and Politics from Grant to Coolidge (1927) and IT COSTS TO BE PRESIDENT (1938), Mr. Stoddard has drawn on his rich memories of a long newspaper career. Inevitably he was attracted by the story of one of the first great American newspaper men, Horace Greeley, who was so influential a voice in his period that he was once appropriately characterized as "the drumbeat of the nation."

For years Mr. Stoddard, who has himself exercised no small influence on the men and events of his time, has devoted himself to a study of Greeley and his times. The present book is the result of his years of application to every phase of that varied and exciting life, and it fills the great need for an accurate, interesting, and sympathetic biography of the great American editor.

By education and background Greeley had little to start on. But from the outset he thought for himself and knew almost by instinct what

...l to be right. He never

...he common people of ... him for their man, ...er of the *Tribune's* edi- ...beyond that of any of his

..., "Go west, young man," ...ed through the decades as ... folklore, and never was ...thusiastically followed, ...emendous and far-flung

...rd follows the course of ...blic career and of his ...ustrated personal life ...nding and illuminating connections with the experiment and with ...re carefully and amus...ed, and the tense and course of his relations ...is a dramatic chapter of ...s reluctant yet gallant the presidency, with its ...nent, provides a fitting ...ivid and immeasurably ...e lived.

...be reminded of Greeley Stoddard does the job

...h of Horace Greeley
...y Constance Jones Naar

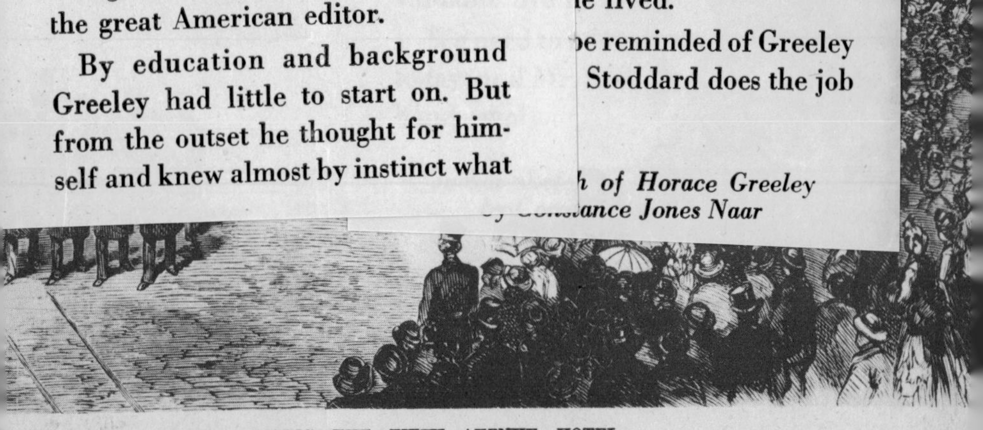

FUNERAL PROCESSION PASSING THE FIFTH AVENUE HOTEL.

HORACE GREELEY

Horace Greeley

HORACE GREELEY

PRINTER, EDITOR, CRUSADER

by Henry Luther Stoddard

FOUNDED 1838
GPPS

G. P. Putnam's Sons

NEW YORK

Designed by Robert Josephy

Manufactured in the United States of America

VAN REES PRESS • NEW YORK

IN cordial tribute to the many editors I have known who since Greeley's day have advanced journalism in America to its present power and independence; and in the hope that those yet to become leaders in that profession may be inspired to repeat, as a covenant of good faith with their readers, Greeley's character-building words, "I do no man's bidding."

Acknowledgments

Much gratitude is owing the curators of the following public and private collections: the William T. Dewart Collection for minutes of *Tribune* staff meetings, the Widener Library of Harvard for the Margaret Fuller correspondence, the Henry A. Stahl Collection for the Margaret Allen letters, the University of Rochester for the Thurlow Weed papers, the Indiana State Library for the Schuyler Colfax papers, the U.S. District Court at Richmond for Douglas bail bond material, the Sterling Memorial Library at Yale, the J. Pierpont Morgan Library, and the James Wright Brown Collection.

Thanks are also given to the following for particular assistance in obtaining Greeley material: the New York Public Library, the Society Library of New York, the New York Historical Society, the Library of Congress at Washington, the New York State Library at Albany, the Huntington Library at San Marino, California, and the libraries of the New York *Herald-Tribune, Times, Sun* and *Editor and Publisher.*

Appreciative thanks for their interest and co-operation are tendered to Roscoe C. E. Brown, William Harlowe Briggs, William F. Leggett, Francis W. Leary, S. S. McClure, William H. Stephens, Charles Willis Thompson, Francis A. Young, Miss Margaret L. Douglas and Miss Margaret E. Lippencott.

Contents

Contents

Illustrations

Why I Have Written

I CANNOT recall the exact date but certainly I was not quite ten years old when, after climbing two high steps to the door at the rear of a Broadway coach and floundering through the deep, dirty straw that in winter was then always used to cover the aisle floor, I sat with my mother opposite an old man whose white hair and thin fringe of white whiskers like a collar rimming his pinkish cheeks presented a strange picture to me. Looking up over his newspaper he raised his broad-brimmed felt hat in courteous salute, smiled graciously and spoke to her once—only once. Immediately the page he was reading was again held close to his nearsighted eyes; he knew us no more. My mother had met Horace Greeley several times while visiting my uncle Henry Luther Stuart, who then lived in a Gramercy Park house near the Greeley home at 35 East Nineteenth Street, and for many years had been on terms of friendship with him.

That was seventy-five years ago, yet I still have clearly in mind the kindly face that for an instant smiled also at me across the aisle—just once—but the abiding impression made upon me was the spectacles. They seemed so big and the eyes behind them were so little and so blue! They held my wondering attention until at Canal Street we left the stage.

"The man didn't say good-by," I commented to my mother as we reached the sidewalk.

"No," she replied, "he didn't see us getting out."

Of course not even a boy's wildest imagination could have

lured me that day to foresee that my first job in life was to be a printer on the newspaper Greeley had founded back in 1841; that I was to become proofreader of Whitelaw Reid's editorials and of dramatic critic William Winter's worse-than-Greeley handwriting; that I was to be a space reporter under long-remembered city editor William F. G. Shanks; or that during the past four years I would be writing a life story of the man whose big spectacles aroused my youthful interest in that Broadway stage so many years ago. As my thoughts turn back to that distant time, recollection seems to me more like a dream of phantom figures of the future than a review of men and events during a career I have ended.

Obviously, any portrayal by me of Greeley must be a tribute to an editor who loved his profession beyond every other calling, who reflected its highest character by his integrity, his courage of opinion and his use of its great power to urge thrift, education, justice, opportunity and patriotism. Greeley had but one chief purpose in life—to be helpful; and in that ceaseless effort there was no yielding by him to the calumnies of opponents or the pleadings of too timid friends. In his many battles for the causes in which he believed, he surrendered to no conqueror but death—sought no rest until rest eternal came to him in the needed repose of a timely grave.

I do not offer this volume as the work of a historian or skilled biographer; I claim no such talent. What I have written is more a tale told in his twilight years by one newspaperman of another whose challenging spirit gave to American journalism its first independence and sole reliance upon "my own thoughts"; "I do no man's bidding"; "I mean to make something of myself."

During the lifetime in which I have been engaged in every department of a newspaper I have listened to and read many estimates of Greeley, his influence, his motives and his peculiarities. They varied as naturally estimates must vary even when they mean to interpret fairly such a provocative and conspicuous figure as he was throughout more than thirty years of passionate agitation. The finest tribute to any man's activities, however, is that his sincerity is attested by those who knew him best. Greeley won that tribute. As to his judgment, that is another matter. Time and events had to vindicate it, and they often did.

Greeley inspired the confidence of his readers because he was known to be an editor without concealments or subterfuges—an editor unafraid to turn from an outworn past with its hopes denied to so many people and to demand a future with promise for all—an editor unafraid to denounce conditions and practices that masked selfishness and injustice—unafraid to be called revolter, socialist, visionary—yes, even wrecker.

"I believed, and therefore have I spoken" was as true of the one reason prompting Greeley's utterances in his newspaper as it was of Paul preaching at Corinth.

No man, no power, no fear of consequences could command silence by him when it was a duty to speak. His "terrible candor," as his frank, positive words were frequently called, dismayed the timid but they also exposed and thwarted the stealthy. More than that, they did much to prepare and unify the people of the North for their tragic struggle. His readers knew that they had a covenant of good faith with him to tell them the truth precisely as he believed it, and they accepted his unhindered words in his newspaper as their dependable guide.

If this were not so, if Greeley had not been trusted by the many, the free, frank flow of his mind would not have been so disturbing to those whose selfish unconcern for others he persistently denounced and whose only rejoinder to his attacks was to characterize them as emotional and unsound. On this point his critics were well agreed!

But equally well agreed were the people in upholding him!

His "Weekly Try-bune" was their newspaper Bible.

It could have been said with truth of Greeley in his day as General Edward S. Bragg, of Wisconsin, in the 1884 Democratic national convention said of Grover Cleveland: "We love him most for the enemies he has made."

The Greeley I have always had in mind is the fifteen-year-old boy who alone gamely walked from a home of poverty eleven miles to the East Poultney *Spectator* to ask, "Don't you want a boy to learn the trade?" But the Greeley of history, properly enough, is the Greeley of the *Log Cabin,* the Greeley whose *Tribune* led all other newspapers in demanding social betterments, the Greeley having Henry Clay as his pattern of statesmanship, the Greeley calling for tariff protection and for homesteads in the West, the Greeley arousing the North against the slave power, the Greeley demanding in 1860 "any candidate but Seward," the Greeley who often God-blessed but as often "greatly bothered" Lincoln—finally, the Greeley who, in 1872, in a patriotic effort to bring together in a restored Union all of his countrymen estranged by four years of war, became a candidate for President who "if elected will be President of the whole people and not of any party."

With broad patriotism he said of the South in those days of anger: "Theirs is a lost cause but they are not a lost people." In his plea to both sections of the country to "clasp hands across the bloody chasm," Greeley met what in politics is called defeat, yet three weeks later he won a tribute far more significant in its meaning than the unstable, partisan verdict of the ballot box. By the presence at his grave of the nation's President and his cabinet, of the Chief Justice, and of New York's governor and two Senators, as well as the leaders of his profession, you get a true appraisement of this master journalist of his era.

The purpose of this book is to recall that value to the people of today.

H. L. S.

HORACE GREELEY

CHAPTER I

Dwellers at the Grey Lea

IN THE EARLY 1640's three brothers, "dwellers at the Grey Lea," not many miles from Nottingham, England, landed at Boston. They called themselves Greeley. On arrival there each brother promptly went his separate way.

Benjamin, ancestor of Horace, settled as a farmer and blacksmith at Salisbury on the Massachusetts–New Hampshire border. When or whom he married is not known. His son Ezekiel, who moved a few miles farther north to Hudson, New Hampshire, seems to have been the only Greeley in four generations to be regarded as hard and crafty. At his death he divided his acres among thirteen children including Zaccheus Greeley, great-grandfather of Horace. Zaccheus lived to the age of ninety-five—long enough to realize that he had an unusual boy in his great-grandson Horace, familiarly called "Hod."

The second Zaccheus, like *his* father, year in and year out plowed the fields he had inherited, but with no result other than an ample table for the family and barely enough money to buy a supply of rum and tobacco to pass around evenings among visiting neighbors. Hospitality in that form was regarded as imperative; too often it came before expenditures for home or clothing.

In time a third Zaccheus appeared in the world. He was the father of Horace—"born, I think," wrote Horace, doubtfully, "in Londonderry." This Zaccheus knew his Bible thoroughly. He added to it an equally deep knowledge of tavern drinking. He worked farms on shares and also contracted to cut timber, until by 1808 he had saved enough money to marry and at the wrong time to buy eighty acres in Amherst near Londonderry. They were burdened with a mortgage he was never able to reduce. Hard times came, many farmers went bankrupt; families sold all they owned in their efforts to respond to the lure of a more promising west. By 1820 the sum of twelve years' struggle on that Amherst farm was that a sheriff took possession of it. So "Zac" moved his family to Westhaven, Vermont, in a new effort for a livelihood.

Throughout a century and a half, life for every Greeley had been hard, ceaseless struggle. Farming, lumbering and blacksmithing cleared no primrose path financially for any of them. It was the same with the Woodburns, who were Horace Greeley's maternal ancestors. But they were more prudent; they kept out of debt. They were of the Londonderry, Ulster, Scotch-Irish Presbyterians who in 1689 defended that city through its long siege by the army of King James II when he attempted to return from exile.

Derry folk remained loyal to the kingdom they had helped to preserve, but they were in constant turmoil with the Catholics of Ireland on one side and the Established Church of England on the other. Neither sect recognized Presbyterian pastors as clergymen nor looked upon their churches as places of worship. Many Derry-ites ended their troubles by emigrating to America, "(1) to avoid oppression and cruel bondage; (2) to shun persecution and ruin; (3) to withdraw from a community of idolatry; (4) to have an opportunity of worshiping God according to the dictates of conscience and the rule of His Inspired Word." As a tribute to the courage with which they had held Londonderry against surrender a royal patent was granted them for twelve square miles in the Massachusetts Bay Colony.

In 1718 at least twenty families hazarded a voyage to the New World to select homes for the dissatisfied. Ultimately they made "Nutfield," a settlement in New Hampshire about sixteen miles north of the Massachusetts line, the center of their grant. Perhaps it was shrewdness to buy peace with the Indians, perhaps it was the inherent honesty and fair dealing of the Scotch-Irish, that they insisted upon paying them five pounds sterling for the land title, though years before the Indians had signed a treaty parting with it. The love of the colonists for the old country was shown in the swift substitution of Londonderry for Nutfield.

Four pastors came with them to insure that they would never be forced to listen in church to any doctrine other than their pure Presbyterianism. As these preachers died or were called to other pulpits the colonists sent back to Ulster for clergymen guaranteed to be of the straitest sect, for only "true believers" were ever permitted to interpret their faith. They had no doubts and wanted none urged upon them. Like all else, their church management was on a business scale. The pastor's salary was $200 a year, but if and when the elders thought that they could not afford a sermon a deduction of pay would be made proportionately for each Sabbath on which they had notified their minister that they would not seek his services.

About 1721 John Woodburn, great-grandfather of Horace Greeley on the mother's side, came over from Ulster with many other families. To each was awarded a share of what were called "Exempt Acres"—this being the tax-free land given by royal decree for division. A share comprised one hundred and twenty acres in one plot and an "out" lot of sixty acres additional. The Woodburn family worked their farm for nearly two hundred years, son following father in succession. Title passed from that family less than forty years ago.

Of all our emigrant colonists no sturdier group ever crossed the Atlantic than those who then left Ulster for the freedoms of the New World. They brought with them their spirit of independence, their Irish vivacity, legends and ballads, their rigid Presbyterian convictions and their willingness to endure hardship in order that they might live and think their own way. They accepted the church as their guide but tolerated no other control. Thus their community was in truth a real democracy. But it was also a field for labor—hard labor. Few of the settlers had any vision beyond his long day's work, his log-hut home, his school, his town meeting and the family jug of rum. For them each day's dawn inspired no new or greater hope than other workers elsewhere had when they heard the shrill blast of a factory whistle—just another summons to ceaseless toil. There were no pretensions to superiority; no social inequalities; all shared a simplicity of living that knew no extravagances and no idleness.

There were none so rich in acres that they did not have to work and none so poor in spirit as to seek maintenance from others. "Of genuine poverty there was plenty," wrote Greeley, "not beggary nor dependence but the manly American sort." Each day's labor ended with evening merrymaking in which both young and old participated with much song and dancing as well as much drinking. The very wilderness they had undertaken to subdue gave them keen realization of a spiritual freedom and of individual sovereignty that back in Ulster had been like a dream of another world.

So went years of rugged labor, years of stern religious faith; years of indifference to a world beyond their own horizons. They desired that outside world to keep its distance, and they certainly kept theirs. The Indians surrounding them were their only concern. They treated them fairly, but never trusted them. There were constant minor depredations; sometimes a kidnaping, but only for ransom. Often a gun was taken to the fields in the morning to be within reach during the day's plowing; in the early years guns were also carried to church and stacked near the pulpit, prepared to do the Lord's bidding at sight.

When John Woodburn settled there he was the father of twelve, of whom David Woodburn, a son by John's second wife, was the grandfather of Horace Greeley. This wife was also Ulster-born. From all accounts she loved to read and write although able to do but little of either. Pridefully Greeley attributed to his mother and his grandmother credit for his early desire for learning.

People of such character naturally flocked to the patriot cause when the first call of the Revolution came. "I was born of republican parentage, of an ancestry that participated vividly in the hopes and fears, the convictions and efforts of the American Revolution," Greeley replied to an inquiry.

What could be more amazing than that the ruddy-faced, white-haired, restless man whom the nation knew as Horace Greeley should have sprung from such lusty stock? For he was a direct reverse to it in physique and spirit; even in childhood he turned resolutely from the deadened life of his family—"thinking nothing, dreaming nothing, destined to nothing." He was the one Greeley who ever had an ambition beyond the acres they plowed for more than a century. Nor did the Woodburns develop any men save farmers during the ninety years prior to February 3, 1811, on which date Mary Woodburn Greeley gave birth to Horace "on that farm near Amherst four miles northeast of the village or 'Plain,'" as Greeley described his birthplace, "in the last house on the old road before you pass into Bedford to Manchester." When he came into the world there was serious doubt whether he would remain more than an hour or two; the breath of life came so slowly and so faintly that it seemed not at all. He was what doctors know as a "blue-black" baby. At school he was called "Ghost," a name that followed him throughout his sixty-one years.

Horace was a second son, the third child of seven, and the first to survive birth. Two brothers and two sisters subsequently born grew unresistingly into the life pattern of their ancestors. Horace shared with them its bareness and its hardships; though frail and quickly tiring no one ever heard him complain of his tasks, but even before he realized it others knew that farming was not the career for him.

His mother was anxious that he should have early schooling. The nearest schoolhouse was an impossible mile and a half walk for so small a boy; therefore for three winters he lived in his Grandfather Woodburn's home at Londonderry and attended the near-by school. His mind ran toward spelling, reading and arithmetic. "Grammar came hard to me and geography I never studied at all," he wrote from New York City to Moses Cortland, at Londonderry, "but I cannot remember when I did not know the multiplication table; it seemed to me just play." Greeley also confirmed the story that at evening spelling bees "it was difficult to keep such a babe as I awake. When the 'word' came to me I had to be waked up to spell it, and I have lately found the story current that I could and did spell just as well asleep as awake!"

Still another way to education was found for Horace—a way that never lost its sentiment with him. He would sit on a low bench at his mother's knee while she carded wool or knitted as she sang ballads, interrupting her work to tell him stories and to smoke her pipe while he spelled out his first words. As the book was spread on her lap he had to look at its pages from every angle—sideways, upside down and right side up. He got to know the alphabet that way. "There I learned to read," wrote Greeley. "I faintly recall mother seated at the little wheel with the book in her lap when I was taking my daily lessons. The first book I ever read was the Bible, under my mother's guidance, when I was five."

When eight years old he no longer wintered at his grandfather's home. His parents considered him equal then to the walk from the Amherst farm to school between chores. Let Greeley tell the life of a farm lad in those days:

> Being the older son of a poor and hard-working father struggling to pay off the debt he had incurred in buying his high-priced farm, and to support his increasing family, I was early made acquainted with labor. My task for a time was to precede my father as he hoed his corn, dig open the hill and kill the wire-worms and grubs that were anticipating our dubious harvest. To "ride horse to plough" soon became my more usual vocation; the horse preceding and guiding the oxen when furrowing or tilling the planted crops. Occasionally, the plough would strike a fast stone and bring up the team all standing, pitching me over the horse's head, and landing me three to five feet in front.

Not all the hours at the Amherst farm were given over to work. He had his schooling—chiefly in winter. The snows were deep. "Many a time I carried little Horace on my back through drifts to school," wrote Silas Parkhurst, the owner of an adjoining farm, "and put my mittens over his to keep his little hands from freezing."

He persisted in his reading too. Pine knots gathered by day were used by him at night as a flare to light the pages of his book; on

Greeley's Birthplace at Amherst, New Hampshire

Greeley's Home at Westhaven, Vermont

Barging on the Erie Canal

wintry evenings both boy and book would be spread out on the floor very close to the stone hearth—*Pilgrim's Progress*, Byron, Burns, Shakespeare. Particularly was he interested in the *Columbian Orator* as well as in the *Farmer's Cabinet*, a weekly newspaper published at Amherst. On publication day he was impatient for the appearance of the pony rider distributing the *Cabinet;* immediately he was lost to all around him until he had read every line of its pages from first column to last.

"A prodigy," declared many who knew Horace—but a prodigy so frail and so "booky" that he seemed unlikely ever to make much of a place for himself in this world, or indeed to last in it many years. He was set apart from others of his own boyhood group because of his modesty, his kindly nature, his earnestness and his respect for his elders. He who in later years was to become one of the nation's most aggressive editors seems to have been one of the most quiet and retiring of youths. His earnestness in study led several family friends to offer to pay his expenses through Phillips Exeter Academy, at Exeter, New Hampshire, but pride still controlled the impoverished father; he refused to be under obligation to others for his son's education. "Hod will have all the schooling we can afford," said the independent Zac, "and that will be enough for him to get along on." Of course, this meant very little schooling—but in after years Greeley was proud that his family was indebted to no one for such education as he had.

The shadow of a sheriff kept deepening over the Greeley household. Almost every third farm in the neighborhood was for sale at any price; "and ours," wrote Greeley, "did not escape. My father and mother were hard-working people but poor managers. Father had a proud spirit and always wanted to entertain. He was too fond of the smiles of great men." In order to avoid arrest for debt Zac was finally forced to go into hiding.

Greeley's sister Esther related that Horace, then nine years old, followed his mother from room to room as the sheriff sold the very modest chattels, begging his mother not to cry as he would go to work and care for her.

With his farm gone there was little hope for Zac in Londonderry, so he secured a job as a lumberjack at Westhaven, Vermont, to which place he took his wife, their five children and the unsheriffed remnants of household furniture. In midwinter they drove one hundred miles in a homemade sleigh that was little more than a large packing box.

Westhaven was a new adventure for the family, but it did not prove to be a new living condition. Indeed, the Greeleys were even poorer than ever. Through the first winter Zac earned about $3.50 each week as wood chopper. When spring came the entire family joined in field work. They were no longer farmers; they were now classed as day laborers. How this family of seven persons lived may be imagined from the fact that the monthly rent for their two-room cabin was $1.50. "Yet," Greeley proudly recalled, "we never ran into debt for anything and never were without meat, meal and wood." The parents ate at a small table but the children sat on the floor around a large porridge bowl into which they dipped long wooden spoons. A straw hat, a linen shirt with wide open collar, trousers that had many stains and patches, no shoes—such was his summer garb. In winter, shoes and a jacket were added, and a felt hat took the place of the straw one.

Here Horace again divided his time between school and farm work; here also at fifteen he was through with both. "Such education as I have since acquired, I picked up on the way through life."

Those years between ten and fifteen had been for him a period of increasing absorption in newspapers, magazines and books. As at Amherst the boy borrowed reading matter from every neighbor who possessed any; despite weak eyes and tiring day's work he read all of it thoroughly. Greeley often said that had there been books on agriculture, with suggestions how to lighten farm labor, his interest in reading them might have encouraged him to continue with his family as a farmer.

"I knew I had the stuff in me," he wrote, but from his own experiences as well as from all that he heard he saw nothing in agriculture then other than what he termed its "mindless, monotonous drudgery." He turned from it "in dissatisfaction if not disgust."

It was at Westhaven that the urge to become a printer really took strong hold of him. He persuaded his father to walk with him over to Whitehall, New York, in an effort to induce the weekly newspaper editor at that place to take him on as an apprentice. Fortunately for the Greeley of the future an older boy was needed; so Horace trudged those eight miles back home to grow up to a printer's apprenticeship somewhere else.

For two years he searched the weekly newspapers for notices of such a job. At last in 1826 he saw one in the *Northern Spectator*, published at East Poultney. Again Horace asked his father to accompany him and to aid him to get the job. Zac, however, had determined to migrate with his family to Wayne, Erie County, Pennsylvania, close to the Chautauqua County, New York border. He expected that Horace, too, would go, though he knew that the boy's heart was set on becoming a printer. He could never understand where or how Hod got that notion.

Had Horace been as expert at tree chopping and plowing as were his brothers, he might not have secured his father's permission. The custom of the time gave parents the right to a son's labor during minority. Fortunately Zac made no claim on his boy, though he refused to go to East Poultney with him—Horace could go there himself "if he had a mind to."

CHAPTER II

"Don't You Want a Boy to Learn the Trade?"

No one was awake earlier in the Greeley household than Hod next morning, nor more eager to finish his part of the early chores. Soon he was on his way alone on the eleven-mile road to East Poultney; at the *Northern Spectator* office he was told to go to the home of the Rev. Dr. Amos Bliss, a Baptist minister who was also the editor. He found him in his garden preparing the ground for its summer work. In early April turning over and breaking the frosty soil is a task for close attention, and Dr. Bliss was hard at it when he heard a voice unlike any other he had ever heard—a voice that would have been unpleasantly shrill if it had much strength.

"Are you the man that carries on the printing office?"

In wonder Dr. Bliss stopped his spading and looked inquiringly toward the low, strange sound. Only a few yards away stood a figure as unusual in appearance as was the voice that came from it—a boy of fourteen or fifteen years, tall and frail in body, cheeks so pale as to seem almost bloodless. The large, round head was covered with blond hair topped by a narrow-brimmed felt hat; he wore trousers that barely touched his shoes, no socks, and a close-fitting jacket like an Eton much the worse for wear and plainly outgrown. Dr. Bliss wondered why a boy so poorly clothed, so evidently destitute, was seeking him.

"Yes, I'm the man," he replied as he resumed his soil breaking, not caring to be interrupted.

"Don't you want a boy to learn the trade?" came the next question.

Again Dr. Bliss paused in his work. He looked the young visitor over—this time in amazement.

"Do *you* want to learn?" he asked.

"I've had some notion of it," came the modest reply.

"It takes considerable learning to be a printer, my boy," cautioned Dr. Bliss. "Have you been to school much?"

"No," came the frank response, "I haven't had much chance at school, but I have read some history and a little of most everything."

"Where do you live?"

"Westhaven, sir."

"How did you get here?"

"I walked over."

"What's your name?"

"Horace Greeley, sir."

It seemed incredible that this odd-looking boy should have a real desire to be a printer's apprentice. Surely he wanted any odd job; the *Spectator* did not need that kind of a boy. Still, after further talk, the lad's earnestness so impressed the minister-editor that he decided to send him over to the foreman of the printing office for his opinion. Soon he returned and handed Dr. Bliss a torn piece of narrow proof slip upon which was scrawled in pencil, "Guess we'd better try him."

Then and there began the career of Horace Greeley, founder of the New York *Tribune*. In the forty-six years of life still ahead of him much was to happen to this ragged printer-apprentice and also to his country.

All that remained to close the bargain was to have the father sign the apprentice papers. Dr. Bliss took the boy back to the *Spectator* office to meet other employees and then to the village inn for a much-needed midday dinner.

That afternoon a proud youth traveled homeward with lighter step than had marked his return from Whitehall three years previously.

Those who can recall getting their first job, especially those who looked upon that job as the fulfillment of a stirring, youthful ambition, know the thrill that must have possessed young Greeley as he hastened to break the good news to his parents. What thoughts of the future must have crowded his mind!

Within a week Horace returned to East Poultney accompanied by his father. Apprenticeship papers were executed. He had hired out for four years in return for board and $40 a year allowance for clothing. He estimated that his allowance for each year was as much as had been paid for all the clothes he had worn in all of his fifteen years.

For Horace, however, the day of indenture—April 18, 1826—was not a day of rejoicing. It meant that he was to part with his family—perhaps forever. Such separations come hardest, of course, when parents and children have gone through straitened times together, as the Greeleys surely had. Parting with his mother was particularly trying. In later years he stated that had she said the word he would have stuck with the family. But a mother's instinct dictated silence on her part. She seems to have been the only one who desired for her son a better future than life on a wilderness farm. Though of all her children he was nearest to her heart, she knew that the moment had come for unselfish sacrifice. She made it.

So the family departed for Pennsylvania by wagon and canal without Horace. "The saddest day of my life as I felt then," said Greeley. "As I was on my way to my cold storage home in East Poultney I was strongly tempted to turn back, but I continued on the slowest walk I can remember."

His apprentice job made Greeley not only a printer but a pressman as well.

On publication day he divided his time between cranking the press and feeding pages of paper into it. It was no easy task for a fifteen-year-old boy, but Greeley stuck to it. He enjoyed type-setting, however, and also evening hours with the "exchanges"—newspapers published in other towns sent in exchange for your own. With no other means of communication, the newspaper education of an editor of that time depended upon knowledge of public opinion gathered in that way. Greeley made the most of the opportunity. "I do not think I have ever read to so much profit," was his frequent comment. The day's work, the evening reading, a debating society and local issues took up hours that other young men devoted to fishing, hunting or dancing. Walking was his only recreation—but always alone. His tall, slim figure with its stooping broad shoulders, still as poorly clothed as when he first sought a job from Dr. Bliss, became familiar to neighbors as he moved along at the four-miles-an-hour pace he had early fixed for himself.

"Why don't you buy some clothes?" a fellow apprentice asked him.

"Because I have no money to pay for them," he replied, "and I won't go into debt."

Even in those East Poultney days Greeley loaned money to others just as he continued to do in New York City. "Borrowed 2 s. from Horace Greeley," "Owe Horace Greeley 2 s/6 d," were items found in the diaries of some of his companions. He seems to have been the only boy with a savings fund—though probably one of the poorest. George Jones, who in 1851 became founder and chief owner of the New York *Times*, was an exception. His parents were successful farmers close by Poultney. James Parton, who in 1855 published the first Greeley "Life," spent several days in East Poultney trying to "find one fact that an enemy could adduce to your discredit," he wrote Greeley, "but I could not." Nevertheless Parton resented the efforts of editor Bliss of the *Spectator* to make Greeley "the primmest, dullest little Moral Philosopher that ever went to church." He was far from that. Greeley played games of chance with other boys who would put up one cent and often three cents on draughts or cards, but the hours given by him to that pastime were solely of the rainy-day order. He learned to swear in old-time printer fashion, however, and he continued to do so through all his years, as the *Tribune* staff had reason frequently to know.

Greeley's chief diversion was walking, but it was never aimless roaming. Often there was some village he wanted to see; more often a spot several miles distant that served the purpose both of exercise to reach it and of undisturbed reading. Books and a lunch were his only companions. It was while on these all-alone tramps that he learned from Burns's poems—as he wrote in his essay on "Poetry"—that "virtue and vice, worth and worthlessness, fame and shame are divided by no social lines—that each may be found in the palace and in the hovel." The psalms of David also thrilled young Greeley; later in one of his lectures he said of them: "This untaught shepherd, this man of a thousand faults and many crimes, knew how to sweep the chords of the human heart as few or none ever touched them before or since. Other thrones have their successions, their dynasties, their races of occupants, but David reigns unchallenged King of Psalmody till time shall be no more."

Even in those apprentice days politics interested Greeley. The *Farmer's Cabinet* had much to say about national affairs; so did the *Spectator*. Though he was not eligible to vote for President until the Jackson-Clay contest in 1832, it was in those years at Poultney that Clay became his ideal statesman and Benjamin Franklin his ideal American. The hotel dinner table was then Greeley's lecture platform. Shirt-sleeved, he would sit through the meal talking rapidly on all questions and eating ravenously.

There might have been no Horace Greeley arriving in New York City in 1831 had the *Northern Spectator* been a profitable enterprise, but it never was; its financial troubles were chronic. Early in 1830 the owners ended them by ending its career. This meant that Horace had to seek a job elsewhere.

If he then had visions of a future other than doing a day's work at a printer's case, he gave no indication of it to others. He never spoke with enthusiasm about a career such as boys often discuss among themselves. Yet no one in East Poultney was surprised when news came of his progress in New York City. There was a sort of "I told you so" feeling among all who had known him.

Though Zac Greeley had been persistently appealing to Hod to "come west" and make his future there, he had made no impression. The boy was more stirred by stories he heard of the nation's "Commercial Emporium"—as he then called New York City—but its giant size made him doubt that he was fitted for its competitive life. He once said that completely out of his mind was any thought that only one year later he would leave his father's forest cabin in western Pennsylvania headed toward that great center.

A visit to his parents was his one definite plan.

He was nineteen years old—and June! He was eager to have a week of barging on the new Erie Canal and then a walk of forty-five miles from Dunkirk southwesterly across Chautauqua County into Pennsylvania. All his earthly possessions were bundled into a large red cotton handkerchief of the bandana pattern, hung from a hickory stick shouldered much as one shoulders a gun.

He left East Poultney as he had entered it four years earlier—a modest, poorly dressed, thin-voiced lad. The one certainty in his mind was that he would never return to the places of his youth. The friendships he had formed there were prized, but through the busy years ahead they had their renewals chiefly in memory, in casual visits and in correspondence. Nevertheless he never outgrew them. "When I go up to Vermont," he wrote twenty years later, "I walk into every house as though I owned it and never dream of waiting for an invitation."

Even while publishing the *New Yorker* eight years later he appealed to his friend B. F. Ransom, "Why don't you send me some Poultney news? Deaths, marriages, courtships, even scandals, would be better than nothing. It can't be that you are merely vegetating up there like oysters. Do stir up something!"

A savings fund of $20 represented Greeley's entire cash capital as he left East Poultney. But in addition he possessed something more helpful, more lasting, than dollars alone—something that could not be handkerchiefed and suspended from a stick—for he had industry, character and convictions. Throughout his boyhood the family was forced to get along with little money—even at times with none; for that reason money never seemed to him as essential as education. The latter he sought eagerly.

With the same horror as Lincoln is said to have felt when he attended a slave auction in New Orleans, Greeley witnessed a slave hunt in East Poultney and joined the crowd that drove the white hunter out of town. The story runs that a negro had escaped across the New York state line following a historic "underground" route to freedom, and had been employed in the village. "I never saw so large a gathering of men," wrote Greeley. "Everything on our side was impromptu and instinctive. Our people hated oppression and injustice and acted as though they couldn't help it." The white man, not the negro, went back to New York.

That experience fixed forever Greeley's attitude toward negro slavery. The picture in his mind never dimmed, yet there had formed from his reading a companion picture which depicted a slavery of white workers as well—the men, women and children employed chiefly in New England mills. Their condition aroused in him even deeper resentment. The "lords of the loom" were destined to hear from Horace Greeley in after years as well as the "cotton kings" of the South. He spared neither. "How could I devote myself to crusading against the distant servitude," he wrote June 20, 1845, "and remain silent when I discern its essence in my own vicinity?"

Greeley's first day's journey out of Poultney covered twelve miles of walking to Comstock's Fording on Lake Champlain, then south by boat and then again walking until he reached the Erie Canal basin below Troy, New York. Next morning he took passage on what was called a canal "liner" to Buffalo, then by boat to Dunkirk, Chautauqua County, on Lake Erie.

"Clinton's Ditch," though much used, was still more of a ditch than a canal when Greeley barged through. Railroads were then only talked about, and stagecoaches were too expensive for a youth with only twenty dollars in his pocket. "A mile and a half an hour, a cent and a half a mile" was the accepted schedule for a "liner." Kitchen, dining room and sleeping quarters were in one cabin below deck usually occupied by drinkers until late at night; at daybreak the passenger was ousted from his shelf—flatteringly called a berth—so that the cabin could be aired and the stove lighted for breakfast. Greeley preferred the deck with his bundle for a pillow. It was cheaper. All possible stops for freight, passengers and "liquoring-up" were made on the way. Travel, however, was not new to Horace, for this was his second trip home. Two years before he had walked most of the five hundred miles, using the canal as little as possible in order to save money.

A liner's passengers were always a roistering lot. They had their own rough stories and songs, most of them not printable. Horace must have heard them all, for evenings on a canal barge were always given over to merriment. However, there were some songs whose rollicking tunes Horace may have enjoyed:

Low bridge! Everybody down!
Low bridge! We're coming to a town!
You'll always know your neighbor, you'll always
know your pal,
If you ever navigate on the Erie Canal.

Oh the E-r-i-e was a rising,
The strap was getting low,
And I scarcely think
We'll get a drink
Till we get to Buffalo,
Till we get to Buffalo.

Drop a tear for a big-foot Sal,
The best damn cook on the Erie Canal;
She aimed for Heaven but she went to Hell—
Fifteen years on the Erie Canal.
The missioner said she died in sin;
Hennery said it was too much gin;
There wasn't no bar where she hadn't been,
From Albany to Buffalo.

"I trust I have respect for the good old ways we so often hear of," wrote Greeley of his canal experience, "but if anyone would recall the good old 'line' boats I object."

Landing at Dunkirk next morning after hours of seasickness on turbulent Lake Erie, the homebound traveler was eager for the forty-five-mile walk to Wayne—a settlement named for dashing "Mad" Anthony Wayne. The Greeley clearing, located a few miles farther west, was merely a slash in dense woods. Tramping a good part of the way from East Poultney, Horace had made the trip two years before at a cost of $12; this time his expenses amounted almost to his $20.

On his first trip he had tried to cover the distance between sunup and sunset, but when night came he was lost in a forest, although actually within a few miles of journey's end. He saw candlelight in a cabin tenanted by a father, mother and their two children. He accepted their invitation to stay until daylight in their one-room home, with bare earth as its flooring, a hole in the bark-covered roof serving as a chimney. "We all slept sweetly," remarked Greeley in telling the story.

On this second pilgrimage, however, he determined to sleep in his own home. Zac Greeley had a record back east of walking thirty miles in a single day. Hod enjoyed the prospect of the longest tramp he had ever undertaken.

All his life he remained a walker of distances—always walking alone. He shared the belief of the English essayist William Hazlitt that "the soul of a journey is the liberty to think, feel and do just as one pleases." Greeley did such walking with the same enthusiasm as did Daniel Webster, another son of New Hampshire, born thirty miles north of Greeley's birthplace and along the same Merrimac River. "My chief recreation," wrote Webster, "was to roam the hills of my county. I liked to let my thoughts go free and indulge in their own excursions alone. When thinking is to be done one must think alone. No man knows himself who does not thus sometime keep his own company."

Greeley was keen for a rapid pace: "He who will measure his walk by milestones will discover that lively and persistent stepping with no stopping to chase butterflies is required to make four miles an hour. Beginning at twenty-five miles per day, slowly but constantly in motion, you may add two to three miles per day until you reach forty miles."

That is precisely what Greeley did from Dunkirk to his family home, arriving there after a fourteen hours' jaunt only to find a condition of living that appalled him. All his pleasurable anticipations of reunion with parents, brothers and sisters were at once shattered. The desolate life of a wilderness had made a worn and weary woman of his mother; his sisters and brothers had accepted its privations, but they could not conceal the imprint on their faces.

Back at Amherst, despite a husband hopelessly in a rut and a sheriff always at the door, the mother had still been able to fight on; she had it in her Ulster heritage to do that. At Westhaven even the worst had been more endurable than this barren cabin on which the sun could shine only a few hours daily because of encircling trees. She now faced a life of endless toil; she could not fight that fate. Greeley wrote: "I never caught the old smile on her face, the familiar gladness in her mood, the hearty joyfulness in her manner, from the day she entered those woods until her death, nearly thirty years later. Those who knew her only in those later years, when toil and trouble had gained their victory over her, never knew her at all."

Promptly the youthful Greeley resolved that he would earn enough money to ease the burden on his mother. Within two months he was at Jamestown, New York, setting type on the *Journal*. There his employers preferred to owe him wages rather than to pay them.

Reluctantly he tramped back to the family cabin; then in January came a chance to "sub" on the *Gazette* at Erie, Pennsylvania. Lest someone get there before him he walked twenty miles in one snowy day. Greeley's experience there must have inspired ambitions that Erie could never satisfy, for in July he declined owner Joseph Sherrett's offer of an interest in the newspaper. Here we have the second evidence of Greeley's dependence even in youth solely upon himself—the first when at fifteen he turned from his westward-bound family to become printer-apprentice; and now at twenty he refuses a tempting offer! Five months before he had been eager to secure a substitute position there. "Upon full consideration I decided to turn my steps toward the 'Commercial Emporium' while still considerably younger than I would have preferred to be for such a venture."

The purpose that had been forming for more than a year had at last reached the time for action; he now knew the move to make! Unfortunately, Greeley never stated his reasons beyond the few words just quoted. Evidently there was no thrill about his decision. He proposed to get ahead in the world and New York City was the only place that tempted. There the center of battle was and there he would test his possibilities.

A parting visit home, turning over to his father all but $25 from his *Gazette* savings, and Greeley was off on his great adventure—tramping, canaling, and getting a day's work in printing shops in Mohawk Valley villages. From Albany he was to have twenty-four hours on a boat towing canal barges down the Hudson River, arriving at Whitehall Slip, the Battery, with $10 of the $25 he had when he left Wayne. On August 17, 1831, he was seeking a livelihood in a city of almost 200,000 inhabitants of whom he knew not a blessed one! Out of his life now were the parents in the backwoods of Wayne, the companionships of youth and the neighbors at Westhaven and Poultney—all were in the past. At twenty he faced alone the tests of ambitious manhood.

CHAPTER III

New York City in Greeley's Day

WHO OF THE present time can picture in his mind the city into which Greeley wandered alone one hundred and fifteen years ago? Or who, at Greeley's beginning in that city, could have dreamed of its skyscrapers, subways, art, music, science and other cultural centers of today? Who could possibly have foreseen those few square miles of squalor and cleanliness, of poverty and plenty, spread over short, narrow, winding streets—only Fulton Street extending from river to river—south from Canal Street to the Battery as the world's conceded center of finance and commerce? Foreign cities had proper pride in their centuries-old buildings, cathedrals and famous leaders, but in 1831 Manhattan Island—only twelve miles long from tip to tip and two and a half miles across at its widest—was chiefly dense woods, high stony hills and small farms between the Hudson River, the East River and Harlem River as well as Spuyten Duyvil. It had no past to match old world cities; it could only dream of a future —but surely not of such a future as has come in a century! The canal that flowed through much of what is now Canal Street was in fact the northern limit of city life; its sloping banks of lawn were an afternoon parade ground for those who lived so far uptown. At the southern end, only one mile and a half distant, was Battery Park—the pride of the city "with a view of the waters more beautiful than Naples"; fashionable folk living on State Street, Bowling Green or Greenwich Street looked upon it as equal to London's Pall Mall or the Champs Elysées in Paris;

to young people its benches and shady nooks were "a domestic bourse where are negotiated many of the love affairs of nearly 200,000 people."

The war department had just moved to Governor's Island from "Fort Clinton," as Castle Garden at the Battery was at first called; after Jenny Lind and many theatrical attractions had been heard there that famous place, later to be used as an aquarium, became the chief gateway into our country for emigrants from Europe—thousands of men, women and children year after year—really millions in all. No other place in the world has ever meant more of freedom, opportunity and hope to people than did Castle Garden in its day. Who can estimate how many young men who later won prominence and fortune walked through its gates as Greeley had walked from the Whitehall dock, with all their possessions bundled on their backs, and in wonder faced the fact that a new world was before them? They had their dreams; so had Greeley.

Then the City Hall, with its front of costly Massachusetts marble and its economical Nyack Palisade sandstone rear, marked substantially the extent of the retail shopping district along Broadway to the Battery; Columbia College occupied Park Place from Church Street almost to West Street with its campus extending south two blocks and covered with tall elms. The state prison on Washington Street near Rector was being transferred to its present location at Ossining. There was not a dock on the Hudson River above Barclay Street nor on the East River above Market Street. Few buildings in the city were as high as four stories; most residences were only two stories and attic. Opera in Italian had the backing of new-made millionaires headed by John Jacob Astor, and actors Junius Brutus Booth, Edwin Forrest, Edmund and Fanny Kemble were bringing the theater into better repute.

Washington Irving, Fenimore Cooper, Fitz-Greene Halleck, Clement C. Moore, S. F. B. Morse and Samuel Woodworth established the Bread and Cheese Club at Broadway and Chambers Street; it then became the Sketch Club and in 1848 the present-day Century Association. They even planned to have commercial New York displace Philadelphia as the nation's literary center before

Boston could establish its claim. Eight stage lines with gaudy red and yellow painted busses starting from Whitehall Slip, Bowling Green and Chambers Street were the sole means of city travel; only two of them went farther north than Fourteenth Street. There was one stage a day to Albany and one to Boston; of course there was not a mile of steam railroad; while Brooklyn's 7,000 population had only the Fulton Street ferry to Manhattan. Steamboats had begun making the trip up the Hudson River to Albany, and there was a line of Long Island Sound steamers to Providence. "Don't blow out the gas!" was a much-needed warning printed in big, red letters on both sides of placards suspended from gas jets just being installed nervously in the homes of the rich. Milk peddlers with deep twelve-gallon cans hanging from the extremes of a yoke across their shoulders paraded the streets at dawn shouting for customers and ladled the fluid to housewives. Shares in a proposed New York and Harlem streetcar line (present Madison Avenue bus) were looked upon as another "Mississippi bubble" and merely a plaything for stock exchange speculators. Not a single public building then occupied is now standing except the City Hall and the Subtreasury at Wall and Broad Streets, and only a few residences remain as specters of the long ago.

"The tongue that is lapping up the cream of commerce and finance of a continent," Oliver Wendell Holmes called this New York City.

To twenty-year-old Greeley it was more astonishing than he had ever fashioned in his thoughts back in Poultney. He frankly confessed his timid feeling when, stepping from the Whitehall Slip landing and looking up South Street, he saw for the first time ship after ship that had buffeted the seven seas; great freighters sailing to every port in the world; their big, broad hulls, tall masts, wide-spreading yardarms crowding one another for room, their long bowsprits projecting far across the roadway along the East River front. To Greeley they were monsters of the deep of which he had read in boyhood with wonder; he now gazed upon them in even greater amazement that they were real.

He walked up Broad Street with his bundle still hung over his shoulder on a hickory stick, his clothes a tattered jacket and open-neck shirt with wrist cuffs tied with string, no stockings, and much-traveled cotton pants. He seemed a wanderer from the wilds. Dwellings and business houses of stone and brick instead of the log and shingle houses of his home villages caught his attention. At many street corners were coal-oil lamps on tall iron posts or hanging from long iron arms extending six or eight feet from houses; at night watchmen with big lanterns patrolled the streets and on the hour struck the pavement with a heavy club, shouting the time and "All's well"; there were public pumps from which householders not fortunate enough to have cisterns on their own property drew pails of water at two cents each for all their needs.

Describing his first appearance on the sidewalks of the "Commercial Emporium," Greeley later pictured himself as a forlorn individual whom people eyed curiously as he trudged by: "I realized then that the world was all before me." He did not blame the landlady of a boardinghouse at the corner of Broad and Wall Streets—possibly where J. P. Morgan & Company are now located—for saying to him, not unkindly, as she opened the door and viewed her caller that her house was probably too costly for him—suggesting that he seek cheaper board over on Greenwich or West Street. Unconsciously she directed him to his place of opportunity, for it was in McGoldrick's $2.50-a-week lodging-house at 168 West Street that one week later he met a man who told him he could probably get a job at West's printing shop located at 85 Chatham Street.

August in New York City was hotter than Greeley was used to; from shop to shop he vainly sought work; thoroughly discouraged, he was ready to abandon his rash venture. As his next hope he had Washington in mind. The only reason he did not move on to the national capital was that he lacked the money necessary—or, indeed, to travel out of the city at all. The man he chanced to meet at 168 West Street settled his career.

And what a career then actually faced this young job-seeking printer from the hills of northern Vermont! If the future could have revealed itself to him in those first days, what a stirring story it would have told him—what an utterly unbelievable story of work, worry, poverty—and, then, of triumph! He did not know, of course, that up in Albany, Thurlow Weed, who like himself had tramped as a printer the Mohawk Valley, was struggling to establish the Albany *Evening Journal* with a few hundred dollars. Nor did he know that a young, red-haired lawyer of Auburn, Cayuga County, New York—William H. Seward by name—was serving his first public office as state senator; nor that the Lincoln family had just abandoned wilderness life in Kentucky and with Abraham, their twenty-one-year-old son—"doing a little of everything," as he said, "but nothing for long"—had wandered first into Indiana and then into New Salem, Illinois.

In that same year of 1831 there entered the United States Army as second lieutenant a West Point graduate whom Greeley thirty-six years later with others was to bail out of a military prison where he was charged with treason—Jefferson Davis, born in Kentucky only eight months earlier than Lincoln and not more than one hundred miles from the latter's birthplace. In Boston that same year William Lloyd Garrison started his *Liberator*—"I will be heard!"—and Charles Sumner came out of Harvard to join in the struggle against slavery. Stephen A. Douglas left his Vermont birthplace, tramping to Jacksonville, Illinois, where he found work in a sawmill at $1 a day. What memories those names recall! What history they wrote!

It was during the afternoon of the last Sunday of August that Greeley was told of the vacancy at the Chatham Street printing shop. He was always a churchgoer. That Sabbath he attended both morning and evening services at the Orchard Street Congregational Church. He was amazed to see heavy iron chains stretched across the cobblestone roadway in front of the church blocking off all traffic—a means of enforcing silence while the sermon was being preached.

On Monday morning the foreman was not impressed by the young applicant too plainly from "the wilds," but he finally said: "We'll fix up a case for you and see what you can do." He gave him extracts from the New Testament to be set in pearl and agate sizes of type—the smallest of a range of type faces—in columns about half the width of a newspaper column, with frequent italics and unusual technical references. It seemed impossible for anyone to earn a dollar a twelve-hour day out of such copy; Horace got the job because no one else wanted it.

"Did you hire that damn fool?" shouted proprietor West to his foreman when he noticed Greeley at work.

"Yes, we need men, and he's the best I can do," came the reply.

"Well, pay him off tonight, and let him go about his business."

But that did not happen. The "damn fool" proved to be too capable. Greeley's task was blinding; he worked twelve hours a day, set what is called a "clean" proof—that is, with few printer errors—and surprised everybody by having $6.84 to his credit at the end of his first week.

In order to be at work early and late he moved from his West Street room to a boardinghouse on Chathan Street near Duane in which a group of shoemakers lived and had a common workshop. Board was still at the $2.50 weekly rate. As on West Street, the new home was over a grogshop. He fraternized with the shoemakers while hungrily awaiting Mrs. Mason's loud-tongued brass bell summoning all to benches at a long pine-board eating table. He declared that one could hear it a block away; at its first clang there was a rush for a seat closest to the most food.

Around the corner on Duane Street was the home of the poet Samuel Woodworth, who wrote "The Old Oaken Bucket" while living there. In front of the house there was a pump noted for its pure cool water. Greeley patronized it instead of the saloons that infested the neighborhood. Of course, Woodworth's "fond recollections" in his poem referred to "the iron-bound bucket which hung in the well" at his childhood home in Scituate, Massachusetts, but it was said at the time that his Duane Street pump had inspired him to recall with so much sentiment the water from the well of former days "though now far removed from the loved habitation."

Of the four editors—Horace Greeley, James Gordon Bennett, Henry J. Raymond and Charles A. Dana—who entered New York City one by one penniless and friendless and were to become leaders of American journalism, only Greeley was there in 1831; not one of their descendants is in the profession today; neither the *Tribune*, the *Herald*, the *Times*, the *World* nor the *Morning Sun* was in existence. Only Greeley and Bennett—the two men up from the printer's case—knew then that in one form or another the making of a newspaper was to be their mission in life. Dana at twelve years of age had just left his New Hampshire home to go clerking in an uncle's store in Buffalo; Raymond was still at his widowed mother's home in Lima, Livingston County, New York. Neither he nor Dana had the slightest idea of a newspaper career. Both frankly said that to Greeley they owed their opportunity. Bennett had been a year on James Watson Webb's *Courier* in 1829-30 restlessly seeking money to start an Andrew Jackson paper. Failing in that effort, he had turned from New York City to Washington as correspondent of the *Courier*.

But it was not in Bennett as it was not in Greeley to work for others; he abandoned Washington and undertook a Jackson newspaper in Philadelphia for the presidential campaign of 1832. That paper survived barely six months. Returning to New York City in 1835, at forty years of age, twenty-four of which had been spent in wandering among newspapers from Boston to Charleston, S.C., and back again without ever having found a resting place for long, the emigrant from Leigh, Scotland, started the New York *Herald* with only $500 in cash and not a friend. "One man in a cellar against the whole world," he boastfully declared in later years. The new newspaper had its office in the basement of 10 Wall Street; the one room had but a small window; its only furniture was a counter made of two wide boards supported by two flour barrels at each end; there was just enough space back of this counter for Bennett to sit as he wrote most of the paper, received advertisements or handed out the *Herald* for one cent per copy. One chair on either side of the boards completed the outfit. Yet year after year for almost three-quarters of a century under Bennett father and son the *Herald* proved to be the greatest money-maker of all newspapers in this country. In that respect for thirty years Greeley's *Tribune* was the nearest approach to it.

CHAPTER IV

"Greeley & Story, Printers"

No vision of such a future was in this East Poultney printer's mind that first year in the big city. Life meant nothing to Greeley then but hard work, a cobblers' boardinghouse for a home, and a few dollars saved each week. Even that small saving could not have been made had he not kept to his early determination to spend no money even for clothes. Though he did not realize it, the old garments did not make a helpful impression whenever he sought a job.

"Be off with you!" shouted David Hale, editor of the *Journal of Commerce*, believing that Greeley was a runaway apprentice. "Return to your master!" Next he tried the *Evening Post;* he was quietly at work there a few days when William Leggett, poet, essayist and then managing editor, noticed him. "For Heaven's sake get rid of such a queer-looking fellow," he declared. "Pay him off tonight!" Thus Greeley lost his newspaper job; he resolved to stick to job printing offices. But his second summer in the city brought a longing for the "old country," as he called it. As work slackened early in July he was off on a journey northward, tramping and hitchhiking most of the way to East Poultney and Westhaven. "A few days amidst the scenes of my boyhood are like a blissful dream," he wrote. "In the hours shared with friends from whom I have been severed, and from whom the setting sun will again divide us perhaps forever, we live the essence of years past and to come." In every house there was cordial welcome for the boy who had dared seek a living in the big city. He returned there in time to cast his first presidential vote; it went wholeheartedly for Henry Clay. Though newspapers did not want printer Greeley, he had no trouble finding a place that fall with the J. A. Redfield firm at the highest wages he had ever had.

"He was queer in looks and queer in his ways," commented Redfield, "but he was the best printer we ever had. He talked aloud so much while setting type that one of the men asked him one day if he had a patent talking-machine in his throat."

It was while working at Redfield's early in December that good fortune and Greeley began a lifelong march together. Francis Vinton Story, foreman of the *Spirit of the Times,* where Greeley had once worked a few weeks, suggested that they establish a printing concern of their own. Each would invest $100. Story had been promised the printing of the *Bank Note Reporter,* a weekly magazine, and a Dr. Horatio David Shepard, then editor of a medical magazine, offered the printing of a morning newspaper to be called the *Morning Post* and to be sold for one cent. No established printing firm would then risk giving credit to a newspaper published at that low price; even Greeley & Story refused to do so until Dr. Shepard agreed to charge two cents.

The printing firm of Greeley & Story was thereupon launched, and Greeley's days of working for others were forever ended. He was twenty-two years old. Two rooms on the second floor of 54 Liberty Street, corner of Nassau Street, housed the new enterprise with its $200 cash capital and a $40.00 credit for type at the George Bruce type foundry—after credit had been denied it at other foundries. In appreciation Greeley eventually bought more than $50,000 worth of type from Bruce. The *Morning Post* made its appearance on New Year's Day 1833. At two cents it had a brief, sorry experience; after two weeks the price was reduced to one cent; the paper then began to take hold. By that time, unfortunately, the Shepard money had been exhausted; the Greeley & Story firm could not carry the burden; "thus died the first cheap-for-cash daily in New York, perhaps in the world," remarked Greeley, "and we printers were hard aground on a lee shore."

They had a sharp struggle to survive. Story found part-time employment in other printing offices while Greeley did all the typesetting of the *Bank Note Reporter* and of lottery tickets. They distributed cards reading:

> Greeley & Story, 54 Liberty street, New York, respectfully solicit the patronage of the public to their business of Letter Press Printing, particularly lottery printing, such as schemes, periodicals, etc.

But fate was against them—at least against Story. In July he was drowned in the East River. Jonas Winchester, a printer who was also Story's brother-in-law, assumed the vacant partnership. Slowly they prospered—chiefly through printing tickets for the lottery, then a lawful enterprise.

Just as surely as the days of his youth in Westhaven and East Poultney had receded into the past so with prosperity in New York City receded the career of Greeley the typesetter—the Greeley swaying back and forth in the fashion of a country printer over his case as he picks each letter out of its separate box and drops it into his stick, all the time talking to himself; just as surely, too, had disappeared the Greeley who only three years before had landed at the Battery gawky and bewildered.

Another Greeley had emerged—no longer diffident, no longer awed by pushing, heedless crowds in the "Commercial Emporium." At last he had found himself; he was writing editorials for the *Daily Whig* and the *Constitutionalist;* his earnings from those two newspapers plus profits from H. Greeley & Company, Printers, left him a savings bank margin restless for venture. He had great ambitions in mind when he persuaded partner Winchester that the firm should undertake a weekly magazine "devoted to literature, the arts and sciences" on the lines of Franklin's *Pennsylvania Gazette* founded in 1728 (the present-day *Saturday Evening Post*). He called the new journal the *New Yorker,* and moved it to 18 Ann Street. This address was on the edge of that famous old newspaper location that had Frankfort Street (at the Brooklyn Bridge) as its base and Ann Street as its apex, with Park Row as the east and City Hall Park, and later the now demolished Post Office Building, as the west. It was known as Printing House Square.

In that center were grimy, timeworn buildings with their creaky, upending wooden stairs going up three or four flights to editorial and printers' rooms or down one long flight into dingy, sweaty basements jammed with the clattering printing presses of that period; pawnshops, gambling parlors, all-night "beaneries" and grogshops crowded both sides of the Park Theatre. From those few city blocks there was issued every type of publication—daily, Sunday, weekly, monthly and just sometimes (whenever there was cash in the drawer, a loan to be had or a trustful printer). In Greeley's day it was a place that not even London's Fleet Street ever equaled in variety of publications, in few fortunes made but many lost, in lives sacrificed to an earnest, restless ambition to prove the power and fascination of the pen.

In the first issue, dated March 22, 1834, readers were greeted with this unusual "Publisher's Address":

> "The New Yorker's" columns will show that it is not and never will be the servile copyist of any of its contemporaries; nor shall we adventure our barque among the whirlpools and quicksands of politics.
>
> Our paper is not blazoned through the land as the cheapest periodical in the world, or any other captivating clap-trap . . . no distinguished literary and fashionable characters have been dragged in to bolster up a rigamarole of preposterous, charlatan pretensions: "You cannot succeed without humbug," they tell us. Our answer is "We shall try."

Greeley later wrote of his venture:

> . . . Young in years, poor even in friends, and utterly unknown to the public . . . we gave to the world the first number of "The New Yorker." We spread our sails to the breeze, backed by the moderate earnings of two or three years of successful industry, the good wishes of some forty friends, a sanguine spirit and about twenty subscribers . . . Heaven bless them for their generous reliance in advance upon our editorial capacities!

Notwithstanding the competition of the *Knickerbocker*, the *North American Review* and other magazines, the *New Yorker* became a channel through which flowed much popular literature. For example, at a time when Charles Dickens, writing as "Boz," was still unrecognized in England as an author, Greeley scissored a Dickens story entitled "Delicate Attentions" from the London *Monthly*, and reprinted it in the *New Yorker*—the first Dickens story ever published in this country. He was also one of the earliest to recognize Edgar Allan Poe's talent, and published several Poe compositions. Evidently he could not pay for them in cash, for in the Huntington Library in California there is a sixty-day note signed Horace Greeley and drawn to the order of Edgar Allan Poe. That note was paid, but a later note for $50 by Poe to Greeley was never paid, and Greeley offered it to autograph hunters for half price.

Better acquaintance with Poe led Greeley to say of him: "Poe is a brilliant writer when neither too drunk nor too sober. He might be somebody if he were not an incorrigible rascal and vagabond. That chap will be getting into scrapes all his life until the sexton gets him into one that he cannot escape."

One feature of the *New Yorker* that at once gained readers was a back page devoted exclusively to the words and music of some song of the day—"Meet Me by Moonlight Alone," "False One! I Love Thee Still," "All By the Shady Greenwood Tree," and "Away! Away We Bound O'er the Sea." Greeley believed so confidently in the song feature that at times when the words and music were too long to be completed on a single page he would follow the practice common to serial story journals and promise "Continued in our next issue." Though he never could sing a note he loved to hear others. Concerts were his one extravagance. He began collecting popular songs which he intended to publish some day in a volume entitled "A Song-Book for the People." Unfortunately he never got to it, though as late as 1870 he expressed a keen regret that he had not.

But the *New Yorker* had another sentimental appeal to young folks. There was always room for poetry, too. Indeed, Greeley led off in several issues with verses of his own composition—one of which was this tribute to the printing press:

The World's a Printing House.
Our words and thoughts
And deeds are characters
Of various sizes.
Each soul is a composition
Whose faults
The Levites may correct
But Heaven revises.
Death is the common press
From whence, being driven,
We're gathered sheet by sheet
And Bound for Heaven.

Before the *New Yorker* came into existence Greeley had sold poems to various publications, especially the *Southern Literary Messenger*. His top price for a poem was one dollar—just that much more than William Cullen Bryant, fifteen years earlier, had received from the *North American Review* for his famous "Thanatopsis."

A Greeley poem that appeared in the *New Yorker* consisted of five verses one of which ran:

FANTASIES

They deem me cold, the thoughtless and light-hearted,
In that I worship not at beauty's shrine;
They deem me cold that through the years departed
I ne'er have bowed me to some form divine.
They deem me proud, that where the world hath flattered
I ne'er have knelt to languish or adore;
They think not that the homage idly scattered
Leaves the heart bankrupt ere its spring is o'er.

H.G.

But Greeley did not progress far with the muses. "Those who imagine themselves capable of becoming true poets are many," he wrote when describing his early rhyming efforts, "but I never even got to that grade. I knew that my power of expression in verse was defective, as though I spoke with my mouth full of pebbles, and I very soon renounced the fetters of verse for unmistakable prose."

That feeling, however, did not prevent him from composing this "Ode to Printing" that was sung at the meeting of the Southern Typographical Association, at Mobile, Alabama, January 18, 1837, to the old-time popular air of "Come Strike the Bold Anthem":

THE PRINTER'S ART

Heaven speed the proud cause of the world's renovation
May Virtue and Truth our Art ever befriend
While from each it may claim, in our deep adoration,
A heart to uphold it—an arm to defend.
Then flourish the Press; Freedom's vanguard adoring
The light of past ages reflecting on this,
And earth shall yet bloom in the freshness of morning
An Eden of Glory, of Knowledge and Bliss.

H.G.

Robert Bonner, of the *New York Ledger*, and historically known as the owner of that wonderful trotter "Maud S.," wanted to include one of Greeley's poems in a book of collected American verse. But Greeley would not have it. He wrote Bonner, February 10, 1859:

You must exclude me from your new poetic Pantheon. I have no business there. I am no poet and never shall be. True I wrote some poems in my callow youth but I was never a poet even in the mists of deluding fancy. They were read by few and those few have kindly forgotten them.

Within the last ten years I have been accused of all possible and some impossible offenses against good taste, good morals and the common weal,—I have been branded aristocrat, communist, infidel, hypocrite, disunionist, etc.—but I cannot remember that any one has flung in my face my youthful transgressions in the way of Rhyme. Do not then accord to the malice of my enemies this forgotten means of annoyance. Let the dead rest.

Nevertheless he never abandoned "this forgotten means of annoyance," though in later years he modestly put his rhymes in his desk and not in print.

"Thunder and lightning," declared Park Benjamin when Greeley read one of his latest efforts, "you don't call that poetry, I hope, Horace?"

"Not if you say it isn't, Park," assented Greeley as he meekly restored it to his pocket.

Poetry and song, however pleasing, without clever business management would not meet Saturday night bills. Many subscribers were deaf to pleas to pay; month after month the profits of the printing company were needed to meet the magazine's deficits.

Still the young editor kept on. The joy of working for an ideal was the joy of living—mind, body and spirit were fused into one great ambition. "I paid off every one to-night," he wrote on July 29, 1835. "Have $10 left and have to raise $350 on Monday. Borrowing places all sucked dry. I shall raise it, however."

Not in the same mood was partner Winchester. He was ready to abandon the venture; partner Wilson (whose one-third interest was solely in the magazine) was also ready to retire, alleging that he was "about to commit matrimony." Actually he shared Winchester's pessimism. Greeley urged B. F. Ransom of East Poultney to take Wilson's place "if you like our concern." He estimated that they could probably divide $1,000 profit the first year and then steadily increase it—"but that," he frankly added, "is purely speculation. . . . My scheme embraces a partner with whom I could eventually find a home and thus reduce somewhat the expense of living respectably."

As Greeley wrote those lines he surely could not have had serious thought of "committing matrimony" himself, or of securing in a wife "a partner with whom I could find a home." Nevertheless, six weeks later—on July 5, 1836—at Warrenton, North Carolina, he married Miss Mary Youngs Cheney, of Cornwall, Connecticut.

His courtship had been a boardinghouse romance. Greeley had listened to a lecture on dietetics by Dr. Sylvester Graham, whose graham bread has now stood the test of more than a century. He was impressed by Graham's argument against heavy meals—particularly against eating meats, drinking tea, coffee or liquor of any kind and using pepper or salt. Pies, of course, were taboo, too, though some puddings were permitted. Greeley had always been a heavy and hasty eater—but he determined to try the Graham diet. It was his first "ism." He went to live at Graham's Hotel on Greenwich Street. There he met Miss Cheney, and there, he confessed,

> Quickly I forgot the printer's art
> And hailed the presence of a Queenly Heart.

All doubt he might have had about Graham's restrictive diet was lost in his admiration for "the fair little maiden so tender and true," as he addressed her in another sonnet. Miss Cheney was a one-hundred-per-cent Grahamite—plus a little more. She had a class in a private school for girls. New York City's climate was too trying for her, however, so she secured a similar position in North Carolina. Before she left the city a romance with Greeley had developed, and she was absent only through the winter of 1835-36 before Greeley's letter writing ended in a proposal. When she consented he lost no time in getting to North Carolina.

Greeley was then twenty-five years old; his bride was three years younger. City life had not yet blurred the picture he presented of health and vigor as well as of the modest ways of country upbringing. He had begun to fill out the lank five-foot-ten frame of his youth. His bride was a contrast. She was a frail little creature—scarcely five feet four inches tall. Her face reflected the pale complexion of a student, her jet black hair worn in heavy curls to her neck, her large brilliant black eyes made her an acknowledged beauty. It was said of her then that "she was crazy for education." Though she had the decisive ways attributed to New England schoolmarms, no one suspected the provocative spirit that later developed.

Nor did Greeley give advance notice of the man he was to be. He was companionable with his fellow boarders, who thought him a hard-working young man with no pretensions and no interest in life beyond his magazine.

The brief public notice of Greeley's marriage was another evidence of his habit of keeping his personal affairs within the family circle. James Gordon Bennett had very different ideas on that score. In contrast with Greeley's modest four lines, the breezy way in which Bennett announced his matrimonial intentions illustrates the widely different personality of those two newspaper chieftains. The Greeley announcement in the *New Yorker* on July 16, 1836, among the usual marriage notices, read:

In Immanuel Church, Warrenton, North Carolina, on Tuesday morning 5th inst., by Rev. William Norwood, Mr. Horace Greeley, Editor of "The New Yorker," to Miss Mary Y. Cheney of Warrenton, formerly of New York City.

Five years later came the Bennett notice. He entertained readers of the *Herald* with an editorial in his own characteristic style of writing. Part of it read as follows:

TO THE READERS OF THE HERALD—DECLARATION OF LOVE—CAUGHT AT LAST—GOING TO BE MARRIED —NEW MOVEMENT IN CIVILIZATION.

I am going to be married in a few days... to one of the most splendid women in intellect, in heart, in soul, in property, in person, in manner, that I have yet seen in the course of my interesting pilgrimage through human life....

I sought and found a fortune—a large fortune. She has no Stonington shares or Manhattan stock, but in purity and uprightness she is worth half a million of pure coin. Can any swindling bank show so much? In good sense and elegance another half million; in soul, mind and beauty, millions and millions, equal to the whole specie of all the rotten banks in the world.... This highest order of excellence must produce some curious results in my heart and feelings, and these results the future will develop in due time in the columns of "The Herald."

Such was Bennett! Such was Greeley!

Marriage did not lessen Greeley's devotion to the *New Yorker*. He ended his partners' fears by dissolving H. Greeley & Co., accepting the unprofitable magazine as his share of the assets—the profitable printing concern going to Winchester. Greeley's interest was now solely in his magazine—"making it the best in America." Time and again during the struggle then ahead of him he threatened in despairing letters to friends to abandon it, but when actually urged to do so his invariable reply was that he would "crawl through an auger hole" with it—"somehow I'll pull through."

The *New Yorker* had more than 5,000 subscribers, of whom one-half paid regularly while others paid when they pleased, or not at all. He looked forward to the end of the year for a better response from his subscribers; unfortunately by that time an industrial depression had begun and cash receipts fell instead of increasing. Facing him was 1837—called the "year of national ruin." Everywhere it ruined thousands; personally it ruined the newly married Greeleys—but it did not ruin the *New Yorker!* In the first two years four business managers had come and gone profitless. But Greeley faced it all.

In his magazine, however, he urged the thousands of unemployed to leave the city—to go west: "Fly, scatter through the country, to the great west. It is your true destination! If you have no family or friends to aid you here turn your face and hopes to that fertile land. Dream not of getting rich by speculation, rapidly by trade, or anyhow by a profession; all these avenues are choked—and ten must be trodden down in the press where one can vault.... If you cannot pay $1.25 an acre for your farm then just 'squat'—for the West is your place." Every issue of the *New Yorker* through 1837 and 1838 carried the same counsel to depression victims, until the young editor became known as "Go West Greeley."

Public questions now had attention in the magazine; also his first editorials declaring the duty of society to the unfortunate. While the depression was at its deepest, and he himself in despair, he asked pointedly, "What Shall We Do For The Laborer?" The inquiry attracted a great deal of attention but not so much as an editorial that followed, entitled "The Tyranny of Opinion."

That article again foreshadowed the Greeley of the future: "The great prevailing evil of the social condition is the worship and the bigotry and despotism of opinion. Whoever ventures to propound opinion strikingly at variance with those of the majority must be content to brave obloquy, contempt and persecution. If political, they exclude him from public office; if religious, however moderately skeptical, from social intercourse. This is the vice of the age."

The twenty-six-year-old editor of the *New Yorker* did not hesitate to invite discussion even with such a figure as eighty-year-old Noah Webster, whose Dictionary had long before been recognized as the leading authority in this country. Greeley did not like to abandon the letters *e* and *g* or the *l* in "traveller." So, despite all his financial troubles, he found time to write Webster these comments:

New York, Dec. 25, 1837

Noah Webster
New Haven, Conn.
Dear Sir:

I have resolved to trouble you with a few casual suggestions respecting the etymology of your language in connexion with your Dictionary. My course hitherto as a general and public defender of your views in opposition to those of Johnson and Richardson will, I trust, excuse the liberty. Bear with me, then, while I suggest a few instances in which I am compelled to depart from your Standard. If you think it worth the trouble to enlighten me on these points, you will do so; if not, it matters little. These are my points:

1. *Judgement* and its derivatives. You spell it without the middle "e", as also abridgement, acknowledgement, and other words of this class. Why so? Many of them you derive from the French, where the "e" appears. As the sole use of the "e" is to soften the "g" preceding it, I see not why it may not be as properly omitted in judge as in judgement.

2. *Wo*—you spell indifferently with and without an "e". I hold the "e" superfluous and very unsightly. The word seems to me just as "go" or "no" would if spelt goe and noe. But you give us woesome with an "e" and woful without it, and use the latter to define the former. How can this be justified?

3. *Acre*—you spell correctly, yet give us theater and kindred abominations. As you trace this word to the French "theatre" and as its derivatives are theatric and theatrical, etc., I think your innovation on the established usage unaccountable.

4. *Bituminous*, etc., from bitumen, do not suit me. I know that others are with you in this instance, but I am not satisfied.

5. *Waggon.* I want it with two "g's" in accordance with the analogy of our language, just in rugged, dogged, bigger, baggage, etc. Can't you help as to a reason? The derivation is not sufficient, as our language often doubles consonants after short vowels, in spite of primitive. I know there is flagon in the way, but that is not one of your Rugged Northman gutturals but (as you have it) an irregular off-shoot of Latinity. But I would gladly spell it flaggon for the sake of waggon. I will give up the point if you say I must, but I hate to do it.

6. *Launch* is the good old way and you restrict it to lanch without a reason except the derivation, which looks questionable. (I would take your word for it sooner than any other man's but lexicographers have so demolished each other's characters in this matter of devising from other languages that I trust implicitly to none. Besides, the derivation is NOT conclusive. You give us laundress from lavendire and laundry from laundero. I think I must still write laundry, launch, staunch, etc.

7. *Traveler* looks horribly, but I am coming to it by degrees. You are probably right in this instance (I mean that your principle is a novel one), but to follow you goes against the grain.

Enough for your patience. Perhaps all my difficulties are solved by your Quarto, but how shall a poor editor indulge in such luxuries? This brings me to the point on which I was first impelled to write you. Several persons around me, in the common walks of life, say they would continue to purchase your Quarto if your publishers would but issue an edition in numbers (like Richardson) at a moderate price and at intervals—bi-monthly, for instance. How does the suggestion strike you? I am sure that many would subscribe for it and much good result from the undertaking.

Yours truly,

Horace Greeley
"New Yorker"
12 Ann Street

To Noah Webster, LLD.

This interesting reply came to Greeley by return mail:

New Haven, Dec. 26, 1837

Mr. Greeley:

Dear Sir,—In reply to your inquiries, I answer—

1. I wrote judgement in my old Spelling book; but I found I did not succeed well in introducing E. English books have the word without the final E, at least most of them. But my principal reason for altering the spelling was the use of a point over g, as in j. This is so printed in my later books, and this point indicates the sound of j. See my Elementary Spelling Book and all my Dictionaries.

2. Woe I write with an E for uniformity with doe, foe, roe, hoe, toe—nouns; go and no are not in analogy with it. Woful is according to custom, and I deviate as little as possible from usage. It is not uncommon to omit letters of primitives in the derivatives. Woesome is antiquated; it is given as obsolete.

3. Acre I cannot spell acer, unless my point on C should be received into common use. So with lucre. These are exceptions to my rule, but at present are unavoidable.

4. Bituminous is wrong; it ought to be bitumenous and I should now write it so, even against universal custom. I wish you would now begin that orthography—I will quote the "New Yorker" for authority. I may perhaps alter my plates.

5. Wagon was always waggon, until perhaps twenty years ago; but all at once the printers altered it. The present spelling is according to the original Saxon, Dutch and German. I believe it must stand.

Yours respectfully,

N. Webster

Note,—

My rules of spelling are not perfectly carried into effect.—There are some difficulties in doing what I wish on this subject. An approximation to uniformity is all that can be expected in a language so abominably irregular as ours.

Such letter-writing diversions, however, could not dispel the thick fog of uncertainty that hung over the magazine. Mrs. Greeley bravely resumed her schoolteaching. To Greeley it seemed as though he and widespread destitution were partners. "We were doomed that year to see the fair fabric of our seeming prosperity fade away like a vision," Greeley later frankly told his *New Yorker* readers, "leaving in its stead nothing but debt and embarrassment and a depression that was almost despair." Fortunately the clouds were rifted in the darkest of the twelve months—December—by a most unusual incident, entirely unforeseen. In one of his frank talks to readers of the *New Yorker*, Greeley did not hesitate to recall this most welcome turn in his affairs: "We have pursued the tenor of our way since the close of that 'year of ruin' and, if never elated with any signal evidence of popular favor, we have not since been doomed to gaze fixedly for months into a yawning abyss of ruin, and to feel all the time that it must be our goal at last."

CHAPTER V

"On the Boiling Sea of Politics"

THE EVENT did more than rescue the *New Yorker* from a "yawning abyss of ruin"; it gave Greeley his opportunity.

One afternoon about two weeks before Christmas two men entered the combined editorial and composing room of the *New Yorker* in a back building at 18 Ann Street—up two flights of narrow, footworn stairs. Shirt-sleeved and aproned, Greeley was there alone—setting type for his magazine. One of the visitors asked to see the editor.

"I am the editor," said Greeley, turning to face the strangers, poising his left elbow in true printer fashion on the frame of his case, with the composing stick, full of types, held firmly in his left hand. Like every busy printer he was ready instantly to turn to his case and resume work if the visitors had no good reason for taking his time.

The callers were as much astonished by his reply as the typesetter-editor was when he heard the taller of the two men say, "I am Thurlow Weed. My friend with me is Lewis Benedict, chairman of the Whig State Committee. We would like to discuss securing your services as editor of a campaign paper to be published in Albany."

As we go through the years most of us have our surprises, but it is doubtful whether many persons have ever been more surprised than was Greeley. "The tall, slender young man with light hair and blonde complexion laid aside his 'stick' of type and greeted us," wrote Weed when describing his visit. "'My name is Horace Greeley,' he said."

Of course by reputation the two visitors were no strangers to Greeley, yet he had never dreamed that the editor of the Albany *Evening Journal* and the state chairman of the Whig party would ever call upon him in his composing room to seek his services.

Just as in 1832 when Francis Vinton Story urged Greeley in Redfield's printing shop to become his partner in a new printing firm—thus starting him on his career in business—so in 1837 the shrewd, discerning Weed turned to Greeley. In neither case did Greeley seek opportunity; in both instances it sought him. Without being aware of it he had proved himself to others.

For several months Weed had noticed that someone who thoroughly understood the need for a tariff was writing for the *New Yorker*. He decided to call on the editor when visiting New York City, and if possible to hire that writer. "I felt sure that he was a strong tariff man and an equally strong Whig."

After he had climbed the rickety stairs to the "office" of the magazine and looked upon the slim, aproned and spectacled figure setting type, with no other person in sight, Weed knew as a newspaper owner that there could be no "staff" in such a place, but he did not even suspect that owner, editor, writer and typesetter were combined in that one young man.

Weed invited Greeley over to the City Hotel that evening.

"Have you a family?" asked Weed at dinner.

"I have a wife," replied Greeley, "but she keeps school and is no hindrance to the enterprise."

"What salary would you expect?"

"Whatever you think my services are worth."

The conference ended in an offer of $1,000 plus expenses to go to Albany in late January and establish "The Jeffersonian"—a title suggested by Greeley. The near-by Christmas seemed to him brighter that night.

Greeley agreed to spend three days every week in Albany during the campaign—reserving the other days for his magazine. Larger compensation was indicated if he would make Albany his sole headquarters. It was a tempting offer—debts and anxieties on one side; relief from them on the other. He faced the first real test of his ambition. Should he abandon the *New Yorker* and enjoy a regular income with no anxieties, or continue to battle "on his own"? He had but one answer—the *New Yorker* must go on! But so did its worries. Money and a business partner were immediate needs. He advertised in the *New Yorker*:

> Any gentleman willing to embark with me in measures calculated to extend the popularity and usefulness of our work, taking an active interest in its future direction and profits, will please favor us with an interview.

Three different "prospects" responded, but not one ever returned for a second talk. It was plain that he would have to carry on alone and that alone he must find the money with which to do so. If he could do both he would go to Albany and keep his agreement; otherwise he would cancel it, for he was determined to continue his magazine. He gave Weed early warning of his uncertainty: "You will see the absolute absurdity of my entering into new engagements until I have made some arrangement to fulfill those already incurred. They have a sacred prior claim upon me which I must not disregard. Give me all the time you can, my friend, and I will turn the corner yet."

Abandoning hope of a business manager with money to invest, Greeley wrote on January 14, 1838, to his East Poultney friend Ransom (1) that "plagued by cares and perplexities" he would sell out; (2) that he proposed to make a better magazine than ever—which, as usual, meant that he really would not sell. "We have not realized for the last month as much as $500 against an expenditure of $1,000," he added. "This will not answer as a general rule; and yet it is the way I am obliged to go through the winter. I have no doubt that the paper will *take* better than it has done. In fact, if I can carry out the plans I now have in my mind's eye, I shall have great hopes of ultimate prosperity."

With such confidence in the future of his magazine Greeley

could not have had the remotest thought that in going to Albany he was drifting into what he had termed in his *New Yorker* prospectus "the whirlpools and quicksands of politics." Yet what do we find in New York's state capital? What was the picture in which Greeley finally became such a prominent figure? Weed, constantly scanning the political skies of the State for signs of the approaching campaign as intently as a ship captain scans the sea horizon for calm or storm; ambitious Seward in and out of the city hopeful that in November he will redeem his 1834 defeat for governor; twenty-seven-year-old Greeley doing all the writing for the *Jeffersonian*, as well as mailing articles and selections of miscellany every day to the *New Yorker*, "until the ice is out of the river and I can go back and forth on the night boat"—throughout that winter such were the activities of these three men who were to be powerful in politics for many years as allies and then as opponents.

All through the Seward-for-governor campaign the following summer Greeley went to Albany on a Saturday night boat, spent the next three days there writing the *Jeffersonian*, arrived back in New York City by boat on Wednesday morning to get out the *New Yorker* by Friday afternoon; he used Saturday for planning next week's magazine and "then packed my valise for Albany again on the night boat." At that time Greeley was living in the Weed home. "He would arrive from the boat two hours before breakfast," wrote Weed, "with his pockets stuffed full of newspapers which he would diligently read until summoned to table."

Here was a schedule of industry and activity which in one form or another lasted with Greeley through life. "Work is not a curse to be escaped," he insisted. "It is a blessing to be accepted and improved. Man must create in order to enjoy. Every man who really loves work and who is content to live by it is essentially honest, upright and humane." Nevertheless, how Greeley found time during 1838 to write for other newspapers in addition to his Albany duties is amazing, though he earned $10 to $12 weekly in that way, too. The *Fredonia Censor* was one to which he contributed an editorial on Seward, for the latter wrote to Weed on July 29: "Make my acknowledgment to H.G. for that beautiful article in 'The Censor.' I have never seen anything better turned out or in better temper or more discreet. I started from my chair as I read it and said to myself, 'no man could believe this was written by any one but myself'."

Frederick Seward in his "Life" of his father gave a picture of Greeley as he saw him in that campaign: "With the indefatigable industry that characterized his career Greeley used to pass one or two days each week at Albany and the remainder in New York City, where he was publishing 'The New Yorker.' 'The Jeffersonian' and 'The New Yorker' were favorite journals in Whig families, and the editor was regarded as having great ability, great industry, much eccentricity, honesty, singleness of purpose, and of no particular ambition save in his own profession."

But even with his earnings his money troubles remained serious. Paying off an 1837 deficit out of another deficit in 1838 was a feat of financing that only a hopeful soul like Greeley would ever undertake; but "ambition in his own profession" at any cost had taught him the art of managing deficits, though to his last days he never learned the equally difficult art of managing a surplus. His embarrassment still came from the neglect of subscribers to pay:

> Friends of "The New Yorker"! Patrons! We appeal to you not for charity but for justice. Whoever among you is in our debt, no matter how small the sum, is guilty of a moral wrong. We bitterly need it—we have a right to expect it. Six years of happiness could not atone for the horrors which blighted hopes, agonizing embarrassments and gloomy apprehension—all arising in great measure from your neglect—have heaped upon us during the last six months. We have borne all in silence. Now you must pay up....
>
> Since "The New Yorker" was first issued seven partners have successively withdrawn without having improved their fortunes by the connection and with the conviction that it was not calculated ever to prove lucrative. "You don't humbug enough" has been the complaint of more than one, "you ought to make more noise." Our course has not been changed by these representations. We are content with the

old course and have never envied the success which merit or pretense may attain by acting as its own trumpeter.

It was while he was getting out two publications one hundred and fifty miles apart, constantly borrowing from Peter to pay Paul, that Greeley had the pluck to write: "We love not the ways of that numerous class of malcontents perpetually finding fault with their vocation and endeavoring to prove themselves the most miserable dogs in creation. Nor do we deem those grumblers more plentiful among the brethren of the guild than those in other professions and we rejoice to say that we find them there neither few nor inconsiderable."

With no dread of overwork or of privations, through three depression years every effort and every dollar went into the *New Yorker*. Mrs. Greeley's wages as schoolteacher were willingly sacrificed, too, though every tomorrow had its doubtful forecast. What a story Greeley told in letters to old friends—the story of his willingness to edit his magazine "for nothing"—"for the love of it" if it will only survive—then of his suggestion to one of his friends, despite his own poverty, "Don't bother about what is due me until convenient."

Sunday, New York, June 8, 1838

Dear Diah:

I have just got a Cape Horn navigation ahead of me for a year and how much longer only God knows.

Don't bother about what is due me till it is convenient to pay it. I had the luck to have $5 in silver stolen out of my vest pocket on the steamboat last night. I deserved it for having so much of the cursed Bentonian stuff about me. My bills in my wallet were under my pillow and escaped.

H.G.

New York, June 30, 1839

Old Fellow: [O. A. Bowe]

I am getting along so-so—working confoundedly hard and existing on $12 a week, which I could do very easily and fatly if I had not every sort of call upon me. For instance, I have spent this week's salary already and not one sixpenny of it enures to my own advantage or belly.

Yours in great trepidation,

H.G.

New York, September 6, 1839

I am hard up as usual—harder than I have been for a long year, and must have money or break—but, of course, I shall fish it up somehow. I am at my old business—trying to buy out or change my partner.

Having very little to do for myself and nothing to get for it, and being badly in want of my daily bread-money, (I owe $50 personal and must borrow $50 more to pay board etc., to-morrow) I am about to undertake two or more little jobs—(I), to edit a Whig magazine; (II), to edit a Whig penny paper for Wilson as soon as the Whig "State" expires of intense stupidity; (III), to edit "The Jeffersonian" when it shall get going again. These enterprises, will, I hope, keep me out of mischief.

H.G.

"My embarrassments were sometimes dreadful," he wrote in later years of his *New Yorker* experience. "Not that I feared destitution, but the fear of involving my friends in my misfortune was very bitter." . . . "I speak of real debt—from all such let every youth pray God to preserve him evermore." . . . "All the wealth of a Rothschild would not recompense for a five years' struggle with the consciousness that you had taken the money of friends and had betrayed their confidence by insolvency."

But Greeley found recompense in every issue of the *New Yorker*. His devotion to it confirms his determination to identify himself with "literature, the arts and sciences." He was not then conscious that deeper in him was a spirit which needed only opportunity to reveal him, in the words of editor Dana, as "a man of genius, marked out from his cradle to inspire, animate and instruct his fellow-man."

The "Tippecanoe and Tyler, too" campaign revealed that Greeley. It was the lure that wedded him to newspapers and politics, and Thurlow Weed was the responsible man. When that ticket was nominated it was not in Greeley's mind to engage actively in the struggle to elect it. More than ever the *New Yorker* was his pride and his life. His reference to "my brief experience on the boiling sea of politics" in the following letter to Governor Seward indicates definitely that he began the winter of 1840 with no idea that before the year was out he would be stirred by a new ambition and actually planning to abandon his cherished magazine. Nor, of course, did Weed anticipate such a future for his young lieutenant. All that Weed knew was that he had a big job on his hands to carry New York against Van Buren; the popularity of the *Jeffersonian* had made another campaign weekly by Greeley a necessity. He must be persuaded—but how? Why not have Governor Seward invite him to dinner at the Executive Mansion? Seward did so and promptly received this reply:

Wednesday, Feb. 12, 1840

Gov. Seward:

Your invitation to dinner on Friday is gratefully received, but I shall not tax your hospitality. I have once already enjoyed the honor you tender me, which is enough for Glory. It will enable me, if it so please me hereafter, to preface anecdotes of my brief excursion on the boiling sea of politics with "Once when I was dining at my friend the Governor's." That will suffice. For dining as an art I have due respect, but I am not proficient therein—I have no taste—no time. I pray thee to have me excused.

Yours much obliged
H. Greeley

Hon. Wm. H. Seward

Was there ever another such letter of declination? Who but a Greeley "of much eccentricity" could have written it? "Dining is an art in which I am not proficent—I have no taste, no time"—are phrases not often used in response to a governor's invitation. The refusal amazed both Seward and Weed. But they needed Greeley. If he would not dine with a governor, why not bring him to the Executive Mansion after dinner to discuss policies? Greeley responded promptly to that suggestion. He liked to attend such conferences; they had real purpose. Of those visits Seward's son Frederick wrote: "Occasionally Weed brought with him to my father's house a slender, light-haired young man stooping and near-sighted, rather unmindful of forms and social usage, and yet singularly clear, original and decided in his political views and theories. This young man was Horace Greeley."

Weed's strategy worked. Greeley agreed to publish a weekly to be called "The Log Cabin" provided he would not be a salaried editor as before but owner. Eagerly he went to work. The campaign was to be a contest on behalf of the common people as against aristocrats. Such an issue aroused his enthusiasm. He was ready with the *Log Cabin* as early as May 2. Even the first number was prophetic of the Greeley "isms" of early *Tribune* days:

> This journal will be the advocate of the cause of the log cabin against that of the presidential palace ... and of the interests of unassuming industry against the schemes and devices of functionaries "drest in a little brief authority" whose salaries are trebled in value when labor is forced to beg for employment at three or four shillings a day ... We hope that our humble pretensions will be regarded with favor not for our sake but for the sake of the cause in which we are engaged with heart and soul—the Old Farmer of North Bend!

The familiar story of the 1840 campaign alleged that Van Buren had furnished the White House extravagantly with deep velvet carpets, satin and gold chairs, damask sofas and gilt candelabra; sumptuous dinners were served on gold plates, and wines of choicest vintages were decanted by liveried attendants. It was charged, too, that Van Buren wore corsets even tighter than those worn by fashionable women; also that he perfumed his hair. In contrast Harrison was pictured as living modestly on his farm in a log cabin. A friendly latchstring hanging from the door and a cider keg at the side were depicted as symbols of hospitality to the wayfarer. Actually they did not exist. History has truthfully characterized the campaign as pure humbug. It exceeded anything that P. T. Barnum ever devised to lure his circus audiences into joyously accepting. No one bothered whether the stories were fiction or fact; everyone wanted to believe them and to sing of them. Harrison obeyed instructions to say nothing, write nothing, deny nothing, affirm nothing. Van Buren always indignantly insisted that he was defeated "without a why or a wherefore"—"sung down and drunk down."

Greeley was responsible for the "sung down" feature. Despite Weed's early protest he insisted upon carrying in every issue of the *Log Cabin* a back page of words and music to be sung at campaign meetings. He is supposed to have written most of the verses himself and to have adapted them to popular tunes. "I agree that the music isn't worth much," he wrote to Weed, "but the people like the swing of it. After a song or two they are more ready to listen to the orators." The back page of the *Log Cabin* soon became the songbook of the campaign. Its editorals thus had a reading audience that could have been secured in no other way, and Greeley became a national figure.

"Now, my Democratic friends," popular Tom Corwin of Ohio—governor, senator and Fillmore's secretary of the treasury—would often say at the close of his speeches, "if you do not believe me you will find it all in Horace Greeley's 'Log Cabin,' which, I take it, is good enough political Bible for anyone and especially for those in need of salvation."

Financially, the "Log's" record was not satisfactory. Its subscriptions ran to 80,000, yet the failure of many patrons to pay kept Greeley in debt. "To those who owe us," he pleaded two months after the election, "we are compelled to say, 'Friends, we need our money! Our paper-maker needs it and has a right to ask for it; we only ask the means of paying what we owe! Once for all we implore you to do us justice and thus enable us to do justice to our creditors."

At the same time Greeley was writing to Bowe up in Herkimer:

New York, Tuesday, Dec. 22, 1840

O. A. Bowe,
Old Soul

What I shall do I'm blest if I know—only *one* thing is certain; I ain't a-going to hang myself so long as the Tories are kept out of power. I s'pose I might have got some wretched claw at the "Spoils"; but I want nothing of that sort; and have told all the magnates that I won't have the smell of anything. So that folly is out of the question,

Horace Greeley. From a Daguerreotype in the Collection of Mr. Peter Gilsey

Thurlow Weed, the Boss of Whig Politics

thank Fortune, and I am at liberty to get my Graham bread in the good old way. I reckon I shall come by it somehow.

Next, before I forget it, don't worry yourself about that note to me. If you have the funds when it is due, very good; if you haven't, don't bother—I can get along without it. I have got in some money for advance subscriptions to the "Log" and am expecting more, and I think I'll do somehow.

Do you see how I am getting up in the world lately? Two or three papers have named me for Postmaster-General and several have mentioned me for P.M. of this city! Of course I am at liberty to look down with contempt on small places, which I do devoutly. I want none of their dirty spoils—so old 'Tip' won't have the satisfaction of numbering me among his army of disappointed patriots. Truly their name is legion.

Well, 'Diah, here's health and prosperity too and a letter from you.

H.G.

As when he left East Poultney possessed of little money but with principles and habits that were to prove of great value, so, too, ten years later, at the close of the Tippecanoe campaign Greeley again had little money but something that was to be far more helpful. He had reputation. A much-talked-about political firm of Weed, Seward & Greeley was in control of New York state, but how was that association benefiting him? Weed was established as the strategist and leader of the Whig-organized forces; Seward was again governor; Greeley alone had drawn a blank out of the triumph which since 1838 he had worked so hard to win.

Was there no reward for him except the reputation he himself had made? Was no helping hand to be extended to the young editor still struggling with his *New Yorker?*

"I'm blest if I know!" Greeley had written to Bowe.

And "I'm blest if I care!" appears to have been the attitude of both Weed and Seward. Weed had not written to Greeley since the election; Seward, though returned as governor, had not even thanked him for his campaign work. Once again it was Greeley's job to look out for himself, just as it had been after the first election of Seward as governor. In fact that is exactly what he had been doing throughout his association with the two men. Both knew Greeley's desperate financial straits with the *New Yorker*. Without much effort either man at any time could have lightened his heavy burden. It was no secret to them that he was constantly borrowing from financial Shylocks, but he was never offered, and, be it said to his credit, he never sought, aid from the two men from whom he had earned the right at least to expect it. What Greeley wanted was voluntary recognition by Weed and Seward for his work; but he would not beg it. He never forgot nor forgave their neglect, as his historic letter to Seward in 1854 revealed.

Greeley, of course, knew their ways. They would have no requests from him. "I want nothing of the sort," he wrote Rufus W. Griswold in Philadelphia, whose newspaper was suggesting him for postmaster-general. Griswold had been with Greeley on the *New Yorker*. "... I will not have the world say that I have given hours to the Whig cause with the expectation or design of getting office. Gris, I pray you to have a care as to your practice with the long bow. It is too venturesome. The things you have said of me are more incredible than anything in Munchausen."

In Pennsylvania, Cameron's Whig machine, appreciating Greeley's work with the *Log Cabin*, was eager to make him state printer, and to employ him to edit three of their party newspapers. But he declined. "I know some of the Pennsylvania politicians too well," he wrote politician Weed—of all men. "They are more rapacious and unprincipled, if possible, than politicians in general. ... I did not know that the 'Log' was not going to you.... I did think, however, that you had forgotten me, but that I did not cry about."

CHAPTER VI

The *Tribune*—Greeley's Pulpit

NEVER SO RESTLESS, never so keenly ambitious, was the Greeley of that winter of 1841. The *New Yorker* and the *Log Cabin* were bringing him some overdue subscription money, and he was still earning by his writings for other publications. It was the first winter since 1836 in which finances were not his serious anxieties. "I am beginning to feel quite snug and comfortable," he informed Weed. "I am now able to look bank cashiers full in the face."

Weed could not understand why the *Log Cabin* was still being published. In the letter dated January 27, previously quoted in part, Greeley answered his query: "I want to print it for one year for my own sake. I feel that my honor and character are pledged that the Whigs will act in power as they have talked when out of power—that they will honestly reform abuses."

Actually he had something much more important in mind—something which he did not care to reveal to Weed: he was planning to establish a daily newspaper! The origin of the *Log Cabin* stamped it as a party organ. It could have no opinions of its own!—no purpose outside of politics. Of course, such a publication could not possibly be a steppingstone to fame such as young Seward prophesied for him. He must stand alone on that stone. Besides, it was not in Greeley's spirit to be a "me, too." Seward took a different attitude. After his election as governor he wrote to Weed on December 14, 1838: "The sweetness of his temper inclines me to love my tyrant. I had no idea that dictators are such amiable creatures. It reminds me of old Hassan's (Fatima's father) expression to Bluebeard, 'My dear terrible son-in-law'." No such submissive spirit ever prevailed in Greeley. "I burn incense at the feet of no man," he declared. And, "I must be myself."

The new ambition forecast the end of the *New Yorker*. In sentiment that meant a great deal to its founder. If man gains perfection through suffering it may be that a magazine of one's own creation—"the kind I have in my mind's eye," as Greeley once wrote hopefully—grips you more and more because of the sacrifices it demands of you.

The "Yorker," as he always referred to it, certainly gripped Greeley even though to meet its persistent deficits had been his torment: "I lived as a miser." However, the "Yorker's" time had come. In September those paid-up magazine subscribers who would not accept the *Weekly Tribune*, or "Try-bune," as it became known throughout the country, in exchange were refunded the uncompleted portion of their subscription, though Greeley was never able to salvage much from the nonpaying group. Almost the only note of discontent in his *Recollections* is his reference to "years that, though full of labor and of exacting care, might have been happy had they not been made wretched by these men's dishonesty. They took my journal and probably read it; they promised to pay but defaulted, leaving me to pay my paper-maker and my type-founder as best I could."

The days seemed too long and too many before he was able to begin his newspaper career. In February he published in the *Southern Literary Messenger* some verses of his own composition, in which he plainly indicated the policies he was to pursue:

A stern high duty
Now serves my arm and fires my brain,
To war on Fraud entrenched with Power—
On smooth Pretence and specious Wrong—
This task be mine, though Fortune lower,
For this be banished sky and song!

Greeley was then only thirty years old. He had had no daily newspaper experience except as an editorial contributor and, of course, none at all as a publisher. Already entrenched in the morning field were Ben Day's eight-year-old *Sun,* James Gordon Bennett's six-year-old *Herald,* James Watson Webb's *Courier and Enquirer,* and David Hale's *Journal of Commerce.* With a total circulation of 60,000, those newspapers seemed to meet the needs at that time of a city having less than 200,000 inhabitants.

But Greeley's venture was not hindered by thoughts of competition. He had a gospel to preach; it was the neediest gospel of the time, and his chosen pulpit was a newspaper. He would name it "The Tribune"—for it was to be a platform from which he would speak to and for the people. There was much to be done in their behalf; in the doing of it he would be assailed as a dreamer—perhaps driven out. Yet someone must protest against existing conditions and he had voice, sympathy and courage. He firmly believed then, as John Russell Young said of him, that "the world was permeated with harsh employers, free traders, idle folk and drinkers. He proposed to convert it to fair employers, high tariffs, thrift and Temperance."

If ever a man was moved "by faith and not by sight" young Greeley was that man when, with one thousand borrowed dollars, he undertook a newspaper proclaiming such a purpose in the nation's commercial center. Yet "only the germ of the newspaper that I had in mind," to quote Greeley's reference to the first issue of the *Tribune,* still survives as the only New York City morning newspaper more than one hundred years old, with the *Herald* and the *Morning Sun*—its only predecessors—buried in its bosom. The *Times,* founded in 1851, is the only other morning newspaper that has stood the test of nearly a century in that city. Almost one hundred million dollars have been sacrificed in efforts to establish newspapers on Manhattan Island since Greeley undertook one with a slender purse, and conducted it until his death thirty-one years later with never a year of loss. Call them what you will, echo, if you will, the derisions of his time, there must have been something vital, close to humanity's needs, in policies that led to such prosperity while so many other newspapers were, one by one, fading away. More than that, in the social welfare legislation of nation and states today you find a heritage of many of the "isms" ridiculed then. If a seven-day work week with twelve hours a day is now a five-day week of forty or forty-eight hours, it was Greeley's *Tribune* that first leavened that lump of inhumanity; if wage earners are now organized into unions, Greeley organized the first printers' union and was its first president; if profit sharing prevails in many corporations, Greeley set the example by selling many of his own *Tribune* shares to his associates; if women now have the right to vote, remember that it was Greeley who was cartooned as a champion of their cause.

Yes—there were other "isms" that Greeley advocated which, reader, you and I probably would not endorse. Unto this late day they afford his belittling critics their opportunity to enlarge upon and discredit him; but on record as the real guide for measuring the man are the great causes for which he stood, the upright life that he led and the nation-wide influence of his *Tribune*—both daily and weekly.

Greeley announced his newspaper without a word in advance to Weed. Frankly surprised, the latter nevertheless, in his Albany *Evening Journal*, gave the newcomer cordial welcome into the newspaper world. Why not? He had been his political lieutenant in charge of publicity; he had followed organization policies without dissent; there was every reason why Weed should regard the *Tribune* as a new asset in his political capital—every reason but one. That one was Horace Greeley—"no man's man." Weed overlooked that reason.

Training, industry and ambition were Greeley's greatest assets. He also had reputation and some credit. He estimated that he was worth $2,000, chiefly in printing materials. He bought paper and type on credit and borrowed $1,000 from his friend James Coggeshall.

Originally the plan was to issue the *Tribune* on March 4—the date of Harrison's inauguration as President; this would have emphasized its national Whig character. Inability to get mechanical equipment in time made that impossible. Finally, on April 3—one day before Harrison's death—the *Log Cabin* carried this "card":

NEW YORK TRIBUNE

On Saturday, the tenth day of April instant, the Subscriber will publish the first number of a New Morning Journal of Politics, Literature and General Intelligence.

"The Tribune," as its name imports, will labor to advance the interests of the People, and to promote their Moral, Social and Political well-being. The immoral and degrading Police Reports, Advertisements and other matter which have been allowed to disgrace the columns of our leading Penny Papers will be carefully excluded from this, and no exertion spared to render it worthy of the hearty approval of the virtuous and refined, and a welcome visitant at the family fireside.

Earnestly believing that the political revolution which has called William Henry Harrison to the Chief Magistracy of the Nation was a triumph of Right Reason and Public Good over Error and Sinister Ambition, "The Tribune" will give to the New Administration a frank and cordial but manly and independent support, judging it always by its acts, and commending those only so far as they seem calculated to subserve the great end of all government—the welfare of the People.

"The Tribune" will be published every morning on a fair royal sheet—(size of "The Log Cabin" and "Evening Signal")—and transmitted to its city subscribers at the low price of *one cent* per copy.

Horace Greeley, 30 Ann St.

A more disheartening time could not have been chosen, for on that day funeral ceremonies for the deceased President were held in New York City. Those who are familiar with April sleet in that city will understand the chilly reception accorded Greeley's *Tribune* by the weather man also. It certainly did not bring much cheer to a Whig newspaper making its initial appearance or to an editor having borrowed dollars at stake in addition to his own last one. "The leaden sky, the wintriness, the general gloom," as Greeley described his feelings that morning, "were not ineptly miniatured in my own prospects and fortunes."

James Gordon Bennett's five-year-old prosperous *Herald* did not think much of Greeley's initial appeal to the public. He recalled his own announcement in the first issue of the *Herald* six years earlier: " 'We know,' says the fair Ophelia, 'where we are, but know not what we might be.' In debuts of this kind many talk of principle—political principle, party principle—as a sort of steel trap to catch the public. We mean to be perfectly frank on this point, and therefore openly discredit all steel traps—all principle, as it is called, all party, all Politics. Our only guide shall be good, sound, practical common sense. We shall support no party, be the organ of no faction or coterie, and care nothing for any election or any candidate, from President down to constable."

Promptly Greeley avowed his keen interest in the election of our Presidents and in Whig principles: "If the advocates of those principles shall see fit to support cordially and actively our enterprise not only by taking our paper but by giving it one-half so much advertising patronage as they now bestow on the deadliest enemies of their Cause, we shall be able to go on successfully and efficiently; if not, we shall persevere as long as we shall be able to do so."

The *Tribune* was housed on the second floor and attic in the rear building at Number 30 of narrow, mud-holed, cobble-stoned Ann Street with its little secondhand bookshops, their dust-covered windows gridironed with wires on which sheets of popular song hits were clothespinned, as well as yellow-covered paper editions of startling tales of tragedy, crime and Indian wars. There, in the *New Yorker* rooms, the type was set and collected into columns and pages with material belonging to the magazine or else bought on credit at Bruce's Type Foundry (where, it will be recalled, Greeley, in 1832, got his first credit of $40 in material for his printing firm). There was neither money nor credit with which to purchase a press. For that reason, the forms—made-up pages of type—had to be locked securely so that they could be safely wheeled to a pressroom several city blocks distant—always a perilous journey for type.

Despite snow and rain, Greeley followed the forms to the pressroom. We may be sure there was a thrill of pride as he read "Horace Greeley, Editor" on the first page of the first copy of the *Tribune* that came off the press while he stood beside it. That first copy marked not only for him the beginning of thirty years of a notable career, but also for another person. On the editorial page appeared a line, "Assisted by H. J. Raymond." Such generous recognition of a young man then in his employ only six months and not yet a year out of college is worthy of immediate attention, for it was to have historic significance for journalism, for national politics and for Greeley personally.

Henry Jarvis Raymond, born in 1820 at Lima, Livingston County, New York, had written several articles for the *New Yorker* while a student at the University of Vermont. After graduating in 1840 he advertised for a position in the South as a schoolteacher or private tutor. He turned to New York City for a bread-and-butter job while awaiting responses. The fact that he was a University of Vermont boy made Raymond welcome to Greeley, though he also carried a letter from Rufus W. Griswold, then in Philadelphia, who in youth had lived at Brandon, a short distance from East Poultney, and knew Greeley there. Raymond wrote Griswold that he had been most cordially received.

To Griswold, Greeley at once wrote of this man who was to be his keenest rival: "I decided to keep him because I believe that I can train him in the way he should go."

He made the *New Yorker* his headquarters—doing odd jobs for the magazine. Shortly he received an offer from a school in North Carolina.

"Want to go, Raym?" asked Greeley.

"No," replied Raymond, "but it's the best I can do."

"What will they pay you?"

"Four hundred a year," replied Raymond.

"Better stay here, Raym," said Greeley. "I'll give you that."

So Raymond remained with Greeley to become six years later in the *Courier and Enquirer* his persistent, harmful critic, and from 1851 to 1869 editor of the New York *Times*.

"He decided the whole course of my life" was the most friendly reference Raymond ever publicly made to Greeley.

Though Greeley was no stranger to work that had no hour limits, he soon became more familiar than ever with it in his new venture. For several months he remained after publication every morning to aid in folding the large sheet—"as big as a turnip field," he said of it—for distribution. "It was not much of a newspaper," Greeley conceded of this initial effort, "but it was the best I could do at the price."

His genius for securing attention was never demonstrated more decisively than in the first issue of his newspaper. At once he opened fire on the depravity of the news and advertising columns of the *Herald* and the *Sun,* thus shrewdly luring those newspapers into a word battle that gave his *Tribune* publicity which it could not have secured in any other way. Commenting first on the *Sun,* Greeley said: "Its editorial department is generally pure in morals and correct if not elevated in its tendency, but its advertising columns exhibit and reflect unreproved every species of depravity."

The *Sun* finally closed the argument by declaring that "Horace Greeley's miserable evasions strengthen our opinion that with all his assumed honesty he is a willful falsifier of the truth. At that we let him go as too contemptible for further notice from us."

The *Herald* came in for condemnation for its daily detailed reports of the trial of a murderer in New Brunswick, New Jersey, "with a most unprincipled and reckless disregard of consequences—nay, eager for the sake of private gain to poison the fountains of public intelligence and to fan with destroying flames the hellish passions which now slumber in the bosom of society...."

The *Tribune* of April 14 continued:

> We weigh well our words when we say that the moral guilt incurred and the violent hurt inflicted upon social order by those who thus spread out the loathsome details of the most damning deed, are ten-fold greater than those of the miscreant himself.... The wretched plea of the "duty of the press to society"—that it is bound to keep the public informed—is urged, but the same hypocrites who stab the public good under this protection turn a deaf ear to the higher duties which they owe to the good of their fellow-men and to the requirements of decent morality.

Bennett replied next day with his "galvanized New England squash" editorial:

Horace Greeley is endeavoring, with tears in his eyes, to show that it is very naughty to publish reports of the trial, confession and execution of Peter Robinson. "It makes one feel like a murderer," says Greeley. No doubt he thinks it's equally naughty in us to publish a paper at all; and if we would stop "The Herald" he might condescend to thank us. "A marvelously proper man." Now this Horace Greeley, BA and ASS, is probably the most unmitigated blockhead connected with the newspaper press. Galvanize a large New England squash, and it would make as capable an editor as Horace.

Thus, through life, Greeley and Bennett muddied the editorial pages of their newspapers with personal abuse of each other.

The cost of publishing the *Tribune* the first week was $510, allowing no income for the editor and owner; the receipts were $92.10. Nevertheless, on May 10, Greeley wrote hopefully to Weed: "I am getting ahead very well but thus far I have not had $30 of advertising from Whigs as such, though I expected more. I don't want to beg any of it, but I shall have a hard fight to live through the summer without some help of the kind. I was offered $50 to move to Wall Street. It would give me advantages but probably not increased popularity for the paper. I think I shall not try it."

Exactly one month later, on June 10, "Friend Griswold," over in Philadelphia, received this letter from Greeley indicating slow progress: "I am poor as a church mouse and not half so saucy. I had losses this week, and am perplexed and afflicted. But better luck must come. I am fishing for a partner."

Fortunately there was a pickup in circulation and Greeley's venture was definitely on its way to success. He was also announcing, "We have a number of requests to blow up all sorts of abuses, which shall be attended to as soon as possible."... "The indulgence of advertisers is besought for this day only—tomorrow their favors will appear."... "We raise our advertising rates from 4 cents to 6 cents a line."... "Everything appears to work well with us."

Real assurance of success, however, came in July when Greeley's "fishing for a partner" brought to him Thomas McElrath, whom Greeley had met while setting type in West's Chatham Street printing shop. He paid $2,000 for a half interest and was made business manager. Later Greeley told this story of their relation:

> From that hour my load was palpably lightened.... During the ten years of Greeley & McElrath, my partner never once even indicated that my anti-slavery, anti-hanging, socialist and other aberrations from the straight and narrow path of Whig partisanship were injurious to our common interest, though he must have often felt sorely that they were so; and never, except when I (rarely) drew from the common treasury more money than could well be spared, in order to help some needy friend whom he judged beyond help, did he even look grieved at anything I did.... Henceforth, such pecuniary troubles as I encountered were the just penalties of my own folly in indorsing notes, etc.

No newspaper could survive through one hundred and five such years as have elapsed since the first issue of the *Tribune* without inviting comparisons that seem like dreams in cost and scope between its $510-a-week beginning and its (estimated solely by the author) $35,000-a-day present cost of publication; between Greeley's $15-a-week salary during his first two years and the pay of a present-day editor; particularly is the contrast startling when made with a newspaper founded while it was still a marvel to cross the Atlantic in fifteen days at best by steam and thirty days by sail; while the telegraph was known only as a laboratory experiment, railroads were few and of limited mileage and speed, and news traveled by "pony express," stagecoach or rumor. Yet news gathering then had its keen and costly rivalries even as they exist today. For example, with the Hudson River frozen over, and no railroad from Albany to New York, the *Tribune* resorted to "our trusty riders who never let the grass grow under their horses' feet," as Greeley boastfully proclaimed after publishing this "beat" on his rivals:

> The Governor's message reached us from Albany last evening at nine o'clock. The contract calls for three riders and ten relays of horses. It started at midnight and took 21 hours for 155 miles. Be that as it may the dispatch is almost, if not quite, unparalleled in history.

Determined as Greeley was to have the *Tribune* first with the news, his deepest purpose was to make it powerful in forming public opinion. Surely there can be no need to state here that a search for wealth had no part in his ambitions at any time. It is plainly written across every act of his sixty-one years that, though every dollar he ever possessed was earned by his own labor, money had but little value as such to him and no staying quality. Not dollars but power was his aim—power to fight the inequities he saw all about him. Greeley really summed up his whole life when in 1842, as he saw the *Tribune* prospering, he wrote back to East Poultney: "I mean to make something of myself." He achieved that ambition—but at what a price!

This page is not the place to do more in estimating it than to glance thirty years ahead to those pitiful asylum two weeks of a brain-tired, bankrupt, defeated pleader to North and South to "clasp hands across the bloody chasm," whose last appeal to the North on behalf of the South was that "theirs is a lost cause but they are not a lost people"—finally, to his incoherent weeping at his loneliness and the futility of his life's efforts. Instead, let us take up now the stirring story of this young, vigorous, unhesitating son of the New Hampshire–Vermont wilderness in his remarkable career as editor of a New York City daily newspaper.

Except for the initial $1,000 loan from his friend Coggeshall he had no financial ties; therefore, he would do "no man's bidding." A quotation attributed to Emerson drifted through newspapers at that time to the effect that "when nature is seriously bent upon accomplishing a result she overloads the tendency. When she wants slavery abolished she provides a William Lloyd Garrison; when she wants a 'Tribune of the people' she provides a Horace Greeley."

Here in this new newspaper people soon found that they had a champion as bold as any knight of chivalry and as ready to throw his challenging glove into the arena of conflict. Promptly Greeley lifted editorial writing out of servility, out of suspicion, out of the commonplace. Earnestly and courageously, he gave it self-dependence, purpose and character. He never forgot the lines from his favorite Burns:

Here's freedom to him that wad read,
  Here's freedom to him that wad write;
There's none ever feared that truth should be heard
  But those whom the truth would indite.

Though Greeley had McElrath as a partner to manage the business of his newspaper he never had a partner in its news or editorial departments. There he reigned supreme. He could write with directness and conviction; if necessary he could put his words into type by his own hand; he could "make up" the pages for the press, and then do his share of the work of operating it—all with the skill that comes only with experience from the bottom up. This thorough equipment for newspaper making, his unresting energy, his desire for a newspaper of character and completeness, infused his associates with the same purpose during all the years he was their chief.

And what a staff that was!

What other editor has ever brought to his side such a group of writers as Charles A. Dana, editor of the New York *Sun*, Henry J. Raymond, editor of the New York *Times*, Whitelaw Reid, Charles T. Congdon, George Ripley, Isaac H. Bromley, John R. G. Hassard, Sidney Howard Gay, Amos J. Cummings, George W. Smalley, William Winter, Bayard Taylor, Junius Henri Browne, John Russell Young, William Henry Fry, James Shepherd Pike, Margaret Fuller, Elizabeth Peabody, Moncure D. Conway, John Hay, George William Curtis, editor of *Harper's Weekly*, and Joseph Bucklin Bishop, onetime editor of the New York *Evening Post*.

Russell Young became notable later as managing editor of the *Herald*, and then as historian of President Grant's famous tour of the world in 1878–79. In his *Men and Memories*, he said of this *Tribune* group: "They were brilliant, capable, irresponsible, intolerant, not above setting things on fire just for the fun of seeing them burn. They attracted Greeley because of their earnestness and charmed his literary sense with their gifts. They were proud to be known as 'Greeley's young men'." "I rejoice that I took my first degree in journalism in such a school and under such a master," wrote George William Curtis.

Unfortunately Greeley never inspired that closer relation that may be termed affection for their leader. Seldom did anyone except Dana ever refer to him in that familiar term "the Old Man." That was a common expression in newspaper offices before the staff became as numerous as an army and the chief as distant from the ranks as a commanding general.

But it was not in Greeley's nature to encourage it. In the day's labor there was for him no time for sentiment. Stern duty ruled; work well done was greeted with pleasant words. But mistakes in dates or facts! They were unforgivable, for his own mind was as exact as his *Tribune Almanac*. He was an unsparing critic of the careless and the lazy; for a mean act he had no mercy, for a clumsy one but little; his explosive words were not of the kind heard in polite society; frequently their coarseness shocked everybody as they sounded through the office like a shriek; often he was full of praises, then of impatience. No one knew in advance which mood to expect, but all knew that like a spring shower the clouds would soon be scattered by sunshine.

Despite these weaknesses of temper Greeley held his associates together in a unity of effort. They saw in him a master spirit—different from any of them, living wholly within himself yet engaged in unending battle for others. Association with Greeley was "a delight," in the opinion of George Ripley, who in 1846 came over from abandoned Brook Farm to begin a thirty-three-year career on the *Tribune*. There he won the title of "father of literary criticism."

Take the experience of Bayard Taylor as typical of the encouragement Greeley gave to all. In 1848 Taylor was advised by poet Nathaniel P. Willis that his talent would have a future if he would abandon a weekly newspaper he was editing in West Chester, Pennsylvania, and establish himself in New York City. He wrote to William Cullen Bryant for a position on the *Evening*

Post but received only a discouraging reply about life in a big city. Taylor also wrote to Greeley. "Stay in the country!" replied Greeley. "All the aspiring talent and conceit of our own country and of Europe crowd our pavements and every newspaper is overloaded with assistants. Life is very hurried and fretful in a great city."

But Taylor made a bolt for what he called "the mighty metropolis"—and Greeley gave him a job! "I think you have done wrong," Greeley told him, "but I'll try you for six weeks." Taylor went to work; he had heard nothing further from Greeley for three months when the latter one morning entered his room and said: "You have been faithful; you need a rest. Take a week somewhere in New England." When Taylor returned from his vacation he discovered that his salary had been increased.

Nor was that encouraging incident the only one which made Taylor's connection with the *Tribune* the basis for his fame as traveler, author and poet. During the winter of 1849 Greeley was in Washington serving as Congressman for the unexpired ninety days of a term. While there he was also giving attention to the *Tribune* as closely as ever; his frequent letters of frank comment were awaited every morning at the *Tribune* office with what may reasonably be called keen interest. What would he commend? What would he condemn—and why? For Greeley never dissented without stating his reasons. One letter, however, though not the only one of praise, had a most cordial reception as it was read to the whole staff by Taylor:

Washington, January 13, 1849

Dear Bayard:

I must not defer to thank you for your article on Pope Pius IX the other day. It was very well done indeed. I wish you would resolve henceforth to write one such article per week, and sign your own initials or some distinguishing mark at bottom. I want everyone connected with "The Tribune" to become known to the public as doing what he does.

H.G.

"I want everyone connected with 'The Tribune' to become known to the public as doing what he does"—how encouraging those words must have been to a staff just beginning their climb to high places in journalism! There you find the Greeley who knew so well how to surround himself with competent men and women and to intensify their ambition. What matters if tomorrow there comes a word of complaint—perhaps a guiding hand to better work! The letter to Taylor is of historic value as the first encouragement by an editor to members of his staff to sign their articles and thereby create an individual identity. The by-lines now so familiar to readers had their beginning in that letter to Taylor about one hundred years ago. It is just another evidence of Greeley's talent as a newspaper builder. Seven years later the letter had a companion piece revealing again his ability in that respect in this instruction to managing editor Dana:

Washington, April 9, 1856

Dana:

I want inventions treated like other occurrences with more or less emphasis according to their importance—not treated as though a new motive power and a new currycomb were of equal consequence. If a man invents a new locomotive that could be profitably used in cornfields and on common roads, I should wish to announce it in a leader on the very day it was patented, whereas by your present method it would probably appear the next month in a supplement buried deep under new raspberries and improved bee-hives. Is that the thing?

I am totally disqualified to judge of the value of inventions in general; you take little interest in them. I believe that the history of human progress is written in them and I want to see history early and faithfully reported in our columns. I want to have less and less to do with politics and more and more with productive industry. I feel that the path of empire—journalistic and all other—stretches in that direction. Let us be first to act on this knowledge. It will win few subscribers today but it will be character that will ultimately be coined. I do believe that our daily with five years of reputation as the first to recognize and honor inventive genius would be a far better property than at present.

H.G.

CHAPTER VII

"Shaking Tyler Over the Warm Place"

THERE WERE MANY discouragements for Greeley during his thirty years as editor and politician, but none that affected him more keenly than the unhappy plight of his beloved Whig party as well as the fading presidential prospects for his still more beloved Henry Clay when William Henry Harrison died one month after inauguration as President. Clay was to Greeley "the eagle-eyed, genial-hearted, living master-spirit of our time." With Harrison in the White House, almost seventy years old and pledged to a single term, the Kentucky aspirant had promise of strong administration support to succeed him as President; until then old "Tippecanoe" would, of course, bear the title but Clay would be the acknowledged "keeper of the palace" and hold the Whig majority in Congress under his leadership. With "Tippecanoe" dead and fifty-one-year-old Tyler in the White House, unpledged to a single term and uncertain in his Whig loyalty, there was no such prospect.

The story of "John Tyler, President" is well known, but the story of the futile efforts of Greeley (aged thirty) and his just-born *Tribune* to hold the "accidental" President to Whig doctrine is not. The situation was ideal for the young editor, for it gave him opportunity to impress his newspaper nationally. Success in that respect, however, was Greeley's only triumph throughout the "roaring forties," as that decade was often termed. Fortunately, that one triumph was big and lasting. During those ten years Greeley was to see Clay go down in a second and final defeat for election to the presidency; he was to begin his long fight for homestead legislation; he was to see the Whig party split into factions that doomed its existence—and, too, he was to meet persistent abuse because of his advocacy of "Greeley's isms"—particularly Fourierism. Still worse, three of his children were to die, and his Turtle Bay home in east-side New York City proved to be what he called a "Castle Doleful."

For the moment, however, we are concerned with Greeley's efforts to hold Tyler in line. He appealed to the country to accept the new President as a Whig: "We hope that nobody will doubt that John Tyler is a thorough-going Whig. Certainly if he is not he has changed since we became acquainted with him at the Harrisburg convention seventeen months since. There was not a truer Whig in the country then."

For the obvious purpose of committing Tyler to Whig policies Clay speeded through Congress his bill to re-establish the United States Bank which Jackson had destroyed. While it was awaiting the President's signature, Greeley advised him to "realize the great responsibility of a veto." At the same time he told Whigs not to abuse Tyler until he had acted. "Let us hear him first," he urged, "and then judge. If he is unfaithful to the principles and pledges on which he was elevated to power let him be visited with public indignation."

To several senators who visited the White House on Saturday, August 14, Tyler stated that he believed his message to Congress would be a veto, but he expected "to go to church on Sunday and there earnestly and devoutly pray for guidance as to his duty." Whatever response he may have received to his prayer did not change his Saturday purpose.

Nevertheless Greeley still clung to Tyler's coattails—still hoped for reconciliation. "The failure of no one measure can destroy the Whig party," he insisted. "If it cannot govern the country usefully we are ready to see it upset by its adversaries, but we do trust that it will not be croaked, groaned and prophesied down by its friends."

All that summer Greeley kept warning the Whig Congress:

"We can destroy Whig supremacy, we may break up the Cabinet, but we cannot depose President Tyler."

When the New York state Whig convention met at Syracuse on October 7 Greeley wrote the resolutions and was proud of the way in which he there handled the refractory President. "We did just right on the main point," he advised his Herkimer editor friend Bowe. "We shook John Tyler over the warm place, but didn't go so far as to say that he should be chucked in—just yet. We leave him space for repentance and tell him how to go about to get it."

Defeat of the Whigs in 1841 in many of the states carried by them in 1840 recalled to Whig leaders Greeley's July admonition, "We can destroy Whig supremacy ... but we cannot depose President Tyler...." In December he wrote: "Our wounds need probing and not plastering. The next session of Congress should witness a cordial reconciliation between the President and the Whigs or a formal and thorough separation." But who could negotiate such a truce? Certainly none of the party leaders in Washington who had been denouncing Tyler! Only one man had been fair enough to qualify as a possible peacemaker.

That man was Horace Greeley—Greeley of the *Log Cabin* with its well-remembered popularity and now Greeley of the *Tribune* who was shaking Tyler over "the warm place" but not chucking him in "—just yet." They called him to Washington to pour oil upon the troubled waters and perhaps to edit the *Madisonian.*

Within a week Greeley had returned home convinced that "Tyler and his 'kitchen' Cabinet do not want to harmonize with the Whig party, do not want peace, or to carry their measures, but mean to keep up the quarrel as long as possible with a view to the succession. There is music ahead."

"Treason is lurking in the Capitol," shouted Greeley when there were intimations that Tyler would veto the protective tariff bill passed by the Whig Congress; when the veto came he denounced Tyler as "a Judas backed by unscrupulous followers engaged in a conspiracy to defeat the overwhelming desire of the country that Clay should be elected President in 1844."

Thus, at last, Greeley chucked him into "the warm place." When readers reminded him of his appeals only a year earlier on behalf of "the old Virginia Whig," Greeley replied: "Men always hate those they have wronged—and Tyler fairly detests those he has betrayed. He stands forth an embittered, implacable foe of the party that raised him to the pinnacle of power."

Tylerism or no Tylerism, there was one issue ever in Greeley's mind—Clay's succession to the presidency. He kept it in the forefront of discussion. To drive Tyler out of the White House would not be difficult, for even Tyler's party, if he had one, did not want him; but to put Clay in his place was another matter. However, Greeley did not think so. He was confident that the people only waited opportunity to make good to Clay for having preferred Andrew Jackson in 1832. His admiration for the Kentucky senator was in line with his own native-born zeal for just such a spirited America as that for which Clay was the leading exponent.

Following the 1837–40 depression there was a firmer faith everywhere in the destiny of this New World land of promise. Emigrants—hard-working, thrifty—were crossing the Atlantic in increasing thousands from Ireland, Germany, England and Scandinavia to clear our wilderness, plow our prairies, open our mines or work in factories that were creating new villages and cities. Many New England families had already led the way to the tempting West, but throughout the "fabulous forties" the movement marked the furthest substantial penetration beyond the Mississippi almost to the Rocky Mountains by natives and foreign-born alike.

Then, too, Maine-designed clipper ships—bigger and faster freighters—were outsailing England's boasted fleet to every port; a message by telegraph from Washington to Baltimore astonished people with a new wonder; our railroad mileage was increasing faster and totaled more than in all the rest of the world combined; in five years New York City had almost doubled its population and its commercial activities had increased in diversity and wealth to figures that cleared all doubt of its future. Boston was proudly pluming itself as the modern Athens. Gaudy showboats had begun their sensational racing up and down the Father of Waters, with wealthy cotton planters risking fortunes in palatial gambling parlors above decks while their shackled negro slaves crowded the pens below; rumors of gold in distant California invested the whole era with a halo of still more hopeful promise.

Yes—even as early as that first half of the 1840's—there was a vision of possibilities for our half-century-old nation that made an "ocean-to-ocean America" an inspiring patriotic prospect. People called it our "manifest destiny." "The two oceans are our boundary fixed by God!" declared young Stephen A. Douglas, serving his first term in Congress from Illinois. "These acquisitions of territory will prove fearful calamities," warned Greeley, "inflating our people with pride and corrupting them with the lust of conquest and gold." From Webster in the Senate came the wish "that our country would exhibit to the world the example of a powerful Republic without greediness for Empire. I resist today and forever every proposal to add any foreign territory north, south, east or west of the 26 states that now constitute the Union." Nevertheless, expansion was what the people desired, slavery or no slavery. Of course—and why not?—despite Clay, Webster and Greeley, the Republic of Texas was taken over by Tyler at its own request! Of course, too, in 1848—and again why not?—after a two years' war with Mexico, we paid that government $15,000,000 for its 500,000 square miles of Indian-ruled wilderness extending from the Rio Grande to Canada. Popular, too, was the slogan "54°40′ or fight," not because there was any deep concern for that boundary line of faraway wilderness Oregon but chiefly because the cry echoed old-time antagonism to Great Britain.

Such were the issues when the Whig national convention met in Baltimore in May 1844. There was no opposition to Clay's nomination, nor did it ever seem probable that Democrat James Knox Polk, of Tennessee—a dark-horse, ninth-ballot nominee whom, it was said, nobody knew—could defeat Clay, a unanimous nominee whom everybody knew. Yet "Little Jimmy" Polk, as they called him down in his home state, did that very thing!

Greeley had really wanted Van Buren as Clay's opponent. "Man overboard!" he yelled when the Democrats dropped their 1840 candidate. "You cried that Van Buren had been 'sung down and drunk down' four years ago," he told them, "and it is but just that you should nominate him now. Why do you flunk?"

"Of Clay's nomination not a word need be said," declared the enthusiastic *Tribune*, as the national convention adjourned. "It had been virtually made a long time since by one million and a half Whig voters. . . . He is a statesman, a Christian and a patriot, and he will be elected by an immense majority of the people."

Greeley advised the candidate to remain at his Kentucky home and build up his health, allowing others "to take care of the country's cause and its champion." And of these "others" no one worked more tirelessly than he.

During that campaign began the headaches, the nervous irritations, the sleepless nights, the peevish temper that continued throughout Greeley's remaining years. They were in fact the cause of his mental breakdown in 1861 and of his death. After his own defeat for President in 1872 Greeley wrote that he was not so keenly affected by that result as he had been by Clay's defeat in 1844—"for then the universe seemed to me to have come to an end. . . . I have admired and trusted many statesmen but I profoundly loved Henry Clay. . . . I loved him for his generous nature, his gallant bearing, his brilliant eloquence, his fervid patriotism, and his lifelong devotion to what I deemed our country's unity, prosperity and renown. . . . He was more fitted to win and enjoy popularity than any other American who ever lived."

CHAPTER VIII

"Greeley's Isms"

More fixed in Greeley's mind than politics when he founded the *Tribune* was his eagerness for what he called progress in social welfare. Denouncing Tyler was just partisanship, but a battle for the common man had all the intensity and high purpose of a crusade. It certainly reflected his spirit. He did not wait to speak out until he was safely beyond the danger of unpleasant financial consequences to himself or to his newspaper! At once he was a target for ridicule and coarse abuse by the many do-nothings. "Let them work twenty years as hard as I have done," responded Greeley, "and feel and know the hopelessness of the great mass of laborers, the emptiness of their lives, the dullness of their few leisure hours as I do before they attempt to lecture me.... Do not stand there quarrelling with those who have devised or adopted a scheme that you consider absurd," he continued. "Take hold and devise something better, for be assured, friends, that this generation will not longer tolerate conditions scarcely better than slavery. It will not pass without the adoption of some method whereby the right to labor and to receive and enjoy the honest reward of that labor shall be assured to the poorest and least fortunate."

"Every age has its heroes," he stoutly declared. "Ours demands those who will labor in behalf of a social order based on universal justice—not on the dominion of Power over Need. We could not retard the great forward movement if we would, but each must decide for himself whether to share in the glory of promoting it or incur the shame of having looked on coldly and indifferently—in preferring present ease and plenty to the pleadings of Human Brotherhood."

The year 1841 seemed to be just the time to impress people that such a new day had dawned; that their hard experiences during the depression would bring rich and poor, employer and employee, in closer sympathy. The old cleavages, however, survived, and Greeley realized that he was only a new contender in the unending battle of the ages. True, there was clamor for all kinds of changes from old ways, but Greeley extended no helping hand to change for change's sake. "Along with many noble and lofty souls whose impulses are purely philanthropic," warned the *Tribune*, "there throng scores of the conceited, the crotchety, the selfish, the headstrong, the unappreciated, the played-out and the good-for-nothing generally who, out of place in this world as it is, rashly conclude that they are exactly fitted for the world as it ought to be."

At the top of the list of "isms" in those "roaring forties" was Mrs. Amelia Bloomer's insistence upon the advantages of masculine trousers—in derision called "bloomers"—in place of entangling hoop skirts. Mrs. Bloomer was the editor of a magazine called the *Lily*, in which she urged this change. Challenged to do so herself, she promptly adopted bloomers:

> Heigh! Ho! in rain or snow,
>   The bloomer now is all the go,
> Twenty tailors take the stitches,
>   Twenty women wear the britches.
> Heigh! Ho! in rain or snow,
>   The bloomer now is all the go!

At the other end of the list of reforms was the anti-meat-tea-coffee campaign of the Graham bread cult. Mrs. Greeley led in that agitation, and Greeley stood loyally by her side.

Between these two extremes were anti-Masons, anti-rum, anti-lotteries, anti-renters, anti-foreigners, anti–free-Irelanders, anti–resistants-to-force, anti–users-of-cooked-food because fire belongs to hell and therefore destroys purity (Bronson Alcott, father of Louisa May Alcott, led that reform). In addition, there were women suffragists, spiritualists, phrenologists, and other groups galore. Lecture halls were crowded with men and women eager to give way riotously to their emotions either for or against.

Many of such activities were news, but most newspapers mentioned them only to ridicule. This was conspicuously true of the first national convention of women suffragists ever held. It met at Worcester, Massachusetts. Greeley sent a reporter to write a truthful story of the proceedings. Other newspapers gibed at it. "The Reign of the Petticoat!" they chorused, and cartooned Greeley in woman's dress. "It is easy to be smart, to be droll, to be facetious in opposition to these demands of female reformers," responded the *Tribune*. "In decrying assumptions so novel and so opposed to established habits and usages, a little wit will go a great way. But when a sincere republican is asked to say in sober earnestness what adequate reason he can give for refusing the demand of the women for an equal participation with men in political rights, he must answer—None. True, he may say that he believes it unwise in them to make the demand, but if they should generally prefer a complete political equality with men it is but the assertion of a natural right and so must be conceded."

Promptly Greeley was classed as a votes-for-women advocate; indeed, he became burden-bearer for all the causes urged by agitators. Good and bad, sincere and silly were bundled together and labeled "Greeley's isms." Subscribers complained and friends feared disaster to the *Tribune*. They pleaded with him to abandon, or at least to modify, his advocacy of so many reforms. But they did not know Greeley. He was no backtracker:

> If anyone would prefer to discontinue "The Tribune" because it is and must remain opposed to every measure or scheme of proscription for opinion's sake, we beg them not to delay one minute on our account. We shall all live till it is our turn to die, whether we earn a living making newspapers or by doing something else.
>
> That a journalist is in any sense a public teacher, that he necessarily has convictions, and that he is not likely to suppress them because they

are not shared by others is evidently not suspected for one moment by these complaining subscribers.

My critics evidently assume that I am merely a jumping-jack, who only needs to know what others think to insure my instant conformity—in short that a journalist is no higher than a waiter at a restaurant, expected to furnish whatever is called for....

Thurlow Weed joined the anvil chorus of warnings; his real concern, however, was that the "isms" would be charged against the Whig party. Greeley challenged him—"Not 'The Tribune,'" he replied, "but Whig indifference to public welfare is the real menace to Whig success." Here is part of his letter dated February 19, 1842:

...To have you join in the cry was more than I could relish, though I did not expect you to look with favor on the new actions of our little band of reformers.

I think you take the wrong view of the political bearing of this matter [Fourierism], though I act without reference to that. Hitherto all the devotees of social reform of any kind, all the advocates of a higher destiny for labor, all the combatants against unjust and false social principles—in short all the social discontent of the country has been regularly repelled from the Whig party and attracted to its opposite. This forms a heavy dead-weight against us.

It strikes me that it is unwise to persist in this course, unless we are ambitious to be considered the enemies of improvement and the bulwark of an outgrown aristocracy in this country.

But I will not ask you to think as I do. I only want a chance to think for myself.

And "think for myself" Greeley certainly did! His spirit and earnestness were armor his critics never could pierce. Already he was a recognized leader of national opinion. Even in New York City the circulation of the daily increased. On April 10, 1844, the *Tribune* celebrated its third birthday without having blacked out a single star in its flag of social betterments. It proudly announced: "We shall print 'The Tribune' on a double sheet hereafter for the accommodation of our readers in general, our advertisers in particular, and ourselves most especially." Has any newspaper but Greeley's ever written in this way to its readers?—

> ... We improve this occasion to return our unfeigned thanks to the Public for the large and steadily increasing patronage which enables and almost compels us to make this Enlargement. Our gratitude is the deeper from our knowledge that many of the views expressed through our columns are unacceptable to a large proportion of our readers.
>
> We know especially that our advocacy of measures to meliorate the Social Condition of the Toiling Millions (not the purpose, but the means), our ardent sympathy with the people of Ireland in their protracted, arduous, peaceful struggle to recover some portion of the Rights of Man, and our opposition to the legal extinction of Human Life, are severally or collectively regarded with extreme aversion by many of our steadfast patrons, whose liberality and confidence is gratefully appreciated.

Note that Greeley here made no apology. If people continued to read the *Tribune* they would have to read the same advocacy of reforms! Nor did he hesitate to prophesy that "although I will not live to see it, the errors, crimes and miseries that have made this earth a place of hell for too many shall yet be forgotten in a reign of truth, purity and bliss," and "thriftless Pretence and Slavery shall no longer prosper while Labor vainly seeks employment even at a scant living wage.... Doubtless the realization of such visions is yet afar. We cannot wonder that Heaven is so distant when Hell is so near."

The day Greeley had in mind was one in which opportunity, work and education would be possible for all; women would be paid at the same rate as men for the same services and also have citizenship when as a whole they desired it; temperance in all things should prevail; labor should organize in its own defense; capital should be made to recognize its obligations to better living standards for all; slavery and imprisonment for debt should be abolished and the death penalty outlawed as barbaric. "Grant that it is but a dream," conceded Greeley; "it by no means follows that it has no practical value. On the contrary, an ideal, an illusion, if a noble one, has often been the inspirer of grand and beneficent efforts. Moses was fated never to enter the Land of Promise he so longingly viewed from afar; and Columbus never found—who can now wish that he had?—that unimpeded sea route westward to India that he sought so wisely and so daringly."

Yet Greeley realized that all that he urged could not be accomplished overnight: "Let none accuse me of the enthusiast's common error—the presumption that the world is to be transformed in a day. I know well how great the interval which ever divides the perception of a noble idea by a few earnest minds from its hearty acceptance.... But the world *does* move, and its motive power under God is the fearless thought and speech of those who dare be in advance of their time—who are sneered at and shunned through their days of struggle as lunatics, dreamers, impracticables and visionaries, men of crotchets, vagaries and of isms. They are the masts and sails of the ship to which conservatism answers as ballast. The ballast is important—at times indispensable—but it would be of no account if the ship were not bound to go ahead."

Did that mean Socialism?

Did it mean that Greeley could justly be labeled "agitator," "wrecker," a preacher of discontent? He had to meet that accusation everywhere, but he pushed steadily ahead toward his goal; that goal, not the side-line jeers, interested him. Yet he realized then how merciless and how wrong public opinion often is.

All that Greeley saw during his first ten years on Manhattan Island, with its disease-spreading slums, its hopeless poverty and its general wretchedness in contrast with the "open spaces" of his youth, stirred him to constant effort to persuade people to abandon the crowded city and, if not going west, at least seek a living where health would be found. "The darkest day in any man's life," he wrote, "is that in which he first fancies that there is some easier way of gaining a dollar than by squarely earning it. He has lost his way through the moral labyrinth and henceforth must wander as chance may dictate."

With such sentiments he was in the mood to urge some form of community life when, in 1840, Albert Brisbane approached him to gain his support for the philosophy of François Charles Marie Fourier. Brisbane, a native of Batavia, Genesee County, New York, had returned to this country after several years in Paris, where he had studied Fourier's theories. When someone remarked to him that the end of the world was probably near he replied: "Damn glad of it, Sir! Damn glad of it! The experiment of the human race has proven a failure!"

Despite this lack of faith in world progress Brisbane was a Fourier enthusiast, and soon convinced Greeley of the philosophy's practical application to everyday life. "I accept unreservedly the views of no man, dead or alive. 'The Master has said it,' is never conclusive with me," wrote Greeley, "and I take nothing on Fourier's authority, though on many points he commands my concurrence." Like Fourier and Brisbane, he rejected communism. "There is a small number, very small it may be but I think it increases," he declared, "to whom the old ways, the old purposes of life, have become impossible of pursuit, who must breathe freely or be stifled, who cannot live longer to merely personal ends.... They find in association a reform that will render this age memorable in the life of man."

He committed the *Tribune* to the cause and became its acknowledged leader. Noah Webster, then in poor health, had his son W. G. Webster write from their New Haven home requesting from Greeley an authoritative interpretation of Fourierism. The distinction pleased the *Tribune* editor. He made a lengthy reply, dated March 30, 1843, from which the following is an extract:

> Fourierism—the system of Charles Fourier, a French writer and founder of a school of philosophy—which now has many ardent apostles in this country and in Europe. Fourier's leading inculcation is that the evils which mainly afflict mankind are social in their nature, and to be removed only by a reorganization of society upon principles analogous to those of a joint stock company. Each community is to consist of 500 to 2,000 persons, living in a spacious edifice, cultivating a noble domain, prosecuting industry in common, but sharing the proceeds according to their capital, skill and labor. By this means vast economies are attainable, and a guarantee of plenty, comfort and expenditures to all

may be secured. For his abstract doctrines with regard to the harmony of the passions, the renovation of the physical globe, etc., see a digest of his works by A. Brisbane; from it you can gather what are our views and objects.

Such was his interpretation of Fourierism when he announced his advocacy of it in the *Tribune*.

About twenty "phalansteries" were established at different places, but two principal enterprises were founded: one at Shrewsbury, near Red Bank, New Jersey, and another at Sylvania, near Lackawanna, in Pike County, Pennsylvania.

The Shrewsbury phalanstery struggled for fourteen years; the Sylvania experiment for three years. Both finally gave up the ghost, but not until all had paid their debts in full and had confessed that lack of management was their fatal weakness.

None of the evils predicted, none of the quarreling, nor the scandal ever happened. Greeley lost several thousand dollars in the Sylvania venture—but, he asserted, with no regret, "because I might have lost more had I bought many of the stocks and bonds urged on me by securities salesmen. I shall make the same disposition of more money as soon as I have it to expend," he added. "I hold myself but the steward of a kind Providence, and bound to use all I may have as shall seem most conducive to the good of the Human Race." He continued to do so even as late as 1871 when he helped to create what is now the prosperous city of Greeley, in Boulder County, Colorado, on the basis of co-operative effort, of no fences, and no rum sold.

Of all the newspaper attacks on Greeley because of his Fourierism the most frequent and heaviest blows came from Henry J. Raymond. The latter resigned from the *Tribune* in 1844 to become editor of James Watson Webb's *Courier and Enquirer*. Webb had come off second best in his controversies with Greeley, and Raymond was engaged frankly to destroy the *Tribune's* influence. This Raymond was eager to do. Finally Greeley offered to debate Fourierism with him in their respective newspapers once a week from November 20, 1846, to May 20, 1847—each newspaper to publish both sides. It was a lost battle for Greeley. With the debate closed, Raymond could not resist pursuing his old chief further by declaring: "The Whig party is one of order and stability, eschewing radicalism in every form, and the better way for 'The Tribune' would be to admit that it is Whig only on the subject of the tariff and then devote itself to the advocacy of anti-rent, Fourierist, vote-yourself-a-farm doctrine." The last reference was to Greeley's homestead policy which later became a Republican party measure and was made law by Lincoln's signature.

CHAPTER IX

"I Do No Man's Bidding"

ONCE MORE Thurlow Weed stood in the forefront of Greeley's too solicitous friends. Only four months had elapsed since he replied to Weed—"I only want a chance to think for myself." That was difficult for anyone to do whenever Weed thought differently, and Greeley was now far out of line. Weed devoted a whole evening to warning him again of the futility of his Fourierism. It was the last time that he ever attempted to control him, for following the politician back to Albany was this plain-spoken declaration of independence!

New York, September 10, 1842

Friend Weed:

I rise from a bed of sleepless thought to make plain my position to you. I trust it is now understood, as I thought it had been before, that we differ radically on the Bank bill and I begin to fear we do on the general policy and objects of political controversy.... You have been pleased on several occasions to take me to task for differing from you, as though such differences were an evidence not merely of weakness on my part but of some black ingratitude or heartless treachery.

I cannot realize that there have been any series of obligations between us which render it proper in you to assume so complete a mastery over my opinions and actions. I am sure I never desired offices of distinction, avenues to fortune at your hands.

You sought me out for our first interview and if I have not been as useful to you as to me the fault has been through my want of ability. I have given you and I have been ever ready to give you any service in my power, but my understanding, my judgment, my consciousness of conviction, of duty and public good—them I can surrender to no man. You wrong yourself in asking. However deep my obligations I cannot pay in these. I am ever ready to defer to your superior experience and judgment—only convince me, but do not assume to dictate or lecture me. Do not ask me to forget that I, too, am a man—that I must breathe free air or be stifled.

Let us now hope that we understand each other better. I would hope also that we may still be friends; but if I can only enjoy your friendship on terms of humiliation, let us be strangers henceforth. I trust we can never be enemies, but better anything than I should feel the weight of chains about my neck. While I remain where I am I cannot afford to despise myself. Besides I owe what little chance for usefulness that I may have to the impression that I do no man's bidding but speak my own thoughts.

Horace Greeley

No one was so well qualified as Charles A. Dana to know how resolutely Greeley lived up to these convictions. After his almost twenty years' association with him on the *Tribune*, and despite their unfriendly separation, he said of him:

Every man who has charge of a newspaper, who controls a newspaper, has to have a moral code by which he is guided in the conduct of his paper. In order that I might not state it inaccurately, I have noted down what I conceive to be the professional code that governed Mr. Greeley:

"Always give a hearing to your opponent. Never attack a man and refuse to let him answer in the same columns. Be always as considerate of the weak and friendless as of the powerful. Waste no strength in advocating that which is intrinsically impossible. Never compromise your own opinions on account of your subscribers. If they don't like your ideas they can always go to another shop."

That was the doctrine of Horace Greeley; and that doctrine he practiced during the whole of his active life. I cannot remember, amid all the controversies (and they were often very bitter controversies) in which he was continually engaged, that he ever violated one of those principles.

In the two documents just quoted—the Greeley letter and Dana's confirmation—there is a challenge to those writers who in later years have been eager to question Greeley's sincerity. No other editor in Printing House Square ever experienced so much of work and worry, of poverty and prosperity, of denunciation and praise as did Greeley. His figure soon became familiar to its habitués and for forty years remained as unusual in appearance as were his ways in life.

That unlikeness would have been noticeable even had it not been emphasized, for frankly there was a good deal of the showman about Greeley. Yet he indulged his vanity with so little conscious effort that it seemed as though he came by it naturally.

"People suppose I wear the same old coat, but I don't," gleefully remarked Greeley to Donald G. Mitchell. "The original white coat came from Ireland. I bought it from an emigrant who needed money and I needed a coat. I paid him $20 for it and it was the best coat I ever wore. They do good work in the Old Country."

No title to office nor any honor conferred upon him could ever have meant so much to him as that of just plain "Uncle Horace." Whenever in his travels he was greeted as such instead of "Mr. Greeley," the kindly gleam in his eye, the broad smile on his face, the warm grasp of his hand left no doubt of his liking for its significant import of intimacy with plain people.

No one ever summarized the self-educated Greeley more incisively than Edwin Lawrence Godkin, Irish-born graduate of Queen's College, Belfast, at one time editor of *The Nation* and later of the New York *Evening Post.* In 1863 Godkin wrote in *The Nation:*

> Mr. Greeley is self-educated, and very imperfectly educated at that—has no grasp of mind, no great political insight, and has his brain crammed with half-truths, and odds and ends of ideas which a man inevitably accumulates who scrapes knowledge together by fits and starts on his way through life.
>
> But he has an enthusiasm which never flags, and a faith in principles which nothing can shake, and an English style which for vigor, terse-

ness, clearness and simplicity has never been surpassed, except by William Cobbett; and I confess that, disagreeable as his ways are, and must be to everybody who hates vulgarity in public life and who would wish to see such power as Greeley undoubtedly wields lodged in hands of nicer touch and more careful training, when we remember that he founded "The Tribune" as an organ of the then small and despised sect of anti-slavery men, and never, for one hour, flagged or grew weary in the great struggle of which we are today witnessing the crisis, it is not fair to criticise too severely either his weapon or his manner of wielding them.

To judge Greeley as an editor solely by his own political writings is to do an injustice to his conception of a newspaper. Dana was the only man on the staff interested in politics; others worked in different fields. Their product broadened the *Tribune* and made that newspaper, according to Luther Mott in *American Journalism*, "the chief influence in the writing of the modern editorial page—a department which discusses in an adequate literary style a large variety of contemporary topics. 'The Tribune' came into full flower in the Fifties; it represented wide information and held to high aims."

Historian James Ford Rhodes observed, "No other man in his time exercised so great an influence." Andrew D. White, president of Cornell University, declared in his autobiography: "There was no trail-blazer but 'The Tribune'; Greeley left a fame that must ever touch the imagination of America."

"Greeley is the spokesman of the most numerous, most independent and most determined body of men ever associated for political purposes in the United States," wrote James S. Pike; or, as editor Samuel Bowles wrote in his Springfield *Republican:* "No man of his generation talked to the common people so forcibly, so clearly and with so much sense and benevolence as he; in his beliefs, his instincts and his enthusiasms he was as thoroughly a representative American as any man of his times." Even in present-day comment, historian Henry Steele Commager, in his recently published book *The Growth of the American Republic,* writes: " 'The Tribune' became a liberal power of the first magnitude."

To Greeley, the soul of a newspaper was in its editorial page. He loved to sign "H. G." to an editorial leader and to know that those initials were accepted by *Tribune* readers with full faith because he, and he alone, was speaking. In 1910, when Joseph Pulitzer, blind and body-racked, discussed his own career with his biographer, he recalled that as Mary Stuart sailed from France to assume her throne as Queen of Scotland she declared that she had left her heart behind. "My heart was, still is, and in spirit always will be in the editorial page," declared Pulitzer.

Greeley's heart was always there, too. So was his own swift and clear judgment—and he backed it with unyielding courage. Now and then in editorial council his associates would suggest a slower approach to the policy he had in mind, but "Action! action! action!" would be his response—always eager to lead. He insisted that if he wandered around seeking other people's opinions he would never have one of his own until too late to declare it except as a single voice in a chorus. His attitude toward men in public life changed from time to time—notably toward Seward and Stephen A. Douglas—but he never abandoned a policy based on principle or a purpose that he believed was right. His appeal was never qualified; he knew no ifs. He struck out with meaning words —no rhetoric, no borrowing of quotations from others to bulwark his thought. "Writing for the common people," he explained, "I have aimed to be lucid and simple. I write for the great mass of intelligent, observant, reflecting farmers and mechanics, and if I succeed in making my positions clearly understood I do not fear that they will be rejected."

His "terrible candor" inspired the faith of the people though it often provoked his friends. He had not been reared to the calculating ways of thinking that too often hold timid men in doubt. He was always willing to try something new; to ignore it seemed to him poorer disposition of it than later to abandon it if need be. "Full of error and suffering as the world is," he declared in one of his lectures, "we cannot afford to reject any plea which purposes to improve the moral, intellectual or social condition of mankind."

"It was Greeley's pride," said George William Curtis, "that every friendless cause had a listening friend in him, and it was that spirit that gave 'The Tribune' its great hold on its readers."

As an editor the role of cloistered oracle never appealed to him. He wanted to see and know his country with his own eyes and by his own contacts. No other editor of his day knew it so intimately from the Atlantic to the Pacific and from the Canadian border to Texas. Since only primary things counted with him he sought knowledge of them where the many, not the few, gathered. He loved to believe that by instinct he knew the thoughts of the masses; he was proud that he belonged to them and to believe that he was their spokesman. Not once throughout his sixty-one years did he ever seek to get out of character. That Amherst log house in which he was born and the still poorer one of his boyhood at Westhaven remained through life his worldly environment. He was uneasy in any other atmosphere; he shunned the ease and comfort of wealth and sought no community with those who enjoyed them. The graces of society had no favor with him—"no taste, no time," as he wrote Governor Seward. It was while in the two homes of his youth that he read and instilled into his own beliefs the sentiments of Burns's two poems, "The Cotter's Saturday Night" and "For A' That and A' That." For Greeley himself was of the soil—and not of topsoil at that—and his inherited devotion to the simplicities it enforces on those who live by it kept him ever close to them in thought and purpose. Their hopes and struggles had been his too, and they sensed it in every line he wrote. To them he became their typical American, bred of the bone, maker and master of his own career—their "Uncle Horace."

That is why through the years, as national issues became more and more intense, there was scarcely a crossroads general store that did not have its evening gathering of neighbors listening to the reading of editorials in "Uncle Horace's Weekly Try-bune"; nor was there a rural post office that did not usually have a group on the porch eagerly awaiting the arrival of the mail stage with their "newspaper Bible."

"Greeley does the thinking for the whole West at $2 per year for his paper," was not written thoughtlessly by Ralph Waldo Emerson from Minneapolis in 1856 to his friend Carlyle across the Atlantic. "Today, between the oceans," declared Rev. Henry Ward Beecher at the time of Greeley's death, "there is hardly an intelligent man or child who has not felt the influence of Horace Greeley."

Constantly he advised young men and young families to "Go west," and soon became known as "Go West Greeley." "Your true home is in the West," he had declared even as early as in the *New Yorker* days. Only Harriet Beecher Stowe's immortal *Uncle Tom's Cabin* and Stephen Collins Foster's "O Susanna!" had greater vogue through the 1850's than Greeley's urgent "Go west, young man, go west!" It is said that others used that phrase before Greeley did, but if so no one heard it. When Greeley said it the whole country heard, and many thousands acted.

Such was the genius of his editorship that every line, no matter by whom written, bore indelibly the stamp of Horace Greeley—straightforward, hopeful, uninfluenced. To every reader the *Tribune* was Greeley. And nothing pleased him more. Fulton could have his steamboat, Morse his telegraph, McCormick his reaper, every Midas his wealth—but give Greeley his *Tribune* and all the rest of the world was to him well lost.

Whether he wrote of politics, farming, labor, education, the horror of debt, the rights of women, temperance, marriage or career-making, people everywhere read him day after day. He upbraided them for their drinking habits—still they read him; he denounced their tobacco habits—still they read him; he flayed the lazy and the thriftless—yet they, too, read him. Even capitalists read Greeley. They resented his ideas, yet they respected the man they could never control.

Unfortunately, in the first years of the *Tribune,* Greeley too frequently engaged in the practice then common in editorial controversy of replying by personal reference to the opponent. "You lie"; "We ought never to notice that old villain again"; "Why don't you tell the truth once in a century for a change?"; "This superannuated renegade from all parties and principles"—such phrases are examples of his responses; naturally he got the same type in reply. However, he used his epithets on the wrong man when he responded to a William Cullen Bryant editorial in the New York *Evening Post* with "You lie, you old villain, you basely, wickedly lie!" The facts were on Greeley's side, but Bryant was not the man to be called a liar and an old villain. The cultured poet never had any further interest in the plebeian Greeley.

Of course, Greeley often had to take epithets even coarser than he used. In addition to Bennett's frequent gibes there was a persistent assault from the Cleveland *Plain Dealer*, until finally Greeley brought suit asking $10,000 damages "in money only." He won the verdict, but only $3.50 damages.

When notified of the suit, editor Joseph William Gray wrote:

> Our first impulse was to give a check for the amount but we recollected that, like most Democratic printers, we had not a single dollar in the bank. . . . How Horace supposed he could ever get so much money as that out of any Democratic editor, especially one publishing a national democratic paper in the Connecticut Western Reserve, is as much a mystery to us as the Rochester Spiritualist Knockings. . . . Ten thousand dollars "in money only" is wanted to make good the damaged reputation of a political editor. What a tearing big hole in an incredibly short space of time our pen did make in the "pheelinks" of this feathered philosopher. We plead "amazement" and "go to the country" on that issue. That we possess such powers of mischief with our unpracticed, unpretending pen is "amazing indeed." That Horace Greeley . . . should presume to have ten thousand dollars' worth of character left is still more amazing.

CHAPTER X

The Brook Farmers: Dana and Margaret Fuller

THE FOURIERIST agitation was not without its compensating gains for Greeley. One that was to prove of great value to him and to journalism was Charles Anderson Dana, later to become editor of the New York *Sun;* another was Miss Sarah Margaret Fuller, organizer and first editor of the *Dial*, a quarterly magazine owned and contributed to by Emerson and a coterie of Boston intellectuals, few of whom ever agreed with what the others published.

For these two acquisitions to the *Tribune* staff Greeley owed thanks to his wife, for it was she who by visiting Brook Farm established contact. There she met Miss Fuller and brought her into the Greeley home and on the *Tribune;* there he met Dana, and brought him also into newspaper life. From that fraternity of idealist experimenters with world problems Greeley also brought to the *Tribune* George Ripley, George William Curtis, Elizabeth Peabody and William Henry Fry—all of whom, "descending from Utopia to Journalism," as Ripley said, typify the earliest effort before the telegraph to broaden a daily newspaper beyond the dull routine of local news, carried by coach, pony express and exchange clippings. Thus the uncultured Greeley recruited his staff with scholars not one of whom had previous newspaper experience and later cleared the way for them, one by one, to positions of distinction.

Though Greeley regarded Brook Farm as "too angelic" for this practical world, he was always in sympathy with it. In Lindsay

Swift's *Brook Farm* Miss Amelia Russell is quoted as describing his first visit as "the coming of an apparition which proved to be Horace Greeley—not in disguise but his own astonishing self. His hair was so light that it seemed white, his face was entirely colorless, even his eye not adding much to save it from its ghastly hue. His coat was a very light drab, almost white, and his nether garments were the same. This Apostle of Light, however odd his personality, was welcome to the community to which he was never disloyal."

"Paradise Plantation" was the popular title for Brook Farm when it was founded by a group of New England Transcendentalists under the leadership of Rev. George Ripley of Boston. They purchased a farm at Roxbury, Massachusetts, where they endeavored to separate from the contentious world and to get along in an environment of their own creation. Everybody on the farm was to work according to his own choosing, but all were paid alike whether for physical or intellectual labor, "since intellectual labor," wrote Elizabeth Peabody in the *Dial,* "involves in itself higher pleasure and is more its own reward than is bodily labor." The chief purpose was to encourage everyone to work with hands as well as with head, thus uniting physical effort with cultural aims, and thereby help answer two questions which Margaret Fuller posed as the whole problems of life: What were we born to do and how are we to do it?

Brook Farmers began by tackling a minor but vexatious problem—servants. This they solved by serving themselves, each doing his or her allotted share of the day's work in house and field. "A man who digs ditches or executes any other repulsive work is not at the foot of the social scale—he is at the head of it," insisted Dana enthusiastically. There was no master and man, no mistress and maid. Women of wealth, culture and social position cooked, scrubbed and attended to the rooms, while scholars such as Ripley, Dana, Curtis and Hawthorne plowed the fields, dug potatoes, cleaned the stables and the cow barn. The women wore short skirts, knickerbockers, blouses, broad Quaker hats under which their hair flowed freely and long. Late afternoon and evenings were given over to intellectual sessions; at these gatherings all wore the usual dress of society. Here Margaret Fuller had her innings. She presided over the discussions. As the meetings were held in the principal cottage, called the Hive, it may be assumed that during her visits she was regarded as the queen bee, for she then held undisputed sway.

What wonder that young, "crazy-for-education" Mrs. Greeley was attracted to the Transcendentalists, and especially to the learned Margaret Fuller. Like others she accepted her as a superior mentality—the only person in fact to whom she ever yielded in opinion. And, as events of the next few years revealed, those two women living in his home were the only persons to whom Horace Greeley ever yielded in opinion.

Miss Fuller was thoroughly New England—Emersonian New England and sure of herself. Born in 1810 as the first of ten children of Timothy and Margaret Crane Fuller in a home in the poorest section of Cambridge, she had much housework to do as a girl. She was a youthful prodigy, however, in her zeal for foreign languages and literature: despite her heavy home duties she educated herself, becoming the best-read woman in the country and ranking with the best-read men. She earned her living by teaching and then by holding "conversations" attended only by women; Emerson called the meetings "parlortorias." Her topics were: Culture, Vanity, Prudence, Ideals, Creeds and Woman—her right to freedom and equality with man.

It was this background that led Mrs. Greeley to refer to Miss Fuller as "my greatly cherished friend," and to persuade Greeley to establish a literary department for her in the *Tribune;* the contract provided that she should reside in the Greeley home. That feature he did not like. "I was barely acquainted with her when she came to live with us," he wrote, "and fortune seemed to place us in friendly antagonism. She was naturally inclined to luxury, while my pride, if I had any, delighted in bare walls and rugged food.... An utter divergence on this and other themes created a perceptible difference between us." Another criticism was that Miss Fuller insisted that she could not do her work in a noisy newspaper office; she needed the quiet of Turtle Bay. Even there she would write only when in the mood—when free of headaches and temperamental sulks. "The notion of waiting for a brighter day or a happier frame of mind appeared to me as fantastic as waiting for a change in the moon," declared Greeley. Besides, she took as long to write one column as Greeley needed to write three—though he admitted that when her column was finally written it was well written. Still her affectations continually ruffled the blunt Greeley to such an extent that when commenting upon a friendly analysis of her temperament, he wrote: "If I had attempted to say this I should have somehow blundered out that, noble and great as she was, a good husband and two or three bouncing babies would have emancipated her from a good deal of cant and nonsense."

Probably no man ever changed his estimate of another person so completely as did Greeley when he read Margaret Fuller's *Woman in the Nineteenth Century*, published a year after she had abandoned Boston for New York City. The book was a bold demand to have every arbitrary barrier thrown down, every path open to woman as to man—not as a concession but as a right. "It is the fault of marriage," she insisted, "and of the present relation between the sexes that woman belongs to man instead of forming a whole with him. Woman, if self-centered, would never be absorbed by a relation; it would be only an experience to her as it is to man. It is a vulgar error that to woman love is her whole existence." When on August 24, 1846, Miss Fuller sailed from Boston to Europe, never to return, she and Greeley were in full accord. She wrote of him: "I like, nay more, I love Horace Greeley. He is in his habits a plebeian but in his heart a noble man. His abilities in his own way are great. He believes in mine to a surpassing extent." While in Rome she wrote frequent letters for the *Tribune*, and Greeley wrote her a series of personal letters of astounding revelations of his home life. Several of them will be found on a later page. But Miss Fuller, at thirty-eight, had her romance in Italy. In 1848 she married secretly penniless Giovanni Angelo Marquis Ossoli, many years her junior; a son was born to them. In his letters Greeley kept asking her why "live eternally in the Eternal City?" Marriage was the answer—but Greeley was not told of it. In fact, she never acknowledged it to anyone until poverty forced her in 1850 to return to this country to earn enough for the family to live on. Unfortunately the ship carrying her across the Atlantic with her husband and son was wrecked off Fire Island and all three were drowned.

Though Greeley had overlooked Margaret Fuller during his first Brook Farm visit, he had not missed out on Dana. An intimacy began which led Greeley, four years later, to employ Dana at $10 a week; four dollars more than he was earning in Boston. From the very beginning there seems to have been a recognition by each man that he complemented the other and that, despite differences, the good of their newspaper was their single objective.

Not so, however, as already related, with Raymond, whom, we must not forget, Greeley rescued from a career as schoolteacher in North Carolina and thus, as Raymond acknowledged, "decided the whole course of my life." Suppose we study both men who owed so much to Greeley and for whose employment journalism owes so much to Greeley, too. Twenty years old, just out of the University of Vermont, Raymond in 1840 was eager for work; Dana, at twenty-six and just married, had no such stirring ambition when he joined the *Tribune* staff in 1846. For over thirty years newspaper history was made by those two men with Greeley and James Gordon Bennett. Had there been no Fourierist agitation by Greeley and no Brook Farm, Dana would never have been on the *Tribune;* possibly also Raymond might not have separated from Greeley so early or in such antagonism. He disliked Greeley's "isms" so thoroughly that separation was only a matter of time.

There was not room on one editorial page for two men of such conflicting opinions—

> Two Dervishes upon one mat sleep well,
> Two Kings within one Kingdom cannot dwell!

When announcing Raymond's resignation, Greeley graciously said in the *Tribune,* "We would not be satisfied to part without publicly testifying the esteem for him which our long association has inspired. . . . We hardly need add that our fervent wishes attend him in his future career." These kindly sentiments were forgotten later when Raymond outwitted Greeley by securing some state advertising for the *Times*. Greeley then referred to him as "the Little Villain!" "He said that so that I could refer to 'The Big Villain' of 'The Tribune,'" retorted Raymond—but "Little Villain" stuck to Raymond.

In Greeley's opinion Raymond always studied both sides of a subject so hospitably that he never could distinguish the merit of either one over the other; hence he was slow to form an opinion that led to change.

Thus the two men differed widely. All may be summed up in a single word: Greeley was a crusader; Raymond never sought to be one. "To Greeley life and its employments were an earnest purpose," wrote John Russell Young of his chief. "There should be no trifling by the wayside—no lolling over vanities; there was no virtue as desirable as thrift." He stuck to his farm, to his office, to politics and to the lecture platform. They were his world. But Raymond loved the companionships found on the sunny side of the road. To him "dining out" was a welcome diversion. Greeley shunned such occasions. An evening dress suit adorned Raymond's figure and was greatly to his liking. To Greeley "this having to live in an evening full dress-suit plays the devil with one's deeper and better personality." Greeley's big boots, rumpled trousers, white overcoat and broad felt hat were always in contrast with Raymond's natty attire—the latest cut in tailoring, Congress gaiters covered by bright spats, a gold-knobbed ebony cane, a high silk hat that made his five-foot-six-inch dapper form seem even shorter, particularly when he walked alongside of Greeley's broad-shouldered, shambling frame almost six feet tall.

Raymond stepped out briskly; though always in a hurry, he would see everybody and everything—affable and gracious to all. Greeley, too, was a rapid walker, but he never got rid of the sway of his young days in the furrows; often he would seem to lurch like a ship in a storm. His nearsighted eyes made it difficult for him to recognize people, so he did not try. Equally noticeable was the facial contrast. There was Greeley's big, round seraphic face, which Bennett always likened to a ripening New England squash. Raymond had a well-shaped head; large, round, dark eyes often adorned with a ribboned monocle; short, stubby nose; heavy black hair and neatly trimmed mutton-chop whiskers. "Hello, Uncle Horace" was a frequent greeting to Greeley from passers-by, even when they knew him only through newspaper pictures; Raymond never inspired that kind of salutation.

Dana's sixteen years with Greeley tell a pleasanter story. He and Greeley were as different as night and day in personality, methods and way of life—the latter impatient to see his country and to talk to its people, the other content in the quiet of his home and library. One restless and explosive; the other deliberate and even-tempered. Still loyal to Brook Farm philosophy, Dana dug up Karl Marx in London in 1851, who for several years expounded his social views in a weekly letter to the *Tribune.* It was Dana, too, who insisted that anything that the Lord permitted to occur on this earth was proper news for publication. Greeley thought not. Yet, they were a great team!

Newspaper tradition has it that Dana was the first man to have the title of managing editor—that it was unknown until Greeley used it—but Greeley's respect for Dana's abilities also took more substantial form; in 1849 he sold him ten shares of *Tribune* stock for $10,000 payable "when, if and as you can." Those shares eventually were paid for out of *Tribune* dividends; they made Dana rich.

Both men were born (Greeley in 1811 and Dana in 1819) in small New Hampshire villages—Dana at Hinsdale on the Connecticut River, not more than fifty miles straight west from Amherst across the narrow state. They were far apart in surroundings, however. Greeley, in youth, as we know, experienced real poverty out of which by hard work he emerged slowly. Opinions rooted and developed in such soil become unchanging lifelong convictions. They did with Greeley.

Dana, though poor, had no such hardening time of it; he had

no "riding to plough," no tree chopping, no printer's apprentice job. He clerked in Buffalo to save money for a term at Harvard. Opinions formed during such a youth gave way easily before the experience of later years. In their boyhood the one thing that he and Greeley had in common was an intense fondness for reading—Greeley for the country weeklies and for any book he could borrow. Dana plumbed deeper; he was absorbed in the ancient philosophies and languages. Both resented the oppressions of capital. The breeding ground of Dana's socialism was Harvard—"where I learned the art of living without means"—and the lectures of Emerson. "They make me think," he wrote to his sister.

Dana's father dreaded what Emerson, Carlyle and particularly Harvard might do to his boy. "I know Harvard ranks high as a literary institution," he wrote to him, "but the influence it exerts in a religious way is most terrible—even worse than Universalism. ... Ponder well the paths of thy feet lest they lead down to the very depths of Hell."

From his sister's home at Guildhall, Vermont, Dana on April 12, 1840, told of his carefree life: "In one corner of my room stands my bed, next a window looking out towards the sunrise is my desk, a side table is covered with books, while your humble servant in dressing-gown and slippers sits near the fire in a great armchair having 'pen in hand.' Here I study 8 hours daily. I am fed, warmed, lighted and otherwise cared for for about nothing—perhaps a dollar a week—taken unwillingly."

From Scituate, Massachusetts, where (for $25 a month and board) while on leave from Harvard he was teaching a flock of sailor lads, "the fiercest and most unruly," he wrote on January 10, 1841: "I am fed, clad and permitted to learn something—and is that not enough? Said Erasmus when a student at Paris, poor and in rags, 'I will first buy Greek books and then buy clothes.'"

Because of poor eyes, poor health and a poorer purse Dana did not return to Harvard for the fall term of 1841. He was disappointed—"so genial Harvard is, and where but for the term bills and washerwomen one would never guess that there were such things as money and money-getting in the world. Indeed I hold it an evidence of human depravity that there are such things, and I dream (nay, it is not a dream but a prophecy) of the time when the cycle of humanity shall be completed and it shall not be said 'God makes man and man makes money.' "

Even at twenty-one Dana was not seriously concerned about his earnings or a career. At that age Greeley lived busily in his work; Dana lived calmly in his books. He was delighted to reside in Boston even poorly because there he could consort with those whom Oliver Wendell Holmes called "the Brahmin caste of New England—its harmless, inefficient, untitled aristocracy." Boston was called more a "state of mind" than a city—and to young Dana it was just that.

The Brook Farm atmosphere therefore precisely fitted his mood. Contentedly he wrote his sister from there on September 17, 1841: "I am living with some friends who have associated themselves together for the purpose of living purely and of acting from higher motives than the world generally recognizes. I earn my board by labor on the farm and by giving instruction."

During Greeley's visit to Brook Farm he and Dana had many earnest discussions as to how to reform the world. At first Fourierism seemed too practical for Dana; it lacked the culture of Brook Farm. But Greeley warned him against the "cant of exclusiveness" he had detected there. "My fear for your system," wrote Greeley, "is that it is adapted only to angelic natures and that the entrance of one serpent would be as fatal as in the Eden of old."

"Fourier's system voids this by having a rampart of equal people in every Phalanstery," he wrote on August 22, 1842. "I have encountered much opposition and ridicule and have shocked the prejudices of many worthy friends by my unyielding fanaticism. All this is nothing, but the failure of your experiment would be something. Don't let anything daunt you—much less destroy you. I hear awful predictions of your overthrow, at which I trust you smile. I hope I shall yet live to see the infidels confounded—no, converted. Do you ever read that quaint, devout old record in Ezra of the rebuilding of the walls of Jerusalem?"

By 1844, through Greeley's constant proselyting, the entire Brook Farm group was in complete harmony with Fourierism. Dana wrote enthusiastically of it in the *Harbinger* and also in the *Dial.* In April 1844 he spoke at a large Fourier meeting in Clinton Hall, New York City, with Greeley presiding. He glorified Brook Farm and Fourierism in words that contrasted sharply with his later sentiments during the many years when the *Sun,* in big black lettering on its first page, assured its readers that "If you see it in 'the Sun' it's so!"

CHAPTER XI

"Castle Doleful" at Turtle Bay

DISCOURAGED by the unexpected defeat of Clay in the presidential campaign of 1844, Greeley turned his thoughts hopefully to the one haven he had never had—a home of his own. That is, a home in the accepted meaning of that word. To him home was now only a cherished recollection of boyhood days when he sat on a stool at the knees of his Ulster-born mother while she turned her spinning wheel, sang her jolly Irish ballads or told him her simple folklore stories. The picture had never faded. He assumed that in sentiment such a scene could be reenacted by a youthful, graceful, schoolteacher wife in that peasant mother's place and in a newly established city home instead of the Amherst log house in which he was born.

During the thirteen years since his first glimpse of New York City, Greeley had resided chiefly in the poorest, dirtiest section close to City Hall; even after his marriage he had not moved far from it and continued to live in boardinghouses. The city had not absorbed him into its typical life; perhaps one reason why he was so conspicuous on its streets was that he never fitted naturally as part of its hurrying, business-minded crowd; he was not of that crowd and never could be. He longed to get away from it. There was another and stronger motive. In March 1844 a son had been born—Arthur Young Greeley by name but for some reason called "Pickie"—to take the place of a son and daughter born there three and five years previously who only peeped into this world briefly with their baby eyes and then closed them forever. Greeley wanted his new son to have a better chance for life. He rented ten acres in a section of the city still called Turtle Bay or Kip's Bay, fronting on the East River and extending west to Third Avenue, then known as Boston Post Road, and from Thirty-fourth to Fiftieth Street.

The Turtle Bay property was historic. Wouter Van Twiller, the old Dutch governor of Nieuw Amsterdam made picturesque and memorable by Washington Irving, had occupied it as his country residence. The quickest way to get to City Hall by public conveyance was by two-horse stage every hour until eleven o'clock at night. The house had been untenanted for years; in its dilapidated condition no one would live in it except a Greeley interested chiefly in the trees, the fields and the extensive East River view. It brought Greeley back to the land. At once he began the tree chopping for which editor Dana years later referred to him as "the old Wood-Chopper of Chappaqua."

"I am a poor tree-chopper," he said of himself. "Yet the ax is my doctor and my delight. Its use gives the mind just enough occupation to prevent its falling into reveries or absorbing trains of thought, while every muscle of the body receives sufficient yet not exhausting exercise. If every youth and man from fifteen to fifty years old could or would wield an ax two hours a day dyspepsia would vanish from the earth and rheumatism become scarce. I wish all our boys would learn to love an ax."

To this new home came Margaret Fuller to live most of the time until she sailed for Europe in August 1846; here in 1847 was born a girl baby frankly unwanted by the mother before it entered the world and unwept by her when it departed less than one year later. "It caused too much anxiety and labor." Here was a home presided over by a wife whose kindliest thoughts were reserved for the spirit world, while to family and friends still on earth she showed so many irritabilities that life in the same house with her was often a test of temper and of nerves. New faces among callers "agitated" her; often she bluntly told them that she did not care to receive them; old friends developed in time "bad magnetism," or refused longer to pretend to hear the "rappings" which Mrs. Greeley insisted that she heard; thereupon, according to Greeley, they promptly fell from grace.

The birth and death of her children, her too rigorous adherence to Grahamite diet rules, her vain search in her own way for health and better sight must, of course, have accentuated Mrs. Greeley's peculiarities and sharp tongue, but she seems to have been of the type that finds pleasure in denying pleasure to herself as well as to others. She was most in character when dissatisfied with everything and everybody. The only exceptions were her too frequent visitors from the group of women she had met among Transcendentalists in Boston and at Brook Farm—in particular Margaret Fuller. The latter had free run of the Greeley home to revive there the "conversation parlortorias" which she had conducted in Boston, and which now brought to her at Turtle Bay in afternoon sessions many women "seeking perfection as our aim and patience as our road." They were in search of the path of the true soul—of a kingdom not only in this world but in particular beyond it. Harsh critics referred to the Greeley household and its visitors as eccentrics, and often wondered how long Greeley could stand it. How far or if at all Miss Fuller shared Mrs. Greeley's spiritualism is not known, but the entire group were more or less absorbed in mesmerism, mythology and the occult in all of its phases. Following his habit of experimenting with the new or unusual, and also prodded by his wife, Greeley had the Fox sisters, who were well-known mediums, give two séances at the house for querulous friends. He soon abandoned even that much interest, however, saying that he was too deeply concerned in the affairs of this world to get mixed up with those of another world. "Besides," he added, "I could see no good in it. I took a disrelish to it." Yet he would never reply publicly to the charge that spiritualism was one of his "isms," nor evidently did he try to persuade his wife away from it, for she never lost her faith. As for Greeley, what he called his "reveries concerning the Unseen World" were with him all his life, and were the subject of frequent discussion with his religious friends.

In his *Recollections*, when writing of "My Dead," Greeley

declared "I do not wear my heart upon my sleeve," but readers of this chapter will wonder where his heart really was while his wife was making their children the victims of her freakish fancies.

Here we find a man who had so impressed himself upon his fellow citizens that everywhere he was greeted as "Uncle Horace," yet in his own home he had no voice "unless I fight for it and not even then." . . . "It is woeful to think how friendless our little blessing was!" he wrote to Miss Fuller of the dead baby. It was on "Pickie," however, that Greeley's affection centered. Nevertheless throughout the boy's five years of life he saw him in constant revolt against the mother's restrictions and whippings and heard without heeding the little one's longing for playmates denied him, his loud cries for food that other children had, his appeals to be permitted to be as other boys. Both parents idolized him as their "angel" child, his pure soul not to be tainted by ordinary earthly contacts; but Mrs. Greeley determined to rule and bend him her way. He was her "dream boy," born to live as such unspoiled. He was kept in baby attire to the last; his golden hair was never cut and reached down almost to his waist; his face was constantly oiled to keep the skin of purest hue, his body thoroughly scrubbed at least twice a day. Pickie resented it constantly and violently but without avail. How tragic were the results is told by Greeley in a series of letters to Margaret Fuller from February 6, 1847, to August 14, 1849.

Among the saddest of family stories, it is the more poignant because Greeley tells it in extenuating and forgiving instead of complaining spirit. He professes to believe that his household tragedies are God's method of "weaning me from sordid ways." The letters to Miss Fuller, however, place responsibility where it belongs, though Greeley's persistent neglect of his home by long absences puts upon him a heavy share. The truth is that Greeley was not a home man; he was not born to the hearth. He was intended for the world, not for family life. It was his nature as it was also his fate to be constantly engaged in battles for others —even though at the time losing one for his own kin. Yet deep in Greeley's heart there must have been a love for his own fireside which to be surfaced needed only the encouragement of a home-making wife. Constantly forming in his mind was a hope for such never-to-be evenings at home as he visioned when in later years at Chappaqua he wrote to a friend: "I have a lot of cedars cut up for firewood. You know how pleasant is the odor of burning cedar. Well, I reserve this to warm and light my hearth when at some future time I can with my family and friends spend three or four evenings reading poems or discussing themes of enduring moment."

Greeley's loyalty to "My Mary," as he often referred to his wife, never lessened. Her wishes were his wishes, her peculiarities were his accepted burden. She dominated him even to the extent that at her frequent suggestion he would abandon Turtle Bay and take lodgings downtown so that she could pursue undisturbed her own way of living for herself and children. And what a home she made of it! Not a note of song was ever heard there; not a musical instrument in sight anywhere; not a picture on the walls (except a portrait of Pickie); not a library space worth talking about; nothing of furniture beyond cheapest and barest necessities; not a window curtain nor a carpet rug—not one blessed thing to extend to family or friends the warmth of welcome and companionship! All such were scorned as unsuited to life as it should be lived. Nor was Greeley himself out of sympathy with this raw condition; he had never known any other. He seems not to have realized the lack in his own house that deprived it of that blessed title, home.

It would be difficult to find another place of such loneliness and bareness, of constant sickness, of too frequent death, of absenteeism by the master and abandonment by the wife of many of the impulses of motherhood because of her slavish devotion to her personal whims; nevertheless that was the Greeley home at Turtle Bay throughout their six years of residence there.

Of course, in the highest sense, a man's home is his place of privilege beyond prying eyes—but the contrast between Greeley of the home and Greeley the great editor is too startling to be overlooked, especially as he himself opened the door wide by his revelations in his letters to Miss Fuller. There he tells of the girl baby sacrificed; of the struggles of Pickie for his own natural way and for "dirty food"; of "Castle Doleful" in which no servant would ever remain many days; of his building the morning fire, milking the cow and doing the housework. His description of the death of Pickie and of his own grief presents Greeley at his best in realistic writing. His own pathetic picture of the home life of this man of the world could be penned by no other. There were more than a dozen letters, but only so much of them as reflects that life is retained:

New York, Monday February 8, 1847

Dear Miss Fuller,

Your long and private letter of the 26th Dec., ... I have read to Mother and Pickie to their entire gratification.... Pray, when you reach Rome ask the Pope to lend you a file of The Tribune. I don't know that he takes it directly, but judging from his policy and spirit there can be little doubt that he ranks among its readers and disciples....

Mrs. Greeley has received your present with gratitude. She is pretty well, though worn down with the care of her two children, having little or no help—that is, only the queerest possible Irish girl in the kitchen, who doesn't know how even to wash or boil a potato, and nobody but me to help her with the children, and I am often away.... Mother was nearly worn out when I returned from Washington, and Pickie was almost sick of hope deferred. He is getting some better of his terrible propensity for mischief, and I hope will overcome it entirely. His habitual temper is very sweet, though his occasional moods, you know, are quite otherwise. He grows still, and his mind and conversation improve somewhat, though not proportionally. He has some very odd ideas, which his mother endeavors to repress when they transcend material and mental conditions. I have been schooled for telling him, in reply to his question whether I had ever seen an angel, that we should only see angels after death. Said he last night, "Mama, I don't remember when I was last dead." ...

New York, July 29, 1847

Dear Friend Margaret:

I returned last Saturday from an eight weeks' journey to the Lake Superior region, the prairies of Illinois, etc., during which I traveled some 3,000 miles, saw a good deal of country, traveled much on foot, worked some, attended to business, had an eye to politics, talked a little in public, and thought somewhat of my health, returning somewhat stouter, browner and more rugged than I went away....

You will have heard probably, of the death of our little daughter on the 6th of May last.... It is a sadness to me that you never saw her, and cannot know how sweet and gentle, how quiet and loving she was. I never saw a creature so patient under suffering and so grateful for kindness; and her love for me was a precious wonder. Alas for us! neither "Pickie" nor Mother realized her worth till called to part with her. "Pickie" regarded her as a rival and an obstacle to his enjoyments, urging that she should be given away; while Mother often said she wished her dead on account of the labor and anxiety she caused—I trust not really meaning it; but it is awful to think how friendless and often, I fear, consciously so, our blessing was.... With proper treatment and care, I am sure my darling would have survived.

Pickie is just what you knew him expanded. A week after the funeral his mother said to him, "Are you not sorry for the death of little sister?" "Yes," he replied, and after an instant's thought added, "but you couldn't take care of us both." His mother says she had a dreadful time with him for the first four weeks of my absence, but that during the remainder of the time he was an angel. Yet the day after I came home (Sunday) he awoke from a long sleep in the afternoon in a dreadful passion, and cried, raved and tore around for *two hours*, until his mother was terribly frightened. When I came home at 10½ P.M. he had been hours in bed but was still broad awake (his mother had whipped him twice in trying to wash him) and was now the sweetest, most loving creature you ever saw. Nothing can exceed his archness, his powers of insinuation, or his propensity to mischief; it is almost impossible that I should write in the house; he is so bent on snatching my paper, upsetting my ink, etc., in a spirit of sheer roguery. Having heard no children's prattle, he uses words picked up from us which sound most oddly from such lips. He enjoys rather more liberty than formerly, and will spend hours all alone at play with blocks, or with pebbles I brought him from Lake Superior, if no chance for mischief offers. When your mother was here, he talked much of you and wanted to take a boat and go over the water to you. He evidently thought you were on the Long Island shore across the East River. It is impossible to be stern with him, yet I feel that he is running to weeds. He does not yet know his letters, and will not probably for a year or so. His mother whips him often but never rules him; and I have no voice in his management and never can have without fighting for it—probably not with it. I have never yet been allowed to bring him downtown; he is unvaccinated, his hair uncut, and in his baby attire, and will long remain so. He grows tall, is very fair, and bids fair, under his mother's excellent regimen, to enjoy health, if his terrible paroxysms of passion do not destroy. Mother is very much as you knew her—I think a trifle calmer and clearer in mind, and enjoying fair health for her. . . .

When do you return? Please write me definitely.

Yours,
Horace Greeley

New York, Sept. 14, 1847

Margaret Fuller:
Dear Friend:

. . . For these two weeks, we have been entirely without help at our house, and what with running after servants downtown and doing their work up at the castle my last chance of leisure even for reading has been dissipated. I rise in the morning and make a fire (always difficult for me, having been accustomed neither to anthracite nor stoves in the days when I learned fire-making;) then I pump water, feed the cow, milk, etc., while Mother gets breakfast first for "Pickie," next for me, until a late hour, when I hurry down to work, and, returning late at night, take hold of the milking, etc., again. Last Sunday night, it rained so hard that I could not keep the road for pitch darkness and floundered badly in the briers and rocks as I went down the hill to the brook. It was some time before I could tell how to get out; and when I came to milk at 11 P.M. I could not see the first sign of the cow while I was walking close behind her to the barn, having found her by running against her and being guided by the sound of her footsteps alone. Nearly an hour was spent by Mrs. G. and I in ludicrous mis-adventures before the milking was accomplished, a light being necessary, yet three times extinguished. So we get on. Today, I think I have secured a servant girl, and shall send Augustus up with her to prevent her escaping, as now that I am to be absent for three days one must be had. Several have promised and disappointed us.

Pickie dear is pretty well physically, but grows daily worse morally, as indeed he could not fail to do so. He will break every dish entrusted to his hands, and though he often promises me that he never again will break my watch crystal he rarely misses an opportunity to do it. Yet he is very sweet and tender for the good part, and yields readily to gentle influences. Your mother was with him a good part of Friday, and their meeting and parting were most affecting. He insisted on making her generous presents from among my agates collected on Lake Superior, and she left him deeply affected.

I have engaged an admirer, if not a friend, of yours (Miss Emma Whiting of Chicago) to come to us and take care of Pickie; from whose ministerings I hope much for him, though it is now decreed that if she comes to the house I must leave it and board downtown. I shall do it gladly if I cannot otherwise procure him this most necessary guidance, though I could better part with almost any one or three beside. I declined to invite Miss W. until I had been fully requested to do so (but, on your brother Arthur's urgent representation) and now I fear the good for Pickie will have to be largely paid for by me. However, I shall gladly purchase it even so....

Let me stop here to say that if you want money, you may draw on us at your discretion or write us where and how to send you....

Yours,
Horace Greeley

New York, Jan. 27, 1848

My dear Friend:

...My life is just as you know it, save that I have now no leisure at all....I have not yet found time to lay my little one's ashes in the earth, though warned that they must be removed from the receiving vault where they have already remained far too long....

Pickie is still very rational, rather beautiful and grows well. He learns better than he did, and talks bewitchingly. His grammar is much better than Murray's—all his verbs being regular and his adjectives ditto—"hurted," "goodey," etc. He has no baby-talk, but says, "Do it promptly," "That's a strange condition," etc. Mother has a lot of his sayings privately written down, which I wish I had now by me. He undertook to dictate a letter to you a few days since, which she was to write. "Tell her the moon shines very bright," says Pickie. 'Well, what next?' "Tell her once there was a little voice," he continued after a pause, quoting the first line of one of Harry Cornwall's songs which

I croon to him, and which has impressed him—he being the one sole admirer in the universe of my singing. Here he stuck, or something occurred to break off the letter-writing.

...Emma Whiting from Chicago was with us for five or six weeks. ...She is a good girl, but Mother could not like her quick motions, abundant talk, her weak and diseased eyes, etc., and complained of "bad magnetism." She left us reluctantly. We have little help now, except in serving, besides an Irish girl who lives in our basement and works for us most of the time. This arrangement works well, and my poor Mary is improving both mentally and bodily. I have rarely known her calmer than for the last week or two. If we could do without servants and live very much alone I think she would slowly regain a state of serenity and moderate happiness. But life is still hard with her, and I rarely reach home before midnight without finding her still hard at work and very weary, though the day's execution has been meagre indeed. I have rarely known anyone but you whose influence upon her was not irritating. But if I could be very much alone with her, and household cares did not interpose to drive her crazy, she would steadily improve....

Pickie's mind is much poisoned with supernatural terrors in spite of our intense watchfulness.

New York, April 4, 1848

Dear Friend:

Yours of the 9th and 25th Feb'y from Rome only reached me on Sunday, when I returned from four days' speaking in Connecticut. I have since been hard at work to raise the money for you to go by steamship from Boston to-morrow. I have just accomplished it, but it has nearly broken my back. I regularly spend all the money I can get and as fast as I can get it; but about once in two years I get behind a long way, through endorsements, etc., and have to resort to some extraordinary course to extricate myself. I have sold, most reluctantly, a part of my interest in The Tribune, and devoted the proceeds to buying off most of my embarrassments, reserving $3,000 for Mrs. Greeley, having promised her so much to buy a house and a piece of ground with. By the time the house is found, I guess there will be nothing left to pay for it with—but that must take care of itself. I obtained $100 from the office (all I could get) on your account; the other $500 is between you and myself personally.— And now let this chief misery of life—money and the abominable calculations and twists it gives rise to—be as though it were not and had not been....

"Pickie" has grown about a head since you saw him, and is quite graceful and winning; but he does not learn anything in the way of letters, nor will he for some time, has very little consideration for others, in fact is thoroughly selfish, though tender-hearted—and is addicted to secrecy. "Don't tell Mother" is quite a common request with him. I cannot imagine where he caught this; for his mother is thoroughly sincere, and our family, though naturally reserved on personal subjects, is not addicted to dissembling— Yet he can be sensible and faithful. I heard last week for the first time that about a year ago, he ran away from me into Palmer's room, and some one there offered him candy. He rejected it decisively, saying "My mother does not allow me to eat candy." That was very well. We shall remain at the old place this summer, I think, and probably until we can buy some sort of a cottage in the country. I dread moving for our trumpery is very hard to move, and our place hard to move from. I hope to get some sort of a country place within the year. I shall then stay in the city except going out some Friday nights and returning Sunday mornings....

Why should you linger in Europe in such miserable health? You cannot enjoy it; you cannot improve your opportunities; you can hardly be useful there to any, and certainly the discomfort and expense of traveling must be serious. Do come home, where you can have nursing and air and repose, such as no traveler among strangers ever did have. Why should you stay?

Yours,
Horace Greeley

New York, June 27, 1848

My Friend Margaret:

...I regret the resolution announced in your letter not to write further for The Tribune, but I do not complain of it. I can well understand that an implied obligation to write periodically to a distant journal must be irksome especially to one in ill health; but I thought in this case the fact that you were to write when you pleased and as you pleased would deprive the engagement of any character of constraint or task-work.... But do exactly what seems most agreeable and don't make your life a drudgery for the sake of a few dollars.— And at all events send us your banker's postage account, and let it be used to your credit on our books. Your recent letters have been far longer than we had a right to expect.... If you will make out a bill against the firm, including postage and a fair extra charge for the extra length of certain of the letters, I suppose it will be passed without difficulty—say $2½ extra for each column over two to each letter. I want the account so adjusted that you shall be entirely satisfied. What we pay you by agreement ($10) per letter is just twice what we pay for any other European correspondence, but we are very well aware that the quality justifies this. Whether you shall write for us hereafter or not, let the past be made fully satisfactory.

I trust you have received the money I sent you, and that it will prove of service to you. Do not borrow trouble about its re-payment; for I presume it will find me just as needy at one time as another. I was a little bothered to raise it, for the demand came in a time of general panic, and I had expected that the concern would make any advance that might be called for, but was disappointed. The money was raised, my trouble was over; and, if you have duly received it, I trust you will think no more of it till the good times come around....

We are still at the old place—or rather, Mother and Pickie are; for I seldom get home at night, though I go up about every other morning for an hour or so. We are all very much as of old, except that Pickie becomes more and more of a Loco-Foco daily. He is governed, and restricted, and cramped till he hates all law and all authority, and takes more delight in mischief than in all his life beside. He can't see my hat without throwing it across the room, and as to crockery-breaking he rarely misses an opportunity to do it. He doesn't know why Truth should be preferred to Falsehood; or as he told his Mother on Saturday: "I don't care for *Truthness;* I like Fun." He cannot quite whip her yet, but he tries it every day or two, in order to do it as soon as possible. When beaten, as he was when we rode out last Saturday, he looks her in the eye with an aspect of indignation and grief, yelling "O you ugly creature." He still grows like a weed and is quite hearty. Page is about to paint him at full length. He does not get whipped so often as he did, for his Mother has adopted the plan of shutting him up in the upper chamber, which speedily brings him to subjection. Mother is in rather poor health, and has just run out of servants again, but expects another to-morrow. We have talked of buying a place, but I don't think we will very soon. I never happen to have the money.

There is very little here to interest you. We live at the old place still, and I hope you will see us there once more. Pickie and that place will not look natural to you if separated. He has all the hair you left upon his head, with the natural additions, is still in long clothes, and still unvaccinated. I am sad at the thought of being away from him this winter, when he needs and relies on me so much. He has often threatened to leave his Mother, but never to leave me. He and I are very needful to each other. He talks about his "Dutch Mother" whom he used to live with before he came to us, and has a head full of the strangest fancies. He evidently don't know the difference between his conceptions and absolute facts. He often loses or hides something, and it is almost impossible to make him tell where he has put them. When questioned his reply begins, "Well, I don't 'xactly know, but I think it is" in such or such a place, where it rarely proves to be. He sometimes tells his Mother, "Mother, I think you have a very strong imagination," when she has said something he believes or wishes untrue....

I had a letter from Thoreau at Concord, Mass., to-day mentioning that he had recently dined at Emerson's with Longfellow and Alcott, who (A) is going to Boston this winter to attempt a course of conversations. No time or room for more.

Yours truly,
Horace Greeley

New York, July 29, 1848

S. Margaret Fuller,
Dear Friend:

We are much as usual at our house. Mother is not well, works too hard and worries too much; but I think is better than she has been. We have had the same girl for over three weeks and I hope she will last another. Pickie grows in grace and in his father's good opinion. He has a wonderful faculty of imagination, and invents the strangest stories of himself and others. One of his latest fancies is that his original mother was a Dutchwoman, very poor, who could only feed him on curds and fruit, whom he left to come and live with Mrs. Greeley; and he will spin away on this yarn by the hour, half in fun, half in earnest, seeming to have no clear idea of the dividing line between perception and cognition. We were down at the Phalanx a week since; and you would have screamed with laughter had you heard him, sitting on Dolly Hosman's knee, describe his mother's peculiarities and insist that he could not abide them and must have another mother—this one is so "particular, particular, particular, particular." He wanted one that would let him "eat dirty food" (such as other people eat) and run about unwatched. He created general merriment....

Washington, Jan. 29, 1849

My Friend:

...When are you coming home? You have already outstaid all expectation. I confidently looked for your return last autumn; and am unable to imagine how anyone could remain wilfully absent from country and kindred so long. The hasty note which reached me with your last gives no hope of a speedy return. I cannot comprehend your long term in such a region of the dead. Come back soon to refresh your eyes with...our young country, or you will grow old yourself. I am sure one must grow wrinkled and mummyish by gazing at ruins—ruins. A very little of that would content me. "A living dog is better than a dead lion."...

Poor Mother gets along badly this winter. She rejoiced at my coming to Washington, hoping that she should do better with Pickie in my absence, but it proved otherwise. She has a man-servant, wet nurse, a female friend (sister of Mr. Nathan whom you know) and a kitchen-girl—she had two when I was home—but still things go badly with her....In her last letter there is a full sheet about the barn being robbed, the man rather indifferent, Pickie sick (though getting better) the nurse lying constantly, Maria an annoyance (by sending for money), and so on. I think this will bring Castle Doleful more vividly before you than anything I could write. It will be a shame if you linger in that old heathen labyrinth until we move away and the old Castle is torn down or metamorphosed into a groggery.— Do you remember Hawthorne's capital story of the youth who ran the world over after three things essential to his happiness, and finally found them all at his boyhood's home? ...

Pickie has no pantaloons yet. He grows capitally. He said the other day—"It is funny that everybody laughs at my sayings."

Yours ever,

Horace Greeley

S. Margaret Fuller,
Eternal City—but why stay there eternally?

New York, June 23, 1849

My Friend:

...You ought to see Pickie soon before he is wholly spoiled. The attitude and manner of his saying to his Mother, "Don't you dare to shut me up in a room!"—"A'int you ashamed to strike me, you ugly creature!" would be a study for a tragedy queen. And though Mother dares and isn't ashamed two or three times a day, yet Pick repeats with the same impressiveness of mien and gesture on the very next occasion. You must see him and our dear quiet, sensible, good-natured, common-place daughter ere long. Don't you consider one young child a greater treasure and wonder than all the old walls and old daubs in the round world?

Yours ever,
Horace Greeley

Coney Island Beach, near
New York, July 23, 1849

Ah Margaret! the world grows dark with us. You grieve, for Rome has fallen; I mourn, for Pickie is dead! The one sunburst of joy that has gladdened my rugged pathway has departed, and henceforth life must be heavy and rayless. I have never had an intimate friend—my life has been too intensely busy and my aims not entirely common; but this one dear being already promised to be my friend in every trial, my solace in every care. To him my form and features were the standard of beauty, and even my singing was music. He was my one auditor who never tired—my companion on whom my leisure hour was ever spent and never wasted. I had no hope, no dream of personal good or distinction of which his delight, his advantage, was not the better part; and now he is dead! Ah! my friend! did I not realize that my Father in Heaven has dealt this terrible blow not merely to punish my sins but to wean me from sordid ways and low aspirations to purity and Him, I should indeed be most wretched. But I know He doeth all things well, and will strive to be resigned. Nay, I think I am.

You have spent years in Europe and reveled amid the treasures of Art and genius that Rome encloses—I have known Pickie meantime and would not exchange with you. You knew something of him in his infancy, but you left three years ago. He was nothing then but an infant of two years; he was five last March—a tall, fair, glorious boy, his golden locks uncut, his grace, wit and even wisdom surpassing all you can imagine. Some of his observations were really keen and searching. No youth of twenty could receive strangers with a more engaging mixture of modesty, manliness and sweetness. He was selfish and violent at times—you know whether he had good reason to be—but he was generous and tender-hearted, and always laying by or begging some coin to give to the poor. O he was a dear child, and it is very hard to leave him in the cold earth and go back to struggling with the mean for ends which seem too like them.

I have written a full account of his last bright days and that one day of blackness in a letter to Emma Whiting, of which I have kept a copy, and hope you will read it when you come home. It is quite too long to send to Rome; beside, you must come home before you will feel how great is this loss for us all. He never forgot 'Aunty Margaret,' though his recollection of her grew fainter toward the last. Ah! had we dreamed of this loss when you left us! Even as it was, your tears were prophetic!

We had not the least premonition of this blow. I last saw him in health at 10 A.M. on the 11th, when I went downtown leaving him as hearty and joyous as ever in the world. His mother went down too; he, on account of the heat, was persuaded to stay at home. Mother bought him a small *real* fiddle, which greatly delighted him; he hated to lay it aside at bed-time, but finally did, delighted with the idea of coming upstairs in the morning to play me a tune on it before I got up. I came home and went to bed at 11—still no complaint or alarm. At 2 he had a call, and his mother got up with him—still no alarm. At 3, he was called up again by violent purging; now his mother came up and called me. Very soon he was vomiting as well as purging—the awful rice-water! We doctored incessantly, but not efficiently; it was 7 o'clock before we got a physician; more potent remedies were now resorted to; the discharges were stopped, and at 9 a reaction seemed to be established; but our doctor was called away at 8 by a sudden and dangerous illness of his own wife; he did not return until after 12, and meantime (perhaps through mismanagement) the reaction had been lost and our darling had for two or three hours been sinking; we went to work desperately, but the only effect was to torture him; at 2 he was hopelessly sinking, and for the first time became conscious of it himself. He had struggled with superhuman strength all day to throw off the clothes that we held upon him, trying to produce perspiration (he sometimes asserting that he was well, and only wanted to be let alone)—even biting the fingers by which we were holding him down under the clothes, and constantly struggling to get up in the bed; and at last the inflammation in his stomach striking to his brain he struggled up on end repeatedly, exclaiming at intervals,—"O it's no use trying to do any thing for me! ... I am afraid! ... I am afraid! ... I am sinking! ... I am sinking! ... I am dying!" He then sank down in the bed, and offered no more resistance to whatever we chose to do. I think he was not rational afterward, though it was more than two hours before the spirit took its flight from that beauteous, wasted tabernacle to one still more glorious. The next day his cold ashes rode between his father and mother to Greenwood, as his sister's had done two years before. I carried the new coffin down into our vault and laid it beside the other—the mother going down into the narrow house and directing, with a burning heart but a tearless face. Ah me! Ah me!

Mother has been well and strong throughout, though you know that, compared with him, all the world beside was nothing to her. The next day we were compelled to begin (or rather resume) a struggle for the life of our last remaining child, now eight months old, whom Malaria, Teething, Diarrhea and finally Sprue came very near carrying off. To save her, the doctor ordered us here.... Our neighborhood is *very* bad with cholera and mostly fatal. This is a sad letter for us—not for long life, but for Heavenly faith and life.

Horace Greeley

New York, August 14, 1849

Margaret:

Why should I write you again, when I know not that you have received any of my recent letters, and fear you will not receive this? And yet I cannot help writing just this once more about our lost angel boy. My Pickie! My Pickie! How sad is this world without him! Don't forget to ask for and read my long account of his last days on earth when you come home. If I had a copy I would try to send it by some private hand, but the labor of copying is too great.

I must transcribe for you from Mother's memorandum book a letter from Pickie to you, written by her (at his dictation) more than a year ago, but I think never sent. It is *verbatim* as follows:

"To Aunty Margaret that has gone to Europe:

"I want to see you very much. When will you come home? Write me about the beautiful things you have seen. I like to play a great deal. I make a noise and make Mama nervous, but you know a little boy can't be very still.

"I had a pretty little sister. We called her Dotty (Doddy). She was so little. She had very bright eyes. She looked at me so still I did not like her eyes. She has gone to another world and I am very sorry.

"In the summer the Narcissus is very pretty. I saw very pretty things at Mrs. Springs. I have got your rose-pin. The angel has got nothing but one wing. The other is broke off.
Pickie"

It is your first and last letter from our darling.... He will never trouble you again. Alas! your tears at leaving were prophetic! And yet he was nothing then to what he had since become—so sweet, so arch, graceful, loving—so bewildering even in his very faults, for his temper, you know, was violent and his disposition strangely selfish; yet you cannot know how generous he became, and how anxious to give to the poor and suffering. O, my father has sorely afflicted me, yet I know it is in love. Pray for me that this judgment may be sanctified to my present and everlasting good. Should you meet the dear cherub in the spirit world before I do, beseech him to love me tenderly and intercede for our early union in that world of abiding realities, in spite of my unworthiness. Even Heaven would seem desolate to me if he were not there....

I have nothing else to write. We deserted our home three weeks or more since, and went to the seaside (Coney Island), but had to come back for a new wet nurse; so a second time; another staid one night; the next left us yesterday—her husband would have her. We have been stopping at the Astor but went up to our desolate home last night and had a hard night with our lovely baby; and today Mrs. G. has gone downtown selecting another nurse. I hope she has chosen a good one (the ninth) and that she may be able to go to the country soon.
H.G.

CHAPTER XII

"The Philadelphia Slaughterhouse"

It is refreshing to turn from Greeley's own revelation of the tragedies of his home life to events with which he had so much to do and that forecast so definitely the future of the nation. He was to be the title-maker of the new Republican party, and the rallying and most influential force in prewar politics. But he did not gain that leadership without periods of baffled activities and ignored suggestions of policies and candidates. Keenly disappointed and depressed by the 1844 election, he was fated for a still more unhappy time as he saw his beloved Whig party losing its vitality under the guidance of his two partners in politics—Weed and Seward. Clay's second defeat for the presidency had given his leadership the character of a lost cause; its vigor was sapped; in 1848 "availability" was to be the test for a presidential candidate and platform silence on the great issue of the day was to be the feature of the campaign. Greeley disliked intensely the prospect of either Taylor or Scott as the Whig candidate for President—the former called by Webster "an illiterate frontier colonel" and the latter described in Greeley's own words as "an aristocratic, bombastic fuss and feathers." He appealed to Weed to nominate "anyone but a soldier with Seward as vice-president." He insisted that such a ticket would surely win—"the country doesn't deserve to have as President that pot-bellied, mutton-headed cucumber, Lewis Cass," the Democratic nominee.

Such utterances are typical of his protests through the two years preceding the convention. A war hero was to be swept into the White House on a battle cry of victory over Mexico—and with no other qualification! Instead, Greeley urged a platform squarely endorsing the historic Wilmot Proviso, excluding slavery forever from all territory taken over from Mexico. He insisted to Weed that that attempted legislation—the first challenge to slavery extension—would win and give the party the power to restore tariff protection, to enact homestead laws to settle the West, and to bring about other greatly needed reforms. "Capital invested in reform movements draws no dividends," was Weed's curt response. "I like to have a victory when we win one and not to be Tylerized again," persisted Greeley. "I want to have some element of progress in the ticket." It galled him, too, that the demand for Taylor came chiefly from the "Cotton Whigs" of the South, led by Alexander H. Stephens and Robert Toombs of Georgia. The future vice-president of the Confederacy boasted in his *Autobiography*, "It was I who nominated Taylor."

It was then that Greeley began his frequent prophecies of Whig disintegration. In two letters to Beman Brockway, editor of the Watertown, N.Y. *Times,* he referred to the campaign as a "farewell scuffle" by the Whigs. Ten years earlier, Brockway had called at the *New Yorker* office looking for work. He found Greeley "seated at a table in the composing room writing furiously" and "the greenest specimen of an editor I had ever looked upon." He did not get work, but a lifelong friendship began.

Under date of November 13, 1847, Greeley replied to Brockway's inquiry about Seward as a candidate for President: "We couldn't get Seward nominated by our party. We may nominate him for vice-president.... He has made bitter enemies alike by his faults as by his virtues. I think we shall try Clay and fall back on Corwin. But no one can guess where any of us will be next June."

In a second letter to Brockway a week later Greeley made this historic prophecy of "the best party ever yet seen," though he did not then have the Republican party by name in mind:

Old Friend:

What you suggest is entirely right, and must come to pass, but I think the difficulties in the way of immediate accomplishment are too formidable to be overcome. It looks to me as if the contest of 1848 is to be a kind of farewell scuffle after which we can see how and where to find a place.

The basis of union of the true democracy for the next twenty years is to be land reform [home-steading]. With this goes labor reform or the 10-hours regulation.

To these articles I hope another will naturally attach itself—abolition of the army and navy.

On such a platform, peace being assured and our boundaries clearly defined, I think the best party ever yet seen in our country can be rallied in abundant time for the presidential election of 1852. Who will lead I neither know nor care.

Knocked about from pillar to post as to candidate and platform, Greeley turned to Clay in November 1847 for counsel. He found that the old flame for the presidency still blazed. Clay was then seventy-one years old, broken in health and heavily involved in debt, yet he wrote: "I will decide next spring or earlier, if necessary, whether my poor name may be used as a candidate for the Presidency.... If I should be a candidate, I mean to write no letters, make no speeches and be mum. I expect if that emergency should arise to be as much abused for my silence as I have been for my writing or speaking.... Taylorism is on the decline with us. It was a burst of enthusiasm which was of a nature not to last. Many now regret having yielded to it."

But Greeley knew that Taylorism was not "on the decline." To offset it, he began in the *Tribune* what Seward in a letter to Weed on January 30 termed "Greeley's quixotic battle against war heroes in politics."

Soon came the nominating convention—June 6 at Philadelphia. It was the first in which Greeley battled "on his own." In 1840 he had been simply a Weed lieutenant; in 1844 the Clay nomination had been made by acclamation. Now that he was the editor of a newspaper of recognized national influence, Greeley determined to use that influence to prevent a nomination so meaningless as that of Taylor.

But the first ballot ended his hopes. He did not even get consideration for Seward for vice-president. Another New York man, Millard Fillmore, won that prize without an effort; it led to the presidency.

Two colorful human interest pictures of Greeley during the convention battle are to be found in the reminiscences of Oliver Dyer, official reporter of the Senate at Washington, and of Alexander K. McClure, famous editor of the Philadelphia *Times*. Mr. Dyer wrote:

One evening, after an adjournment of the convention, I was in the office of the Philadelphia "North American." Morton McMichael, the Editor, was talking over the situation with several Taylor men when who should come tramping into the office, carpet bag in hand, but Horace Greeley. On seeing who were present, Greeley scowled upon them, turned around and started for the door.

"Where are you going, Mr. Greeley?" McMichael courteously asked.

"I'm going home!" snarled Greeley.

"But there's no train tonight," McMichael suggested.

"I don't want any train," Greeley snapped out. "I'm going across New Jersey afoot and alone!" And away he went.

As I withdrew my gaze from Greeley's retreating form, it fell upon a dark young man of small stature, with a large and fine head, who was standing at the foot of the table at which I sat. He had been watching Greeley, and his countenance was convulsed with scorn and detestation, somewhat relieved by a sinister gleam of triumph. He soon left the office, and I said to McMichael: 'How that man hates Greeley! Who is he?'

"I thought you knew him," McMichael answered. "He is a fellow townsman of yours. He is Henry J. Raymond, Editor of the New York 'Courier and Enquirer.' "

Editor McClure's book *Our Presidents* adds this companion picture:

I met Greeley as he was hurrying out of the convention. He was mad clear through. His low-crowned, broad-brimmed, fuzzy hat set at an angle of forty-five degrees on the back of his head, his profusion of shirt collar protected from wandering over his shoulders by an immense black handkerchief that he used as a necktie, with the awkward knot resting under his left ear, and his immense baggy, black swallow-tail coat and the carpet bag he held by one handle while the other handle lay down by the side of the bag—it did not contribute to genteel appearance!

In the *Tribune* next day the Whig convention became "the Philadelphia Slaughterhouse," wherein Whig principles were butchered. The party was skulking behind a Major General of whom it was accurately said he did not know whether he was a Whig or politically just nothing at all. How, then, could voters know? The *Tribune* would take time to decide.

Greeley's heart was really with the free soil movement. Its convention at Buffalo on August 9 was one of the most earnest, enthusiastic political gatherings ever held, with Salmon Portland Chase, Charles Sumner, Joshua Giddings, Charles Francis Adams, John P. Hale and others who later were to be leaders against slavery. Greeley liked their spirit—"For the sake of freedom, forgetting all past differences, we inscribe on our banner free soil, free speech, free labor and free men, and under it we will fight on until a triumphant victory." Though its vigor and its purpose appealed strongly to Greeley, he had denounced the third party movement responsible for Clay's defeat only four years before and he could not follow that example. He did not endorse it editorially, but the *Tribune* news columns gave it abundant space.

Finally, on September 15, Greeley gave his fellow editor Colfax this revealing picture of his mind:

September 15, 1848

Dear Friend:

I am going to vote for Taylor—at least I think I am, and I am not clear that this is right. If I could make Van Buren President tomorrow,

I would. I don't like the man but I do like the principles he embodies now, free soil and land reform.

The Free Soil Party is the only live party around here—it ought to triumph, but God works out his end by other instruments than majorities; wherefore it will fail but fail gloriously.

I could have been the oracle of the Free Soil Party with any extent of circulation had I chosen. Party fidelity—or rather fidelity to men I love who still cling to the putrid corpse of the party butchered at Philadelphia—has withheld me. So I cling to a party which never loved me and am helping elect a President who will shun me. I could shake down the whole rotten fabric by a bugle-blast, yet will not sound it because some good men I love would be crushed within the ruins.

Taylor will be elected and I, cussed by those I serve and deserted by subscribers for the most opposite reasons, shall be where "he that doubteth" belongs! Well, who cares? ... If the Whig carcass wins this election it will not soon win another. Mark it!

H.G.

And history did!

Of all the likely places in which to find Greeley, the last one a person knowing him would guess would be the inaugural ball which for more than a century ended the ceremonies attending the induction into office of a new President. Yet with true newspaper instinct Greeley was there on March 4, 1849, to witness the welcome to Taylor. In his published story in the *Tribune* he could not avoid comparing its mild character with the "thunderous applause" that would have greeted Clay had he been walking "into the midst of three thousand of the elite of the beauty and chivalry of the Whig party"—"how the rafters would have shivered!" ... "Taylor seems a good, honest and not unwise man who will do his utmost." ... "And yet had the dancing part of my education been less shockingly neglected I should not have liked dancing now! I would wish to see farther before exulting genuinely over the new era....

"I turn from this imposing pageant so rich in glitter, so poor in feeling, to think of him who should have been the central figure of this great panorama—'behind the mountains but not setting.'

Let the exulting thousands quaff their red wines of the revel to the victor of Monterey and Buena Vista, while Wit points the Sentiment with Epigram, and Beauty drowns it with her smile; more grateful to me is the stillness of my lonely chamber, this cup of crystal water in which I honor the cherished memory with the old familiar aspiration, 'Here's to you, Henry Clay!'"

> I hear a lion in the lobby roar,
> Mr. Speaker. Shall we shut the door
> And keep him out? Or shall we let him in
> And see if we can turn him out again?

With these lines Greeley greeted the historic 1850 Compromise proposal of his greatest statesman, Clay. He did not share the Kentucky senator's faith in the new legislation. Every southern state had defiantly declared for slavery extension wherever it chose to go. A solid South stood firmly for its "rights." Clay's bill upheld some of those "rights," withheld others; settled none. "As well try to shingle a whirlwind," commented Greeley. Nevertheless after an absence of seven years Clay had returned to the Senate for this one purpose. "I go to serve my country. My health or my life is of no consequence." Had any other Senator sponsored the measure it would have met vigorous opposition from Greeley; but loyalty to the Kentuckian led him for the only time in his career to withhold from *Tribune* readers his real opinion. He gave the bill what he called "qualified support," yet he also made his first bold challenge of the slave power:

> If any Rip Van Winkle be still dreaming of a speedy and harmonious adjustment by compromise of the slavery question now agitating the Union, we beg him to rub his eyes, at least half way open.... We are in for a struggle, willing or unwilling, and our adversaries proffer us no alternative but defeat or victory. We must preserve the new territories intact to freedom or surrender them to slavery.... Our answer is unequivocal ... — Let the Union be a thousand times slivered rather than we should aid you to plant slavery on free soil.

Of course, a Greeley would not be content in his editor's chair merely reading the debate; he must hear it, hear all sides and over his "H.G." initials give *Tribune* readers his interpretation. Here you have again the reason for Greeley's understanding of public questions and his unusual ability to convey it to his readers—he was always his own reporter at the scene of action. In that spirit he was present in the Senate when Clay arose to begin his two days' plea for an era of peace between North and South through compromise—"give and take." "Such a brilliant constellation of wisdom and worthy age and excellence, youth and loveliness," wrote Greeley, "will rarely be seen anywhere. Clay, perhaps the tallest man in the room, stood upon the floor calm and serene . . . clear-headed as ever."

For dramatic intensity it was a scene without equal in our parliamentary history and one of the moments of decision vital to our national life. In that debate we see the statesmanship of America at its greatest. Slumped in his chair, almost helpless, unable to speak for himself, sat John Caldwell Calhoun, Senator from South Carolina, listening intently to Clay and grimly determined to oppose all legislation that challenged, or even fixed limits for, slavery. Across the aisle sat Webster, also studying every word as it was uttered. Here were three men who had served their country in Senate and House for nearly half a century; and all three soon to be in their graves alongside their thwarted hope to be President. Two of these statesmen were pleading to save the life of a nation which had come into existence about the time of their own birth. Calhoun, the third member of the group, had also come into the world with the nation which he was under oath to maintain and protect. He sat now in the seat he had occupied so many years, insisting, justifying and predicting, in the last words he ever addressed to the Senate, that the end had come for the Union which his own South had helped to create, and for which it had then furnished every President except John Adams, his son John Quincy Adams and Martin Van Buren—only twelve years during which the White House was out of southern control.

Crowded to the doors, in gallery and on the floor, was the Senate Chamber, everyone present thrilled by the prospect of a Clay speech. People everywhere were confident that Clay would find a way, as he had found one in 1820, to halt indefinitely the creeping "irrepressible conflict." It was the last effort by legislation to hold North and South together. Clay's opening words reflect his deep feeling: "Never so oppressed, never so appalled, never so anxious, I pray God to avert disaster. It is passion, passion and party, that I dread. Solemnly, I ask you to pause at the edge of the precipice. . . . Let us think only of our God, our country, our conscience and our glorious Union. If any state should choose to place itself in military array against the Union, I am for ascertaining whether we have a government or not. Even if my own state of Kentucky should attempt it, I would not go with her!"

On March 7 came the eloquent Webster—he who only a few years before had called slavery agitation mere "rub-a-dub." "Secession—peaceable Secession? Your eyes and mine will never see that miracle! It must produce war, and such a war as I will not describe."

Greeley did not hesitate to endorse the opposition speeches by Salmon P. Chase and Seward. It was Chase's first speech in the Senate. "The cry that the South will dissolve the Union neither astonishes me nor alarms me. We of the West are in the habit of looking upon the Union as we look upon the Arch of Heaven, without a thought that it can ever decay or fall."

But Seward's historic "higher law" speech aroused Greeley's greatest enthusiasm. In an editorial he endorsed exultingly the memorable paragraph: "The Constitution devoted the domain to Union, to justice, to defense, to welfare and to liberty, but there is a higher law than the Constitution which regulates our authority over the domain and devotes it to the same noble purpose."

"Isn't it sound?" Greeley asked Colfax. "If Seward can only maintain that position he is our hope for 1856. When the right time comes we can elect him on a clean, square issue, thus winning a victory that is good for something." On April 10 Greeley wrote Colfax again from Washington:

"They are likely to make some sort of a fix-up on slavery that won't do. I am looking on. It will not break us down, for we are that, but possibly keep us down for the next four or five years, and kill the last chance for making Clay President. I wish he had not come back to the Senate, for I wanted him to run in 1852. I won't give up."

Three weeks later, with Taylor dead and Fillmore in the White House, the *Tribune* boldly declared that "neither Mr. Clay's plan nor President Fillmore's plan nor any other plan can stop slavery agitation so long as slavery shall not merely exist but insist on extending its domain. . . . The slave-catching fugitive slave bill will make a hundred Abolitionists oftener than it catches one slave. Doesn't the South understand that they cannot get their escaped slaves no matter how many laws are crowded upon the statute book? For the North does not and will not return them. They hide them and send them to Canada."

CHAPTER XIII

Greeley Practices His Creed

ONCE AGAIN, as after Clay's defeat, Greeley despaired of politics. The *Tribune* was now established beyond all uncertainties, and Greeley was the nation's best-known citizen. Though idling was not his forte, the time had come for him to relax from the old activities. He busied himself in giving reality to some of the "isms" for which he had fought his early battles—particularly the sharing of profits and ownership with those who had helped to make company success, and protection to wage earners by organization into a union. He applied his creed to the *Tribune* and endeavored to persuade partner McElrath that they were not entitled to hold all the stock of the company; they should sell, equally, as many shares as their associates cared to buy at the original incorporation figure of $1,000 per share. This was one-fifth of the price he had recently refused from outsiders. McElrath had paid only $2,000 in July, 1841, for fifty shares of the company's one hundred shares, but he was not willing to part with any of it except for cash and at present value.

Greeley decided to live up to his own convictions. At a meeting of the firm in December 1849 he offered as many of his fifty shares as employees desired to purchase. The official minutes of this meeting (still in existence in the library of Thomas W. Dewart of the *Sun*) read that "*each subscriber will receive his stock at once, whether he has the means to pay for it in full or in part, and time will be allowed to accumulate from the dividends money sufficient to pay for it.*"

At the close of the meeting, publisher McElrath owned one-half of the company and Greeley less than one-third—which later was reduced to 21½ shares by the sale of ten shares to Dana, who could make no initial payment at all. Here was "association" with a vengeance!—a foolish sacrifice of the fortune Greeley had worked so hard to create. At the first opportunity to secure himself financially he thus turned from it and knowingly placed himself again in the hands of moneylenders—this time for the remainder of his life. Yet no one ever heard him regret that nearly all the money return from the success of his own efforts was going into the pockets of others.

Never less than twelve employees, and usually as many as twenty, representing every department, were stockholders who paid for their stock out of dividends. There were several years in which each shareholder received as high as $1,700 return on his original $1,000 investment. Whitelaw Reid estimated that the average annual dividend paid over the thirty-one Greeley years was $566.66 per share. In 1872, even after Greeley's death, the stock brought $9,400 a share.

But employee participation in ownership was only part of Greeley's plan for the full recognition of the worker. He believed in a union of wage earners, and again led the way by organizing the *Tribune* printers. He presided over the first meeting of the New York Printers' Union, held in Stoneall's Hotel, 131 Fulton Street, on January 19, 1850. There he was chosen president.

As such he issued the first union card to a printer. It read:

No. 1. Established January, 1850.

New York Printers' Union

This is to certify that C. W. Colburn was admitted a member January 1, 1850.

Horace Greeley
President

W. H. Prindle, Secretary

Greeley did not stop there. He became the first negotiator of collective bargaining, for he immediately agitated for a fixed scale

A Greeley "Ism"—Votes for Women

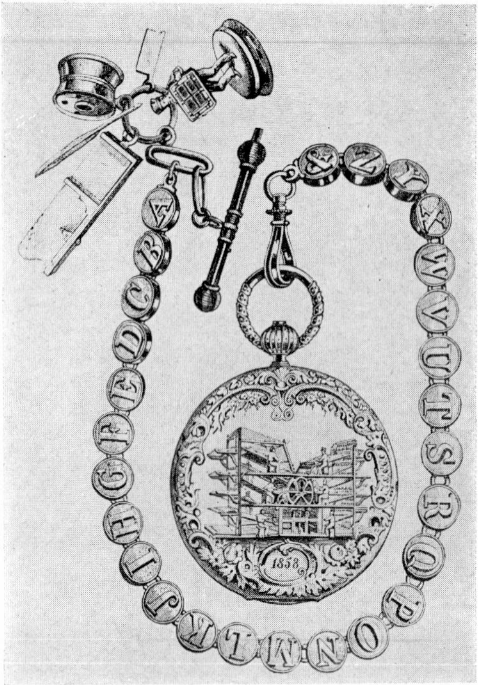

This Unusual Watch Is Described in Detail in the Text

INTERIOR SECTION, SHOWING THE INSCRIPTION OF THE WATCH PRESENTED TO HORACE GREELEY.

OBVERSE OF THE WATCH PRESENTED TO HORACE GREELEY.

of wages and hours for printers. "It is idle to talk of the freedom of labor," he said, "when a man with a family is told 'if you can work thirteen hours a day, or as many days as we see fit, you can stay; if not, you can have your walking papers'." In six months' time he had the union established in most printing offices and was chosen to represent it in conferences organizing unions in other trades.

Sixty-one years later, on February 3, 1911, the centennial of Greeley's birth, Typographical Union No. 6 held a "Greeley Celebration" at the New York Theatre on Broadway, at which President James Tole, using a printer's expression, declared that "no grander character than Greeley had ever come up from the case.... Our fondest thought of him," continued Mr. Tole, "is of the man of simple earnestness, thinking of himself merely as Horace Greeley, printer."

Printers, however, did not wait until Greeley's death to show their appreciation. Greeley chapels and Ben Franklin chapels were organized in the composing rooms of newspapers all through the country. In May 1858, those employed on the *Tribune* presented to their "editor and fellow-craftsman" a unique watch—the most perfect timepiece that Appleton, Tracy & Co., at Waltham, Massachusetts, then could make; "one which will bear comparison with any watch ever produced anywhere," the company proudly claimed. It was the conception of an American artist, the materials were the products of American mines and factories, and the Waltham firm was one of the earliest of American watchmakers. The watch and chain were regarded as a triumph of American workmanship—a fact which made the present all the more acceptable to Greeley.

The photographs on another page tell the story of this remarkable timepiece. It weighs six ounces as against the two or three ounces of present-day timepieces. There are twenty-seven links in the chain, each link a type face representing a letter of the alphabet plus "&." The pieces attached to the ring are a quill, an inkwell, a thin brass rule or blade used to separate the lines of type while being set, a printer's composing stick and a page form of type locked and being carried to the press. The last was evidently intended to be used as a paperweight. The watch is now owned by Mr. H. A. Stahl, living at Chappaqua, a retired member of the engineering staff of the New York Central Railroad.

It was in those years following "the Philadelphia Slaughter-house," while out of sympathy with Whig policies and candidates, that Greeley advanced to the front rank of popular lecturers. The freedoms of the lyceum platform were a relief from partisan wrangling. He could talk of higher things—and he did.

"Horace, how do you figure when a lecture is a success?" asked the Rev. Henry Ward Beecher, famous pastor of Plymouth Church, Brooklyn, himself also a popular lecturer.

"When more people stay in than go out," shot back Greeley.

Going-out was an experience which Greeley had to undergo at the beginning, for he painfully lacked voice and poise.

From the office of the *Log Cabin*, he replied to an invitation to speak at Poughkeepsie on the Fourth of July 1840:

"I am a wretched speaker, lacking voice, confidence and command of language. I am astonished and vexed at myself that I cannot say what rises so clearly in my mind and what I can write so readily, but such is the fact. If you have men who can talk I shall be silent; if you have nobody I shall try to show my good-will at whatever cost of time and mortification."

But as the "Weekly Try-bune" gained circulation, people wanted to see and hear the young editor who was arousing their keen interest. As early as November 20, 1841, he wrote to his old friend Obadiah Bowe:

Companion in Adversity:

I've been writing a Lecture, I've got a dozen invitations on hand—very flattering; only they don't pay. I shall lecture for nothing this winter, and next I'll strike for wages. I've written all the old ideas I could get for a week past in a lecture for which I shall perhaps get a little soap and perhaps none. That doesn't pay, does it?

Last night I was scratching on my lecture till 10 P.M. When I got through and, going on my way, I found myself hard up against two oak folding doors, locked on to other side. The clerk had supposed nobody above and shut up. So I had to come back, fix my fire, read till I was tired, and then try to sleep, which was the only foolish part of the business. It was bitter cold; the fire wouldn't more than half burn and a bed of newspaper files and no blanket was not the thing. I wasted several hours in hard trials, and then turned on the gas, built a wood fire and went to reading again. This I followed till half past 7, when I was let out. I was as good as wheat all day. Nevertheless, it is better than card playing all night, I charge ye! *That* gives a headache and a fogginess of perception.

Greeley's first lecture on a lyceum circuit was delivered on January 3, 1843, in what was called the Tabernacle, located on the east side of Broadway, between Worth Street and Catherine Lane, New York City. It was popularly known as "the Cave," because of its amphitheater; Jenny Lind called the place "an old tub" and refused to sing there. "Human Life" was the subject. "If those who care to hear him will sit close to the platform they will favor the speaker's 'weak and husky voice,'" was the advice given in the advertisement. That occasion was probably the only time when Greeley ever apologized for himself. "You must not, my friends, expect fine words from a rough, busy man like me, yet such observations as I have been hastily able to note down I will now submit."

Unfortunately he read most of his lecture and delivered it in such a manner that he almost emptied the house. That night he was given the title of "Squeak Greeley." "Did you ever hear such a tedious, terrible speaker?" asked one who had sat through the lecture; "but what he said enchanted me." "Horace had better stay at home and look after his newspaper" commented Bennett's *Herald*.

It was several years after this first lecture before Greeley achieved even a measure of the success he described to Beecher; ultimately he became so popular that Ralph Waldo Emerson, writing of his own lack of an audience in Minneapolis, said, "Greeley preceded me by a few days and the people gathered together, coming thirty or forty miles to hear him speak."

As usual, money-making was not Greeley's chief purpose. He

liked to be out among the people, especially among church and social organizations. A typical letter was evidently in reply to a suggestion to him of an unusual fee because of the distance he would have to travel. Greeley replied:

N. Y. March 6, 1850

Rev. H. Farrington—Lawrence, Kansas.

I would like to earn the money, if you are perfectly able to pay for the lecture, though hereabouts I never am paid, and away from here only about one-half the time. On the whole, though, the places that see fit to pay me make up for those that don't—so that I lose nothing pecuniarily for what lecturing I can find time to do. I never make any terms but take pay when it is offered and take nothing when that is more often agreeable. You must take me when I can come or let me be. I can speak to your folks (D.V.) on last Friday of this month. I hope this time will suit you. If it does let me know; if it doesn't no matter.

Horace Greeley

To Schuyler Colfax, then in Congress, he wrote from Baltimore ten days later: "I am urged and almost driven to come here and fill three lectures, but no man says 'thank ye' and my tavern bill is $5.60 and with gratuities to the servants will go over $6. I must change my last bill to pay my fare home. Everybody supposes that since I live in the City and print an extensively circulated newspaper (though I own but a quarter of it) that I can hand anybody $100 and never ought to be paid; so I am eternally in pecuniary hot water and never see a dollar that has not a dozen mortgages. About half the world likes to get the use of the money of other people on these terms. Well, I can afford it, but it is all I can do."

CHAPTER XIV

"Editorial Rooms. Ring the Bell"

GREELEY LEAVES FOR Europe until September," wrote Dana to Washington correspondent James S. Pike, under date of March 26, 1851, "and I shall have the paper on my shoulders. I hope you will send us a rocket occasionally to flash up to our sky. You will thus save the country, not to speak of saving me from making a stupid paper. It must be better than when the 'Old Man' is at home, or they'll say that Dana's a failure, which God forbid!"

Yes—strange news it certainly was! For at least four consecutive months the *Tribune* is to be published without its founder at the helm or within guiding distance. That surely will be a new experience for the staff! They are to miss that familiar figure bent over his desk, his nearsighted eyes almost buried in the page on which he is writing—lost to the world—his shrill, sharp complaints of poor work, his gracious compliments for good. Vacationing had come none too soon. In the twenty-five years since the morning on which he timidly asked editor Amos Bliss in East Poultney, "Don't you want a boy to learn the trade?" Greeley had known no rest from work, no freedom from anxieties. He labored with a might that resented every hour snatched for food or rest; such interruptions of duty were tolerated only as regrettable necessities. Too frequently of late he had been found asleep at his desk—quill pen in hand, an uncompleted sentence on his page of copy plainly marking where resistance to weariness had at last ceased—just fagged out.

Before he touched pen to paper Greeley always had definitely in mind what he wanted to say and the precise words he was to use. He wrote rapidly, as though eager to catch up with his thoughts before they escaped him. He would rest his left hand at the top of the sheet to keep it firm, his fingers nervously drumming on it as he drove his quill pen with its heavy scrawl; often it would catch in the sheet and then a flow of ink made big blots which editor Amos J. Cummings said were "like mashed spiders or crushed huckleberries." Deeply absorbed, he seemed unconscious of all else, particularly of visitors. When interrupted it was his habit to keep his left thumb on the page exactly where he had stopped writing, so that he would not waste time hunting later for the place. When a sentence had been completed Greeley rarely changed a word. He was most particular to punctuate. Woe betide the printer who failed to include Greeley's commas, semicolons and periods! To Greeley each one had a meaning as significant as the marks on his score have to a musician. "Follow Copy!" was the standing order; as the saying then was among printers, "Follow Copy!—even if it blows out of the window!"

No doubt the "worm fence" handwriting was difficult for a stranger to decipher, but *Tribune* printers and proofreaders were familiar with it. Others compared it to gridirons struck by lightning. Yet Joel Benton asserted in his *Persons and Places* that, once you learned its "alphabet," its illegibility was not so apparent as its homeliness. "Good God!" exclaimed a friend to whom Greeley had written hurriedly, "if Belshazzar had seen this handwriting he would have been more terrified than he was."

Think back over the Greeley career so far outlined and you will not fail to realize the solicitude of his associates that he should travel to new scenes and among new people—and travel alone! Recall the seven years' struggle with the *New Yorker*, the night-boat trips to and from Albany week after week, the *Jeffersonian*, The *Log Cabin* and the first ten years of the *Tribune*—what an experience! But what a drain on body, mind and nerves!

Even when Greeley arrived at his office as late as noon, to remain usually—except for a hasty restaurant dinner—until eleven o'clock at night, he would throw on his desk out of his coat pockets a bunch of newspapers he had already partially read; frequently as he took off his hat all kinds of letters and memos would flutter out of it to the floor. That famous hat was his "reminder box" as well as his post office! He always kept it on his desk inside up, so that he could throw memos into it.

Fatigue of body was never so evident as fatigue of mind. Often he hadn't even a good-morning greeting for those about him; quick of temper, nerve-worn—"scold like a drab," declared Dana, "as ferocious as a baited bear." When Beman Brockway asked him if they should give unusual space to a particular Beecher sermon his tart reply was: "Why not? We give space to the damned theatres and the damned race tracks—why not to a sermon?" Fortunately, after a few moments of sleep in his chair, a different Greeley would awaken—cordial, placid, looking for things to praise instead of things to condemn, ready to resume his quill-driving, as he called it, even while visitors were talking to him—or, rather, at him—and awaiting his reply. Indeed, he seems to have had the faculty of conversing and writing at the same time, often not even looking up at his caller as he answered his questions.

In illustration, an incident is related of a visitor who once seated himself beside the desk and kept telling his story to the writing Greeley, until the latter finally turned toward the man and exclaimed: "Now, tell me what you want; tell me quick and in one sentence, for I haven't a moment to spare."

The visitor stated that he was seeking a subscription to a cause, as he put it, that was designed to save thousands of our fellow citizens from going to hell.

He got no further!

"Not a cent!" interrupted Greeley impatiently. "Not a damned cent! Not half enough of them go there now!"

Swiftly he swiveled his chair around to his desk, and the existence of the would-be hell-saver was forever out of mind.

Another story is told of a visit by William H. Vanderbilt to whose son Greeley had made several loans.

"You think that I'll pay those loans," declared Vanderbilt hotly, "but I tell you I'll never pay a damned cent!"

"Who in hell asked you to?" shouted Greeley, as he turned to his desk and forgot the presence of his millionaire visitor. However, the debt was voluntarily paid to Greeley's children after his death as a tribute to "my friend."

Visitors would climb the one flight of circling iron stairs and enter his office merely by opening a door lettered on its glass panel: "Editorial Rooms. Ring the bell." Seldom did they obey even that request. Politicians, would-be farmers, social reformers, borrowers, good men and bad with all kinds of schemes and notions, swindlers, visitors from the West and from other cities—all crowded in, robbing him of his money as well as of his time. "There's just a bare chance that my little gift will do good for some poor devil," he would say, "and I am willing to take that chance."

Two windows of his office afforded a wide view of City Hall Park. On the wall between the windows hung a lithograph of Henry Clay and another of "Pilgrims Landing at Plymouth Rock." His swivel chair stood on a small rug, but no carpet covered the pine-board floor; a high stool at a reading desk and two narrow cane-bottomed chairs did little to relieve the bareness.

That well-remembered desk! how many stories have been related of it; how many memories for all familiar with it! It was larger than he actually needed, yet had it been twice the size it would still have been completely covered with all sorts of things. He permitted no one to touch a book or paper upon it. Though absent a week or even longer he wanted to find it on his return exactly as he had left it. Books and pamphlets full of old election returns were conspicuous; "Congressional Globes" for many sessions were piled high on the top; letters answered or to be answered and newspaper clippings were scattered all over it.

Suspended from the ceiling on a sort of pulley, almost over his head, but just within arm's length, was a big heavy pair of scissors which he pulled down when needed; they would have cut tin; a bell cord to summon a copy boy hung from the ceiling too; at one corner of the desk there was always a paste pot and at the other end a box of sand which he peppered over the pages to dry the ink.

It was a marvel to others how he ever found whatever data he needed, but he always did and he never thanked anyone for presuming that he could not.

The bareness of this Greeley office was in keeping with the entire *Tribune* building erected in 1845 at Nassau and Spruce Streets immediately after fire had destroyed the original Ann Street quarters. "We would not indulge in unnecessary sentiment," wrote Greeley of that destruction, "but even the old desk at which I sat, the ponderous ink-stand, the familiar faces of files of letters, the pamphlets—can they all have vanished, never more to be seen? And our boots and Webster's Dictionary!"

The new *Tribune* building did not take long to complete, for it was just four walls of brick enclosing a workshop. There was no unusual design or decoration and particularly no mortgage; every dollar of the cost came out of earned surplus. The presses and other plant equipment were the best that could be purchased, but the office appointments were cheap and scanty—often repaired but never replaced. This scantiness of furnishings was in line with Greeley's theory that it did not matter what kind of chair you sat on, or what kind of desk on which you wrote—all that counted was: What did you say and how well did you say it?

It was not the absence of comfort in his office, therefore, that made Greeley a tired man. It was a mind restless to instruct the world and certain of its premise. His associates knew how real was his affection for the *Tribune*. Though that attachment was under constant challenge by his love for the soil, the newspaper he founded was a living thing—his own creation. He turned to it every morning as a parent turns to a newborn child. For years he actually read every line of it every day. It was his life, and in its pages he wanted what to him seemed to be perfection in fact and expression.

Is it surprising that he had no joy in anticipating that an ocean would soon separate him from it, and particularly that during his absence his "Weekly Try-bune" might not seem the same to its readers?

That is why Dana, Ripley and Curtis at once set about making a newspaper that would continue to reflect his leadership. That desire was back of Dana's efforts to tie James Shepherd Pike permanently to the newspaper. Pike was a Maine man who had made a reputation as Washington correspondent of the *Boston Courier*. He was one of Greeley's "discoveries." On April 24, 1850, Greeley started negotiations:

Dear Pike:

Will you write me some letters? You are writing such admirably bad ones for "The Courier" that I fancy you are putting all your unreason into them and you can give me some of the pure juice. Try!

What I want is a daily letter (when there is anything to say) on the doings of Congress, or on anything spicy or interesting, letting the readers do their own thinking rather than see that you are doing it for them.

Three days later—April 27—the Greeley of true news-gathering instinct wrote:

Dear Pike:

I will thank you to send by telegraph rather than the slower way. Bear in mind that expense is no object in the matter of early advices. Can't you guess out for us somebody who can fish out executive session and committee secrets? If you can, set him to telegraphing. Everybody from Mother Eve's time down has been especially anxious to know what ought not to be known, and we must get some of it in "The Tribune" or we will be voted dull, indolent and behind the times!

H. G.

The year 1850 had been so prosperous for the *Tribune* that Dana suggested that Greeley's weekly wage of $50 should be increased; but a reply came promptly from Greeley, at Washington: "As to salary I am indifferent. Spend it on the paper."

And Dana did! In his efforts to persuade Pike he revealed to him the rich mine that Greeley generously opened for his associates when he sold them his *Tribune* stock for $1,000 a share pay as pay can: "Of course, we would prefer to have you one of the proprietors. I know of no way in which you could invest money better. In 1849 the company divided $25,000; in 1850 it divided $50,000, and in 1851 it is sure to divide between $40,000 and $60,000. The first quarter has salted down $20,000. The price at which we youngsters were admitted on January 1, 1849, was $1,000. Several shares have since sold for $1,500, but if McElrath will sell ten shares for $20,000 I shall buy them—or 25 shares for $50,000. Greeley is of the same opinion."

But Pike was obdurate—he would write for the *Tribune* from Washington but he would not invest.

When Greeley stepped on board the ship *Baltic* to cross the Atlantic he had labored with the *Tribune* ten years to a day. He had recently shared its ownership with others; the time had now come to have others share its burdens and direction. Nevertheless he turned to his great adventure reluctantly. He dreaded three thousands miles of ocean, but he bravely packed his capacious carpetbag—he never owned a trunk—tied his cotton umbrella to it and faced the torments of a boisterous April Atlantic. He had experienced Hudson River night boats and Erie Canal "liners," but an ocean steamship was a new thrill—he kept to himself just a little doubt of getting safely to the other side. During the voyage he made what he termed "an unloving acquaintance with the sea"—and wrote in his first letter, "he who would teach us to banish seasickness will be one of the greatest benefactors of the human race."

What Europe thought of the carpetbag vacationist we shall never know; what he thought of Europe was frankly told in letters to the *Tribune* such as only a Greeley could write.

Those who recall actor William Hodge almost forty years ago as "Daniel Vorhees Pike" in a popular Booth Tarkington play entitled *The Man from Home* will have no difficulty in picturing the wandering Greeley during his four-months' tour of England, France, Austria, Italy and Ireland.

After the leading character, Pike—the Man from Home—had spent several weeks abroad viewing old castles and noted ruins he turned to a Russian prince with the friendly suggestion that if

His Highness wanted to see something worth while in architecture he should go to America and look upon "our new county court-house in Kokomo, Indiana."

"It beats all holler all the ruined ruins you have over here, Prince," declared "Daniel Vorhees Pike, Attorney-at-law, Kokomo, Indiana," as his visiting card read in big black type. While he was in foreign lands, Pike's Hoosier mind would turn irresistibly to scenes back home along the banks of the Wabash, and in comparison Europe's historic attractions usually lost out.

So it was in spirit with Greeley. All his "glances" brought a "back-home" thought. He reached London in time for the opening on May 1 of the famous Crystal Palace Exposition there given to prove that glass and iron could take the place of stone and timber in buildings.

As a juror representing America, Greeley saw Queen Victoria during one of her visits. Here is his impression of the royal entourage:

> The Queen was here by Divine right of Womanhood, by Universal Suffrage, or anyhow you please; but what have her Gentlemen Ushers of Sword and State, Ladies in Waiting, Master of the Horse, Groom of the Stole, and such uncouth fossils to do with an exhibition of the fruits of industry? What in their capacities have they ever had to do with industry except to burden it? The Mistress of the Robes would be in place if she ever fashioned any robes.

And when he saw the "gee-gaws, dainty carvings, rich mosaics, articles of finery from European countries," he thought that "one such plain, odd-looking concern as McCormick's reaper in comparison with an inlaid table or a case of Paris bonnets is of more practical account than a Crystal Palace full of the latter of them."

The McCormick reaper made its first appearance abroad at this exposition and was "greeted with derision by 'The London Times' as a cross between an Astley chariot, a flying machine and a tread-mill."... "When it was taken out into the field for demonstration it was confronted by a tribunal prepared for its condemnation," wrote Greeley. "Before it stood John Bull, burly, dogged, determined not to be humbugged. Nothing disconcerted, the brown, rough, home-spun Yankee in charge jumped on the box, set the blades of the machine in lively operation, and commenced raking off the grain in sheaf-files ready for binding. There was a moment, and but a moment, of suspense; human prejudice could hold out no longer; burst after burst of involuntary cheers proclaimed the triumph of the Yankee tread-mill."

And Greeley was patriotically proud to have witnessed it!

Here are some of his comments on England: "I do not like these cold and stately English, yet I think I am not blind to their many sterling qualities. They would have rendered them wealthy and powerful though they had been located in the centre of Asia. They are a race to make their mark on the destinies of mankind. ... In London's 'prison house of woes'—the county poorhouse—there are not many hogs in America who are not better fed and lodged than these poor human brethren and sisters. It made me feel that hitherto I have said too little, done too little, dared too little, and sacrificed too little, to awaken attention to the damnable wrongs and abuses of civilized society as now organized."

Greeley saw Paris through different eyes—"The Paradise of the Senses, a focus of enjoyment but not of happiness." He wrote: "Nowhere are youth and its capacities more prodigally lavished; nowhere is age less happy and less respected. Paris has tens of thousands who would eagerly pour out their heart's blood for liberty and human progress, but no class or clan who ever thought of denying themselves wine.... Having an evening on my hands, I spent a share of it at the opera. But what grace, what sense, what witchery, there can be for instance, in a young girl's standing on one great toe and raising the other foot to the altitude of her head, I cannot imagine. Such a medley of drinking, dancing, idol-worshipping and Delilah craft I have never before encountered. I came away after the second of five acts."

"In Chanberry, Savoy, I did not understand why I was charged more for breakfast than others, but to talk English against Italian or French is to get a mile behind time. So I got into the stage and turned to my neighbor and asked why I was charged three francs for breakfast and the rest of them only two and one-half.

"'Don't know—perhaps you had tea or coffee?'

"'No, sir, I don't drink either.'

"'Then, perhaps, you washed your face and hands.'

"'Yes—I did.'

"'Then that's it! The half franc was for towel and basin.' . . ."

At last, as he embarks on the steamship *Baltic* for home, Greeley closes his *Glances at Europe* with thoughts of his native land: "Let me see once more the scenes so well-remembered and beloved; let me grasp, if but once again, the hand of Friendship and hear the thrilling accents of proved Affection, and when sooner or later the hour of mortal agony shall come let my last gaze be fixed on eyes that will not forget me when I am gone, and let my ashes repose in that congenial soil which, however I may be esteemed or hated, is still

"My own green land forever!"

"I am glad to find myself back home," wrote the European tourist to Seward on his first day at his *Tribune* desk. "Ruins and antiquities are well enough when taken in small doses, but a daily newspaper at the breakfast table is preferable as an ordinary matter." Greeley soon found more than his breakfast table newspaper to occupy his mind. Fillmore, Webster and Scott were the only contenders for the Whig presidential nomination, and time had not changed his lack of confidence in any of them. In his opinion, "Fillmore lacks pluck. He wants backbone. He means well, but he is timid, irresolute, uncertain and loves to lean. There will be no Thermopylae in his life and there has been none in the life of his Secretary of State Webster. Nature bestowed no intrepidity in making up either's composition. It was the omitted ingredient. Would the name of either be mentioned as the leader of a forlorn hope? No—we do not hate—we lament and grieve that northern spirit and northern sentiment and northern conviction are not honestly represented by these men."

How to remain in the Whig party and yet deplore its candidate and its platform was his problem. The old fire with its stunning retort came back to him in full flame, however, in 1852 when Fillmore announced himself against the renomination of every Whig Congressman who had voted against the Clay Compromise. This was the first effort of a President to purge legislators of his own party who differed with him. "Have we arrived at the parting of the ways?" inquired Greeley. "Do Whigs who uphold the fugitive slave law propose to make it their shibboleth and strike down every Whig candidate who deems that enactment unworthy of a free people? If new tests are to be imposed, new conditions exacted, which bind us to acquiescence in what we deem wrong, we reject the manacles and whether in or out of the Whig party will live and die free."

To Colfax he wrote early in 1852: "I reckon you see how hopeless things look in the political way. We shall probably run Scott for next President and get flogged at that. I hate it. Win or lose with old 'Fuss and Feathers'—either will be disastrous. He is a Know-Nothing, body and soul, an aristocrat, and anything else but wise and winning with any amount of dough plastered all over his face." Thus, we got the now familiar term—doughface.

Scott, of course, was nominated and, as Greeley predicted, "flogged." No words were minced in analyzing the defeat: "When a man's head is taken off by a cannon ball, it does not matter whether he has a bullet also in his leg or arm.... By Scott's overwhelming defeat the Whig party is not merely discomfited, it is annihilated. We have no prophetic ken and make no pretense to reading the future, but we do not see how the Whig party as such can ever be rallied again."

Raymond at once disowned Greeley as a Whig. " 'The Tribune' considers the Whig Party shivered to atoms and is not inclined to expend much labor in exploring for its fragments....All the Whigs have to do now," insisted Raymond, "is to carefully preserve their organization, to watch the tendency of public affairs, and to wait until they are wanted."

The Troy *Whig* joined with the *Times*: "Now, if Mr. Greeley and his crew will...get out of the Whig party...and keep out for all time to come, the Whig party will come up again. Go where you please, Horace.... Claim to be anything you please. Join the Mormons, if they will let you. Do anything—be anything; but, for God's sake and your country's do not claim to speak or act as a Whig!"

To which the *Tribune* defiantly replied: "We mean to stay in the Whig party and not to keep silent about slavery nor acquiesce in the fugitive slave law."

To Colfax he wrote: "I have ceased to expect wisdom from the Whig party. It is like the duelist whose brains couldn't have been injured by the bullet through his head—'cause if he had any brains he wouldn't have been in such a predicament."

"I have had enough of party politics," wrote Greeley to his friend Bowe. "I will speak for temperance, law and agriculture but I am not going to stump the country again in the interest of any party or candidate."

He turned to farming.

CHAPTER XV

Chappaqua—"Greeley's Bog"

As hopefully as when after Clay's defeat in 1844 Greeley sought a home at Turtle Bay, so, early in 1853, he made a second effort to get out of city life—this time, however, he did not call it a home but "my farm." There can be no doubt of his sincerity when he wrote, "I should have been a farmer. All my riper tastes incline to that blessed calling whereby the human family and its humbler auxiliaries are fed. Its quiet, its segregation from strife and brawls and heated rivalries, attract and delight me. I hate to earn my bread in any calling which complicates my prosperity in some sort with others' adversity—my success with others' defeat."

Greeley settled in Chappaqua, Westchester County, a village founded by Quakers in 1730, about thirty miles north of New York City, there to seek the rest he had never known—indeed that he was never to know.

The place was "substantially," to use Greeley's word, Mrs. Greeley's selection. She had stated her requirements: she wanted "(1) a peerless spring of pure soft water; (2) a cascade or brawling brook; (3) woods largely composed of evergreens." The Indian name Chappaqua suited Greeley, too: "There is comfort in the fact that the village was not called 'Clinton or Washington, Middletown or Springfield', nor any of the trite appellations which have so often been re-applied that half the letters intended for one of them are likely to bring up front or back of some other." He deplored the naming of our cities after foreign places; he believed that New York should have remained Manhattan, and that, as with Chappaqua, the Indians had furnished us with names that had a native significance. Neighbors called the farm "Greeley's bog," but he idolized it. He was a countryman, and the contrast with city streets won him. "As for me," he explained in an address just after settling there, "long tossed on the stormy waves of conflict and endeavor I have begun to feel the weary, tempestuous voyager's yearning for the upland. And so in the sober afternoon of life I have bought a few acres in the broad still country and, bearing thither my household treasures, have resolved to steal away from the city's anxieties and to revive as a farmer the memories of my youth."

In Chappaqua the Greeleys lived their remaining twenty years. "My woods are the pride of my life," he said jubilantly of his new land. "Without them it would never have been my farm. The trees cover about twenty-five acres; over and over again I say to them with Oriental courtesy 'may your shadow never grow less!' . . . I am tired of glaring at brick walls and glistening steel; I want trees close up to my windows in front and rear of my home."

The new home proved to be a place from which Greeley could keep out all but those he invited there. He lived with his farm neighbors, discussing crops past and to come, rejoicing over first or second prizes at the Westchester County fair for his turnips, his pumpkins or his apples, and thus, as he said, bringing back memories of his boyhood. He absolutely barred politics. His midweek absences from home must have meant uneasy times for Mrs. Greeley, for she persistently demanded a revolver for protection. Greeley refused for several years but finally acquiesced, as this letter testifies:

February 17, 1853

Gentlemen:

I received yesterday your box containing two smaller boxes having respectively a pistol for Mrs. Greeley and one for myself. Thank you for sending them. I hope never to make use of them myself. Possession of one by my wife will give her confidence and assurance of safety because of their presence in the house. We live—that is, *she* lives—in a small house surrounded by woods and far from the reach of any help. There is seldom a man in the house. Though her pistol will never be loaded I know that it will be flourished a great deal in the sight of all who come near the house, and who must guess whether it is loaded or not. She has often asked for a pistol, but I have never found it convenient to get one. She may now have both if she chooses, and I hope she will sleep sounder therefor.

Sincerely,
Horace Greeley

To:
Colt's Fire Arms Company
Hartford, Connecticut

Everyone in the *Tribune* office knew without a calendar when it was Friday, for on Friday morning Greeley would arrive in jovial mood, eager to be through with his share of the day's work and to hasten up to the Harlem Railroad station, then at Fourth Avenue and Twenty-sixth Street, bound for his week end with farm and family, and struggling with a heavy market basket.

And now look upon the picture at Chappaqua on those home-coming Friday afternoons as described by his eldest daughter, Mrs. Gabrielle Greeley Clendenin, in the *Ladies' Home Journal* of February 8, 1892:

Friday evening was always the busiest and happiest of the whole week for then father would come home for over Sunday. All day the whole house was alive with happy preparations. As a little girl, I would be dressed in my prettiest frock and at train time I would hasten down the lane to meet him.

The faces of people are children's books and they always read them searchingly. I read happiness and joy in my father's face the instant he caught glimpse of me; the market basket that he often carried, or the half-dozen bundles of all sizes, would be dropped to the ground as he would take me in his arms.

The first place he always sought was mother's room, where for years she lay ill.

Fully half of Mrs. Greeley's time at Chappaqua was spent in bed; when strong enough to travel she sought comfort in Europe or in Cuba. As she always took one or both of her daughters on these trips to care for her, it was their fate to sacrifice their youth for their mother. This they faithfully did, even unto the last in 1872 when they sat by her bedside day after day comforting her as she slowly faded away. Greeley's absences from home, the hours every day that he devoted to work or to reading, made their ordeal harder for Gabrielle and Ida; their father had no time for real companionship. Several years later Greeley wrote: "Ida's life has been given to her invalid mother and has been a hard one, but trial has not hardened her nature nor soured her disposition." Neither Mrs. Greeley by her exactions nor Greeley by his neglect seems to have been conscious that their daughters were being deprived of the normal way of a young girl's life. In one of his letters to a friend, Greeley confessed that after the death of his son Pickie, in 1849, he sought solace in his work and public affairs. Plainly the mother and two daughters led one life and Greeley a separate one, yet an affection undoubtedly existed in the family—an affection which on the part of both parents was blind to its highest duties.

It was also from his Chappaqua retreat that he wrote to Margaret Fuller's mother of the death of his son Raphael, the final tragedy in his domestic affairs; a letter the despair of which was only slightly palliated by its news of a daughter's birth:

New York, March 28, 1857

My dear Mrs. Fuller:

It were idle to wait for Mrs. Greeley to write you as she rarely writes to any one, and I should have answered your letter days ago but for waiting to announce to you our new daughter now two days old. I ought to be thankful for this gift, but I seem to feel the loss of our darling just gone even worse than before. It has been necessary to keep up Mrs. Greeley's spirits at all events, and I have tried hard to do so; and she is quite interested in the newcomer, as I try to be but am not. I am not sad nor despairing, but simply weary, indifferent, willing to go to my children and hopeful that I shall not much longer be away from them. Ida is now eight years old, and clever in her way, but never intimate with me; while Raphael and I were boys together . . . and saw everything through the same eyes. I do not remember that we ever differed on any subject whatever; whatever seemed best to me was always satisfactory to him; and we mutually regretted the hard necessity that kept us so much apart. Our greatest happiness was to be with each other. I left him brave and hearty on the 14th of January, and went west . . . to Madison, Wisconsin. . . . I was giving my last lecture at Scranton, Pa., when a telegram reached me that looked ugly. I did not open it till I closed, when it told me that Raphael was dangerously sick and I must hurry home. I did so but only arrived . . . to find his mother washing his dead body. He had died of malignant croup only an hour before. Everything had been done on her part and on the doctor's to keep him alive till I could return; his windpipe had been severed by a surgeon and a tube inserted, which kept him alive some hours, but not long enough; he was choked to death before I could reach him. And now I pray God to let me rejoin my brave and beautiful boys ere many more weary years shall have rolled away, though I am willing to live and strive so long as that shall be best. . . . Mother does not follow your counsel respecting spirits, though she had not consulted or paid any attention to them for years till Raphael died, but since then she has done so. She is comforted thereby, and I believe no evil results have yet been experienced.

Yours,
Horace Greeley

The farm afforded all the pleasure that Greeley anticipated; he rejoiced in every acre of it; the boggier he found it, the greater joy he had in working it over into tillable condition. In the house, however, life was different. Greeley often tried to rouse his wife from her bedridden indifference to everything, but seldom with success. Time and again he sought to persuade her to enjoy the farmland she had selected. "I have been weeks coaxing her to go up a hundred rods to the upper part of our little place," he wrote Mrs. E. M. Newhall at New Lebanon, New York. "Yesterday, by taking her in my arms and carrying her part way up the steep hill I did win her to the crowning edge. When there, she owned that she felt a little better, that the move had done her good. But she will not be coaxed there again in a month. She labors under a physical paralysis of will that is discouraging. She plans to go to Europe early in October and I think she will. She will not go to see you at New Lebanon. I am sorry to say it but the fact is so. She thinks she cannot, and 'as a man thinketh so is he'."

Editor Beman Brockway's experiences during an overnight stay at Chappaqua give a realistic picture of life there as a visitor saw it. When introduced, Mrs. Greeley accepted his hand solemnly without speaking a word. There was little expression in her face, but that little was rather against her. During the evening she spoke quickly—not angrily nor peevishly—but her words had a kind of crack like a pistol shot. Brockway then continued:

"Things have gone pretty well on the farm, Mother, while I have been away," remarked Greeley.

"They haven't gone well in the house, Mr. Greeley," shot back the wife. "The roof has leaked and everything is being ruined."

"No, Mother, I don't think everything will be ruined," replied Greeley. "You know you will not allow anyone but Mr. C. to repair the roof and he is away."

It was dark when supper was over—if a meal composed of bread, butter, milk, apple-sauce, custard and cocoa can be called a supper. My efforts to see the time from my watch resulted finally in the light of about two inches of a tallow candle.

"Could Mother not furnish a better light?" asked Greeley.

"That one is good enough," came the reply like an electrical discharge.

Greeley happened to say that it was difficult to find help that would have a deep interest in the work.

"If I had charge of affairs," spoke up Mrs. Greeley, "I would give my directions and they would be obeyed."

"Why, Mother," said Greeley, "you have charge here—in my absence."

"Damn it, I haven't!" was the quick response. "I'm a cipher here—a mere slave! I've no rights; no respect is shown me."

But the real disclosure of temper came when Greeley took the cover off a big willow market basket containing things he had bought in the city to please the family. He was plainly proud of his purchases. First he produced a fine calf-skin.

She held it to her nose and then threw it under the table.

"Horrid!" she exclaimed. "It smells like a beast."

Then came a pair of shoes.

"These will never do," said Mrs. Greeley, "they are too large."

"How do you know, Mother? You haven't tried them on."

"I don't want to try them on! Haven't I got eyes to tell whether a shoe is a rod too long for me? You can carry them straight back!"

"Well, Mother, here is a pair of rubbers for Ida," said Greeley, handing them over for inspection.

"What horrible things!" exclaimed Mrs. Greeley. "They are too heavy; they would kill the child! She will never, never wear them! You don't seem to exercise the least judgment in what you buy. If you had any sense you wouldn't bring anything of this kind into the house."

And so, in about the same strain, the evening hours slowly passed. Brockway wondered how Greeley stood it, but no complaint was ever heard.

Week ends at Chappaqua were restful periods for Greeley, and he enjoyed them. Toward noon every Saturday he would take his ax and swing it for a while or help to build a runway of field stone to drain his swamp, or clear the bed of his brook so that its current could flow freely and swiftly—"brawling"—through the meadows, as his wife desired.

Thus that day always meant for him a few hours of outdoor labor with its healthy tire, creating a keen appetite for a midday dinner of plenty—"farmer's fare" he called it—at the village inn, since a hearty meal was not to be had at home. Joel Benton, who was Greeley's lyceum manager, relates that when traveling the editor often called at breakfast for highly spiced sausage and buckwheat cakes!

A little cottage in the woods when he bought his farm remained forever "my" house in Greeley's affection. Later he built a larger house on the border line of the village, but in the older place he did his writing and reading. There he lived again in the serene atmosphere of his *New Yorker*, the "kind of magazine in my mind's eye." That ambition never left him. Nor did any other. "As yet I am a horse in a bark-mill and tread his monotonous round"—but he lived in a dreamy tomorrow. For Greeley had many aspirations foreign to the clashing world of which he was such a restless part—visions of brotherhood and of justice among the people as well as of literary achievements for himself.

Donald Grant Mitchell ("Ik Marvel") was a visitor at the cottage on one of Greeley's at-home Saturdays. The two men had their usual discussion about literature, when suddenly his host said: "I am going to work with my ax." Then he added jokingly, "Perhaps you would like to join me," as he pointed to another ax in the corner of the room. It was Greeley's polite way of bowing a visitor out. "He did not realize," wrote Mitchell of his experience, "that I, too, was a woodchopper. Promptly I picked up the indicated ax. I think that I never enjoyed a triumph more than that over my host with my ax—not only on the score of time but in showing in my scarf that even distribution of right and left strokes. Greeley's pleasant face beamed with acknowledgment—he even doffed his white hat in recognition of good wood-chopping work well done."

It was from the cottage that Greeley kept up his letter writing to the few friends to whom he ever unburdened his mind. One of this group was Mrs. Margaret Allen, of Jamestown, New York. Greeley had met Mrs. Allen at the home of Mr. and Mrs. P. T. Barnum in New York City, where her church work in association with Mrs. Barnum had made her a frequent visitor. Greeley, too, was interested in religious activities and was a close friend of the Barnums. Exactly when the correspondence between Mrs. Allen and Greeley began is not known, but it lasted until he wrote her eight years later "out of the depths" when he had less than two more weeks of life. The letters were entrusted to Joel Benton for editing on the advice of Barnum and Charles A. Dana. He published only a few. Several of them appear on later pages. "Of this attachment formed first by religious sympathies," wrote Benton, "Mrs. Allen was eminently worthy. By her benevolent character she holds a circle of noted people who cannot say too much of her philosophy and her virtues. Here Greeley laid his whole heart open to be read as an open book." An interesting letter to her on religious creeds was written from Chappaqua in 1864. That year Greeley's sister, Esther, had joined the Catholic church. Evidently Mrs. Allen had expressed her surprise. To her the tolerant Greeley wrote his creed:

You think that my sister Esther is queer in turning Catholic. So do I; but on different grounds from yours.

For my part, I believe God's truth is higher, wider, deeper, longer than all our creeds and includes what is best in each of them. I do not believe that it will ever be asked in the world to come what we believed while here, but what we did, and what characters we formed. Faith is simply knowledge of the right way; you might know that New York is east of Jamestown while another is ignorant of that fact, but if that other started eastward and you westward he would be nearing and you distancing New York, in spite of his ignorance and your knowledge.

My creed is very short. I think Jesus of Nazareth was sent by God to enlighten and save our race; but precisely what or who He was beyond this I do not know; and I do not expect to know in this imperfect state of being. I apprehend He saves us mainly by instructing—renovating, purifying, and making us like Himself in moral character. I think He was truly Divine, yet I do not realize that He who said, "My God, my God, why hast Thou forsaken me?" was Himself the Eternal Source of all things. And my affirmation creed is mainly summed up in the belief that God is infinitely good and wise, and that all evil is temporary and finite and to be swallowed up in the end by Universal Good. I enclose you a few lines of Tennyson that state this truth more fully and remain with love and gratitude to all yours and you.

Thine,
Horace Greeley

The verses were from Tennyson's *In Memoriam*, closing with these familiar lines:

Behold we know not anything.
I can but trust that good shall fall
At last—far off,—at last, to all,
And every winter change to spring.

Greeley's joy in putting his land into productive condition was always too real to be concealed. His references to "my maples," "my pasture land," "my evergreens," and "my brook" had the genuine farmer tang. He was as proud of the results of his farming as he ever was of any *Tribune* editorial. "I wish you could see my corn," he wrote a friend. "I have two fields of about four acres each and mean to have 600 bushels of sound ears. I like the look of it. I have four acres of pretty good oats and will send you a bag for seed."

He was especially anxious that Mrs. Allen should see the place, urging her frequently to make up a party of friends for a day's outing. Finally in May 1871 she did so and her description of her host, the farm and its absent mistress is worthy of closest reading:

May 1, 1871

Darling Sister:

Mrs. Barnum, Mrs. R., Mr. Greeley and I are sitting around the centre table—[Greeley's home on 19th Street] the latter immersed in letters and the others talking about people I don't know. So I capture some paper to give you a sketch of life as it has been with me since I came here.

Saturday morning we left the city depot for Chappaqua. Only Theodore Tilton and wife were of the party and Mrs. R., Mr. Greeley and myself.

The day was one of the happiest in my life. There was lots of fun abroad. Dear old Horace's face fairly beamed with happiness. We rode all over "Mother's Land," up hill and down ravines and over to see the woodland where he spends every Saturday chopping. I'll never again say that Mr. Greeley is not queer. He drove slow, of course, and such driving you never saw! His old horses knew him, no doubt, and they paid not the slightest attention to his chirps and gentle shakes of the lines. He held one line in each hand with elbows sticking out and his hat on the back of his neck, while the horses went all ways but on the road, and sometimes took us over stumps.

From there we visited the cascade and drank from the spring as in duty bound. Mr. Greeley has firm faith that this is the very purest and sweetest water in the world. From thence we drove up by the field Mr. Greeley is so proud of which "used to be the wickedest frog pond you ever saw, all covered with miserable, useless hassocks and skunk cabbage and so springy that you could not walk over it." It is a beautiful field now, but the old man's face, beaming with pride of it, was much more attractive to me.

Back to the house we went, sat a few minutes before the fireplace and looked at the fire of that precious dry cedar, then over to the hotel for dinner. Mr. Greeley lamented that we could not dine at his house and told me more than once in a confidential way it was a sight worth coming to see Ida get dinner there.

Do you know that they have built three houses on the place and that only one of them is inhabited? The man who works the farm uses the back part of it. Besides Mr. G. and "Mother" have each a barn of their own. Mrs. G. would not have a tree cut not even for trimming, around the first house. So they left that and built another in the sunshine to be more wholesome. This second one we entered. But they now have a third partly built which they propose to use if Mrs. G. ever returns—which he thinks she probably will do in the fall. They have lots of old stock which they keep for the good they have done—old cows which "Mother" says will never be killed while she lives because they have given milk to the children. "They fell down sometimes and wanted to die, but 'Mother' would not let them and kept a man to lift them up and care for them."

We rode over to Sing Sing and took the cars back to the city. We rode home, had tea and then Mr. Greeley told us to come up into the sitting room, where he produced some books from his pocket and read poetry to us all the evening. The first was Whittier's "My Psalm"—read it and see how appropriate it was to close such a day. Then he took "Jim Bludso" from his familiar pocket-book and gave us that.

M.

To a visitor walking with him over his acres Greeley said: "There are many to tell you how much I lose by my farming. I only say that as yet no one else has ever lost a farthing, and I do not complain. My part of it has paid splendidly in health and vigor, being all income and no outgo. Who can show a better balance sheet? I don't care how much they may laugh at me as an editor or politician, but when they say my farm is a humbug they are a set of blockheads. Have you ever seen better land made from an old bog? All else that I have done may be of no avail, but what I have done here *is* done—it will last."

What Greeley did as editor and politician has its place in history—but at Chappaqua "what I have done here" will last forever in the proud memory of that little community. The Horace Greeley School, a statue of Greeley in the public square, Greeley Avenue, Woodburn Avenue, are only a few of the tributes by the village to its unforgotten citizen.

CHAPTER XVI

"The Drumbeat of the Nation"

JANUARY 5, 1854, should rank in history with the election of Lincoln in 1860, for on that day Greeley's editorial in the *Tribune* became what George William Curtis called in *Harper's Weekly* the "drumbeat of the nation," summoning the people of the North to unite against the determination of the South "to make the West pastureland for slavery." In the Senate Stephen A. Douglas, the "Little Giant" from Illinois, had introduced his bill organizing into a territory the vast wilderness known as Kansas and Nebraska, giving its inhabitants the right to decide by vote whether or not slavery should be lawful within its boundaries. Douglas called it "popular sovereignty," but Greeley's prompt retort was "squatter sovereignty." "What kind of 'popular sovereignty' is it," he asked, "that allows one class of people to vote slavery for another?"

Here at last was a plain, direct issue that no one in the North could ignore. It was a challenge that had to be accepted or future opposition to slavery extension abandoned. If ever a man sensed instantly and bespoke the spirit of a people, Greeley now did. With the instinct and boldness of courageous leadership he called for a new political organization to take charge of the battle for freedom and the Union. There were confidence, enthusiasm and prophecy in his first editorial:

The passage of the Nebraska bill will arouse and consolidate the most gigantic, determined and overwhelming party for freedom that the world has ever known. We may already see in the future its gathering groups on every hillside, in every valley and on every prairie in the free states. We hear the deep and ominous murmur of the earnest voices of its myriad slow-moving masses. . . . It sweeps along with the force of the tempest and the tornado. The spirit of liberty animates, the spirit of progress impels, and a spirit of solemn religious duty inspires and leavens the old mass.

An invincible army bears aloft the motto: "God is with us!" . . . The decisive events of history come but slowly. They have their source as the great rivers have theirs in the hidden recesses of the plain and the mountain. But we cannot hide from our vision the vital fact that this new party . . . will not fail in its duties.

. . . We urge, therefore, unbending determination on the part of the northern congressmen hostile to this intolerable outrage, and demand of them in behalf of Peace, in behalf of Freedom, in behalf of Justice and Humanity, resistance to the last.

Greeley's words sounded across the continent with a vigor no other possessed. Every issue of the "Weekly Try-bune" was eagerly awaited by the people and read as though an instruction. His editorials became the inspiration of a new party that was to be called Republican; their defiant tone enthused its organizers and raised their efforts from a mere political faction struggle to the loftier plane of purging a nation of slavery and dedicating it to freedom. To quote *Harper's Weekly* again: "Greeley at once became the banner-bearer of a new party, the herald and harbinger of a free Union. The daily issue of 'The Tribune' was a startling drum-beat and 'The Weekly Tribune' became an incessant broadside."

To timid Northerners who at first thought that his forceful words were too severe, he replied: "No other language than we use would faithfully express our convictions. We must treat it as we do other gigantic perfidies and crimes. The conflagration it threatens is not to be extinguished by jets of rose water."

"Greeley's role in this particular drama which ended with the Emancipation Proclamation was as great as any statesman's save Lincoln," declares Allan Nevins in his *American Press Opinions*. "No Free Soil leader, not Chase, nor Sumner, nor Seward, and probably not all three combined, did so much to rally the north in unyielding opposition to the spread of slavery."

There were five months of bitter debate in Congress before the Douglas bill was enacted; Greeley fought every step of its progress. On January 26 he wrote: "The only question to be answered is whether northern sentiment can be aroused and consolidated in solid phalanx against the atrocious proposition. The fools at Washington believe that it cannot. We believe that it can! *The United States will extinguish slavery before slavery can extinguish the United States.*"

But "popular sovereignty" in the proposed territory was not legally possible so long as the Missouri Compromise of 1820 remained on the statute books. That law prohibited slavery north of the historic Mason and Dixon line; only by its repeal could Kansas and Nebraska have any option. Here were the roots of the great controversy just breaking through ground into the plain view of all. Southern senators insisted that slaves had been judicially defined as "property" and that the right to hold property anywhere could not be legislated away. "Would Douglas yield to their demand that the thirty-four-year-old statute should NOW be declared without force?" asked Greeley. "Would he act as Executioner of Liberty in the West?"

"I'll do it! I'll do it!" finally declared Douglas. "It will raise a hell of a storm; it will ruin me—but I'll do it!"

His own words "null and void," written into his bill, gave the deathblow to Clay's old compromise measure, but it raised an issue that armies had to settle.

Then it was that Bob Toombs, senator from Georgia, declared: "Let us carry the bill on the slave issue, since that is what the North wants us to do; then we finally settle the question forever." When at dawn of March 4, after a Saturday night of debate, the bill was carried on roll call while church bells were tolling to early Sabbath prayers, Toombs could not help exulting: "We have relumed the torch of Liberty on the altar of slavery!"

Chase, however, voiced a different opinion. "They celebrate a present victory," said the Ohio senator, "but the echoes they awake will never rest in silence until slavery shall die. It will light up a fire in the country which will consume those who have kindled it."

To which Greeley at once added: "Be assured, be assured, gentlemen disturbers of settled questions, gentlemen violators of sacred compacts, gentlemen robbers of the domain of freedom, that you are provoking a storm of popular sentiment of which you little dream. All will be peace and acquiescence as in 1850? Oh! but you are verdant! We tell you, No! As well expect the waves not to rise when the wind blows."

Again he declared on May 18: "We are in the midst of a revolution—is our response to the proceedings at Washington. The passage of the Nebraska bill is the first great effort of slavery to take American freedom directly by the throat. It is tantamount to civil war and an open declaration of war between freedom and slavery, to be ceaselessly waged until one or the other finally and absolutely triumphs.... The permanence of the Union is predictable only upon one of two conditions, either the South must put an end to slavery or the North must adopt it.... We are now on the eve of a war that has no other real reason than hostility to freedom.... Where it will end, who can tell?"

But the *Tribune* did not stop with mere words. In a black-bordered box on the first page, under the heading "Be It Remembered," were printed the names of all northern senators and congressmen who had voted for the bill. To those who opposed it Greeley declared: "The gratitude of unborn millions is justly due and will be freely rendered to those who, against power, patronage, personal interest and party drill, have fought in either House the Battle of Freedom. Overborne they may be, beaten they cannot be, for on their side are the instincts of Humanity, the spirit of our Age, the hopes of Man and the Justice of God."

Once more Greeley was alone among editors of conservative New York City in asserting that it was "now or never" in the fight against the slave power; they were either Democrat or Whig—not one foresaw the rising tide of northern opinion shaping up the Republican party. "The one thing the South is after," persisted Greeley, "and the only thing, is the extension of slavery.

We are not one people. We are two peoples. We are a people for freedom and a people for slavery. Between the two the conflict is inevitable. Freedom has been betrayed and sacrificed! Who comes to the rescue?"

"Seward hangs fire!" declared the *Independent.* Had Seward at once assumed leadership of the convictions he had so frequently uttered in Senate debates and in public speeches—had he joined with Greeley in making them a platform for a new party organization in New York, the future of both men would certainly have been different. In vain Greeley pleaded with Seward to strike out from Weed and into the new party. "The business of constructing parties and platforms," Seward wrote, "is a difficult one. Let those undertake it who will and those perform it who can." "It was the tide in Seward's affairs, but he did not take it at the flood," is the way historian James Ford Rhodes expresses it. "Had Seward sunk the politician in the statesman the close of 1854 would have seen a triumphant Republican party in every northern state and Seward its leader.... Probably he was held back by Thurlow Weed; his course left an indelible impression."

Six years were to elapse before a leader appeared in Lincoln, but in Greeley the ground swell of defiant opinion in the North at once had a recognized spokesman. It seemed that everyone from everywhere turned to Greeley to say when, how, and by whom the antislavery sentiment should be organized. In February, he had heard from Puritan-ancestored Asahel N. Cole, born at Freedom, Chautauqua County, New York, and editor of the *Genesee Valley Free Press,* published at Friendship, Allegany County. Cole had called a "convention" to meet at the latter place and to organize a political party to oppose the Douglas legislation. He asked Greeley to suggest a name. "Call it Republican—no prefix, no suffix, just plain Republican," came the brief, historic reply from the *Tribune's* editor. And, early in May, the name Republican was "flung to the breeze," as country weeklies then loved to say pridefully, from the masthead of the *Free Press*—the first newspaper thus to display it.

Bovay wrote from Wisconsin: "Your paper is now a power in

the land. Advocate calling together, in every church and schoolhouse in the free states, all the opponents of the Kansas-Nebraska bill, no matter what their party affiliations. Urge them to forget previous political names and organizations, and band together under the name I suggested to you at Lovejoy's Hotel in 1852. I mean Republican."

To which Greeley replied: "I faintly hope the time has come which Daniel Webster predicted when he said, 'I think there will be a North.' . . . But I am a beaten, worn-down, used-up politician and have the soreness of many defeats in my bones. Your plan is all right if the people are ripe for it. I am ready to follow any lead that promises to hasten the day of Northern emancipation. . . . But remember that editors can only follow where the hearts of the people are already prepared to go with them. They can animate and direct a healthy public indignation, but they cannot 'create a soul beneath the ribs of death.' "

Meanwhile, out in Cleveland, Ohio, Joseph Medill, two years later to become editor of the Chicago *Tribune*, was arousing the people. The same spirit that led him in 1860 to declare in the *Tribune* for Lincoln for President stirred him in 1854 to similar activities. The late George Henry Payne, former commissioner of communications at Washington, in his *History of American Journalism,* relates that when Medill and others were considering the name Republican for the new party, Medill wrote to Greeley for his advice.

"Go ahead, my friend, with your proposed Republican party, and may God bless you," Greeley replied. "I hope you will have the best of luck. The time has indeed come to bury our beloved [Whig] party; it is dead. But we have many fool friends who insist it is only in a comatose state and will recover, but I tell them it is dead—still, I dare not yet in New York announce the demise of the party and call for the reorganization of a new one. But do you go ahead on the Western Reserve and commence the work. I like the name for it [Republican]. If you can get the name Republican started in the West it will grow in the East. I fully agree to the new name and the new christening."

Editor Joseph Warren of the Detroit *Tribune* shared Medill's enthusiasm for a new party. He, too, wrote to Greeley and was advised by him to use the name Republican.

Still another conspicuous and typical example was the course of John W. Scripps, then editor of the *Chicago Daily Herald*, for years a Douglas supporter. He bolted the "Little Giant" and wrote to his father in Michigan: "If I am to be ruined at all, let it be from meeting the responsibilities of my position with a conscience void of offense to God and man."

Though Greeley had early given his "God bless you!" to the Republican name and movement in the West, and nationally was its recognized editorial leader, he was in the humiliating plight that he could not urge it in his own state against the determination of Weed, Seward and Raymond to stand by the Whig state ticket. Unity was essential if New York was to be redeemed from Democratic control, for in 1852 it had elected Horatio Seymour as governor.

On June 5 Greeley urged such a course regardless of name: "In the great struggle to resist surrender of the Union to slaveholders we wish to know no party name or divisions. We simply desire to see enlisted under one banner all who want to see Liberty and not slavery in this country." But western readers of the "Weekly Try-bune" pressed hard for a stronger endorsement of the Republican name, and Greeley responded on June 16 with this editorial:

PARTY NAMES AND PUBLIC DUTY

We have not taken much part in the current discussions respecting the name under which the Nebraska inspirators shall be resisted and punished because we feel little interest in the matter. In our view the emancipation most immediately needed in this country is emancipation from party names and party shackles.

Accepting and upholding those ideas of public policy which used to characterize the Whig party prior to 1852, and agreeing substantially with the Free Soil Democratic party in all it affirms with regard to slavery, we could wish to see a union of all those members of the two parties.

We should not care much whether those united were designated Whig, Free Soil Democrats or something else; though we think that some simple name like Republican would more fitly designate those who had united to restore our Union to its true mission—of champion and promulgator of Liberty rather than propagandist of slavery.

Weed objected to any name but Whig. Every attempt at activity throughout the state under the name Republican was promptly stifled. He had editor Raymond attend an anti-Nebraska convention at Saratoga on August 17 to check Greeley. As a delegate Greeley wrote the resolutions, but Raymond succeeded in tabling the name Republican and in adjourning to meet at Auburn on September 25. There the Whigs named Seward's friend Myron Clark for governor and Raymond for lieutenant-governor. Weed thereby denied his junior partner's known desire for either place, but Greeley gamely did his share toward securing for the ticket a scant plurality of 309 votes.

He bided his time to speak his mind. It came immediately after election, when he could no longer be charged with adversely affecting the result. His words had the Greeley directness: "In state after state the antagonists of slavery extension set aside old party differences and united on the Republican platform, and wherever that ground was promptly taken the people have emphatically responded. Amen! The man who should have impelled and guided the general uprising of the Free States lives in Auburn, and his name is William H. Seward. Instead of taking the position which his convictions and his own antecedents seem to require, Mr. Seward, adhering to the vacated shell of Whiggery, has stood aside and has allowed the great movement to go forward without a word of bold and hearty encouragement or sympathy."

Here was the first public break in the relations of the fourteen-year-old political firm. Greeley had really been out of Weed's confidence ever since 1848, and the gulf between them had been steadily widening. "Weed thinks I know nothing about politics in comparison with others," he had written to Seward after the

1853 election. "I won't try any more to overcome his fixed prepossessions on this point. I have held in as long as I can. If there are any plans for the future I want to know them; if there are none, I want to know that, too, and I will try to form a plan of some sort of my own." No reply was ever received to that letter. Silence was indeed a challenge to do as he pleased, and he accepted it as an opportunity to free himself from his old Whig moorings.

He was heart and soul with the new Republican party, and its spirit of victory was reflected in *Tribune* editorials. He proclaimed it the party of the future. In such a mood he wrote three days after election, November 11, 1854, the letter of withdrawal from Weed, Seward and Greeley, which Raymond charged after Seward's defeat in 1860 was the basis of hostility to his candidacy there. At Greeley's request it was then made public. In part the letter read:

> It seems to me a fitting time to announce the dissolution of the political firm of Weed, Seward & Greeley by the withdrawal of the junior partner. As it may seem a great presumption in me to assume that any such firm exists, you will, I am sure, indulge me in some reminiscences.
>
> After your election as Governor you were dispensing offices worth from three thousand dollars to twenty thousand to your friends, and I returned to my desperate battle with pecuniary obligations. It did not occur to me then that some of these places might have been offered to me, but I think it should have occurred to you. I was not the man to ask for it; I think it should not have been necessary. . . . An inquiry by you at that time as to my needs and means would have been timely and even held in grateful remembrance.
>
> . . . All I ask is that we shall be counted out even after the first Tuesday in next February [the date for Seward's re-election as senator by the New York state legislature] and that thereafter I may take such course as seems best without reference to the past.

Greeley did just that. "I am no longer anybody's partner," he declared after making good his promise to aid in Seward's reelection. If he had then realized fully his place in the public mind, he might properly have added that he had become the editorial leader of a patriotic sentiment which was steadily to crystallize into organized defiance of the threat of the South to secede. Thus, the formal dissolution of Weed's old political firm had results far more important to the nation, and to Greeley, than its existence ever had. On November 15, 1880, at a Press Club dinner celebrating Weed's eighty-third birthday, Whitelaw Reid said: "Assuming that one result of the dissolution was the nomination of Lincoln, then I am sure no man rejoices more heartily over it than the venerable member of the firm here tonight."

"Yes, indeed!" shouted Weed—twenty years too late!

All the fascinating uncertainties, plottings and bitter rivalries in politics are to be found in that historic firm of Weed, Seward & Greeley. Its influence, whether exerted together or individually, gave to the nation some of its most historic incidents and leaders, though "the tangled skein of fate" meted out alternately to each of them a crushing denial of his own chief ambition. Yet, in 1838, when Weed brought Greeley to Albany to edit the *Jeffersonian*, it would seem that no other three men could possibly be better fitted to work together. Weed sought the power of politics; Greeley sought the power of the printed word; Seward sought distinction in statesmanship. No one of the three men apparently wanted what the other two desired. Each had his separate ambition; all had youth, earnestness and purpose. Weed was forty-one years of age, Seward thirty-seven, Greeley but twenty-seven. Weed was a suave, velvet-gloved, free mingler among men. In the picturesque words of Theodore Roosevelt fifty years later, he would "speak softly but carry a big stick." Greeley had a youthful, restless energy, and a spirit eager to spend itself in its enthusiasms. Seward was a practicing lawyer, a scholarly orator, far more than a maker of ardent friends in politics.

Weed was the planning, organizing, dominating member of the "firm" that had its actual beginning in evening conferences during the winter of 1839 in the Executive Mansion at Albany, with Seward just in office as governor.

It was a unique association; its origin, its activities and its differences still remain the most interesting story in American politics For Greeley in 1872, the closing chapter was written in a sanitarium where death awaited him; for Seward, in a physically and spiritually crushed man dying at his home in Auburn two months earlier than Greeley; but for Weed, in composed and wealthy retirement in a New York City residence unto his eighty-fifth year.

What manner of man was this Thurlow Weed whose career in politics for nearly half a century has interested so many writers and historians? This man who, of his own keenness, detected in Greeley's *New Yorker* editorials a writer capable later of arousing a nation; this man who foresaw a governor, possibly a national figure, in Seward, then only a first-term state senator from Cayuga County, New York! With confidence in his own judgment of their abilities, Weed started each of these men on his own separate road to fame—a road leading toward the White House for both of them, but not extending into it for either.

Weed's motive? Well, those who knew him best believed that Weed always used men as cards in a great gamble and played them for his own stakes. No doubt he saw in Greeley and Seward the cards he lacked. Whatever they were in his mind was accepted without protest by Seward, but not so by Greeley. The latter never acquiesced in control by Weed—never in fact by anyone!

"The sweetness of his temper inclines me to love my tyrant," wrote Seward to Weed in a letter we have already quoted.

"Do not assume to dictate to or lecture me," wrote Greeley on September 10, 1842; "do not ask me to forget that I, too, am a man—that I must breathe free air or be stifled."

Of course, no power-seeking politician could tolerate as a partner such an independent mind, but Greeley was then too far advanced with his *Tribune* to be stopped or ignored.

The other member of the historic firm—William Henry Seward, the pride of Cayuga County, New York, though born in the village of Florida, Orange County—was in every way distinct from both Weed and Greeley. As a statesman he lacked the essential—leadership. After his retirement, when a visitor in his home library asked him where he got a huge American eagle perched there on a pedestal, he replied that it was given him by some Alaskans and was the only reward he had ever received for negotiating the purchase of Alaska from Russia for the amazing sum of $7,300,000 and battling long with the Senate for its approval. Greeley had said at the time that Seward was "buying a splinter from the North Pole."

Physically, Weed and Seward were contrasting figures—the former tall, straight as an arrow, well-proportioned; while Seward is described in *The Education of Henry Adams* as "a slouching, slender figure with a head like a wise macaw, a beaked nose, shaggy eyebrows, red hair, free talker, perpetual smoker—a hard type to fathom. How much was natural and how much was mock, no one could tell."

Noah Brooks, who knew Seward well in war days, had this to say of him: "Secretary Seward was oddly hostile to all attempts at taking his picture. His manner in public was courtly. He usually wore a dark-colored frock coat and light trousers, and his figure was erect and alert. Like Lincoln, he was fond of good stories. He was also a good smoker. In court his manner was not impressive —he often fumbled with a handkerchief and occasionally blew a tremendous blast on his very long nose."

CHAPTER XVII

The Junior Partner on His Own

FOURTEEN YEARS of presumed partnership by those three men were now ended, but Greeley's letter of withdrawal was not wholly due to their refusal to join him in welcoming the new Republican party into New York state. He had long realized that he figured no longer in their planning. Recall that in the early days of the *Tribune* he had written Weed, "I must be myself." He welcomed now the opportunity to declare it again. Despite his success as an editor, despite his notoriety as a politician, he had always in mind the ambition that was his dream while he struggled with the "Yorker." The old desire for literary reputation rekindled into sputtering flame whenever he wearied of the battles in which he was engaged and of their discouraging outcome, but it died away when events aroused him to the old activities. Always that challenge was too tempting.

A second letter to Seward, two weeks after the one so often quoted, reflects this state of mind. Its frankness, its simplicity—one might truly say its loneliness of spirit—reveal clearly this man who three years before had written that he was "on the downward side of life."

New York, Nov. 24, 1854

Gov. Seward:

I have your letter of the 21st this evening. I write a few words, not to reopen what is past but to make it clear for the future.

My political life is ended. Do not regard me as dissatisfied with what has been done. There was a time when it would have been precious to me to have had some public and palpable recognition that I was accorded worthy among others. But my mother, for whose sake I should have valued this, is now paralytic, almost unconscious, and can hardly live through the winter. I have no other relative for whom I care much or to whom my election would be a triumph, and I only ask to be permitted to glide out of the arena as quietly and as speedily as may be.

I have partners to whom "The Tribune" is a property, and I think it may be rendered much more valuable as a property in other hands than mine. I do not mean to make any parade of withdrawing, but to sell out my interest at some rate (or most of it), pay my debts, retire to my little farm, there to read and work, and thence to write occasionally for the paper. I think I have had my share of contention; and yet I could not remain in my present position without doing more of it. I terribly need rest, but can get none while I remain in my present position.

Understand what I have written, then, as my apology for wishing to withdraw from political strife after the last of February. I trust my doing so will be a relief to the party I have intended to serve. With Myron H. Clark, the bogus Know-Nothing, for Governor, and H. J. Raymond, for Lieut., I think "The Times" will be the proper State Organ in this city and that "The Tribune" in my hands could not be useful. I shall only try to hold the ascendancy to some sort of fidelity on the Temperance question.

If you will understand that what I have desired from you—what I think you have unwisely withheld—is some sort of public recognition that I was esteemed a faithful and useful coadjutor, I need say no more. Office as such is not in my line. I should have no reputation and many enemies in any responsible position. . . .

Plainly Greeley was overdrawing on the reserves even of a burden-bearing, peasant ancestry. For more than a year he had been without family or home. His wife had insisted that she could find health only in Europe; there was not a soul to bid him welcome as he stepped across the threshold of his house. Chappaqua was a deserted home, and living in the city or traveling on lecture tours had no companionships.

As in 1851, Dana and the staff urged him to seek a change abroad, and by May he found courage to renew what he had called on his first voyage "an unloving acquaintance with the sea." "A 'life on the ocean wave' is still surcharged with misery," he wrote after this second voyage across the Atlantic, "and a steamship on the rocking billows is the most intolerable prison wherewith man's follies or sins are visited."

Four months on the Continent more than made up for ocean discomforts. In Les Invalides he saw hundreds of "surviving victims of that 'phantom glory'—wrecks and relics of bygone wars"; the splendor of Napoleon's tomb "repays those whose admiration for military or other despots is stronger than mine," but he deplored the lavish manner with which "millions of dollars were wrested from the scanty earnings of an over-taxed peasantry to honor the bones of him who, while living, was so prodigal alike of their treasure and their blood."

He had one experience in the French capital, however, that greatly interested him. He was arrested and confined more than two days in the Maison de Détention, or Prison for Debtors, because as a stockholder in the fire-destroyed Crystal Palace Exposition, held on Fifth Avenue in New York City on the site of the present Public Library, he was liable under French law for any indebtedness of the company to a Frenchman. Greeley wrote a most interesting description of life in a debtors' "prison," concluding it by saying that among his "fellow-prisoners" he had met more aristocrats of Europe than he ever could have encountered under any other circumstances. And he enjoyed them!

Greeley really had a restful time in Europe—so restful that he forgot his desire to be out of politics and was intent on being in Syracuse in September to witness the formal dissolution of the New York Whig organization and its absorption by the Republican party—Weed leading the way. The exodus of Moses and the Israelites out of Egypt was no more desperate, despairing search for a Promised Land than was this exodus of Weed, Seward and Raymond out of their old Whig organization once they realized from the 1854 elections that it was a place of no power, no patronage and no promise. Thus, it was no longer of use to them. "We go in through two doors but all come out through one," said Seward at the convention. "The Republican party banners are untorn by former battles and unsullied by past errors; it is the party for us!" Had he said that one year earlier!

Here was a triumph for Greeley over his old partners; once more his disregarded counsel had, as in 1848, proved its wisdom. Yet he made no public comment. It was all in the past and he never wasted time with the past. Far more important to him was the approaching struggle for control of the House of Representatives that was to meet for organization on December 3. Here was a new battleground. "For the first time in history," he telegraphed from Washington, "the House has a majority made up of anti-slavery members.... The problem is to unite this loose aggregation of independent thinkers." He was deep in all the wirepulling to elect Nathaniel Prentiss Banks, of Massachusetts, through two months from December 3, and one hundred and thirty roll calls—the longest contest ever waged over the speakership. "It is the first instance," said Greeley, "wherein northern resistance to slavery extension ever won in a fair, stand-up contest without compromise or equivocation." "It does me good," he wrote to Dana just before Christmas, "to see how those who hate 'The Tribune' much, fear it more. There are a dozen here who will do much better for my eye being on them." He failed to realize, however, that others had their eye on him, too, and that he was not going to escape them. On January 17 he again wrote Dana:

"Every traitor and self-seeker hates me with a demoniac hatred, which is perpetually bursting out.... General Shankland, of the Kansas Volunteers, has notified me that he intends to cowhide me the first time he catches me in public.... I trust the man of whom he buys the cowhide will know him well enough not to sell it on tick. I prefer to be the only sufferer by the application."

No blow came from Shankland, but one did come a week later from Congressman Albert Rust, of Arkansas, as Greeley was on his way to his hotel. Unlike most editors of that day Greeley had never before been assaulted, but he managed to defend himself.

He had gone to Washington in fighting mood; to Dana and

others in the home office that meant a complaining mood, too. He was particularly upset when national politics or men in Congress were discussed without notice to him. "Do send someone here and kill me if you cannot stop it, for I can bear it no longer. My life is torture to me. . . ." Soon after the Banks election Greeley again broke out to Dana:

Now I write once more to entreat that I may be allowed to conduct "The Tribune" with reference to the mile wide that stretches either way from Pennsylvania Avenue. It is but a small space, and you have all the world besides. I cannot stay here unless this request is complied with. I would rather cease to live at all. If you are not willing to leave me entire control with reference to this city, I ask you to call the proprietors together and have me discharged. . . . If you want to throw stones at anybody's crockery, aim at my head first, and in mercy to be sure to aim well. . . . I must give it up and go home. All the border ruffians from here to the lowest pit could not scare me away, but you can do it, and I must give up. I am too sick to be out of bed, too crazy to sleep, and am surrounded by horrors.

But to correspondent Pike, who was spending the winter in the New York office, Greeley had another tone. "Dear Pike," he wrote to him from Washington, "do you know what a Delilah of a town it is in which you chance now to be lodged? Have you heard that it is unfavorable to rigidity of backbone? Do you know that men have gone there honest and come away rascals? Have you heard that a virtue less savage than mine would hardly have been proof against its allurements? Beware, oh, friend, beware!"

To Dana, however, there were more letters such as the following:

Feb. 7, 1856

Friend Dana:

What would it cost to burn down the Opera House? If the price is reasonable have it done and send me the bill. I see that you have crowded out what little I sent to make room for Fry's eleven columns of argument as to the feasibility of sustaining opera in New York. I do not believe that three hundred people who take "The Tribune" care one chew of tobacco for the matter.

Feb. 9, 1856

Friend Dana:

Although this is to me the most detestable spot on earth I want to stay here through the Reeder fight, if you will let me. I will stand my chance of being horse-whipped or pistoled if you will keep me clear of being knocked down by "The Tribune." Bear gently on the Know-Nothings while I hope to operate with them here. Do be circumspect and draw no lines of discrimination to our detriment. I am not asking you to do anything—only to forbear doing what can only work harm. I don't pretend to know much but if I don't better understand what is passing under my own eyes than anyone who is 250 miles away I ought to be recalled.... But, remember, I don't expect you to do everything or to see everything. All I ask is that when a thing cannot be done right do not have it done at all.

Despite his threats that he would leave Washington, Greeley wrote on February 15: "Dear Pike: Of course, I shall stay in this infernal hole. Did you ever stay in a place where you didn't dare look in a glass when you got up in the morning for fear of seeing a scoundrel? That couldn't happen to me for I never patronize looking-glasses, but I have seen things here that led me to fear for some of my friends."

Again to Dana on Sunday, March 2, he renewed his protests:

Dear Dana:

If you allowed my letter on Toombs' Kansas speech to be crowded out by the scandal of the Griswold divorce case, why, then, you failed to consider fairly what is and what is not perishable....

You must not get cross with me. You see, it seems hard to stay in this dreary, infernal hole to write letters which mere delay makes more stupid than they naturally are.

Dana was eager to publish a Sunday picture newspaper and kept urging Greeley to agree to it. He received this reply to his last appeal:

March 20, 1856

Dana:

I look suspiciously on that magazine project because I regard "The Tribune" as a great idea just begun to be developed. I don't wish anything to interfere with it. Better do one thing well than several middling well. To make "The Tribune" the first newspaper in America is fortune and fame enough for us, and we are doing that now. Let us try to do what we have undertaken before we apply our energies to printing picture books.

The early months of 1856, however, had more to them than factional squabbles in Congress. The struggle over Kansas had made that territory the first battleground against the slave power. Greeley called it "a rising, threatening cloud." "Slavery—imperious, truculent, encroaching slavery—must be met. Kansas is at the point of the bowie-knife and the muzzle of a revolver; it is time for all in the North to show their colors." Missouri's Kentucky-born Whig Senator David Atchison warned his southern friends: "It means life or death to your institution."

Raiding mobs crossing the state line from Missouri were denounced as "border ruffians" by Greeley, and from the East, to settlers fighting against them, came a load of packing boxes marked "Bibles." The congregation of Henry Ward Beecher's Plymouth Church, Brooklyn, had made up a fund to send arms; but of course such things could not be shipped openly. When the boxes arrived at Lawrence, Kansas, not a single Bible was found in any of them—only Sharps rifles. "We gratefully accept the Bibles," they wrote in acknowledgment to the committee headed by Greeley, Beecher and David Dudley Field, "as the only sure foundation on which to erect free institutions."

Soon there were contributions from many sources to supply "Beecher's Bibles." "They were also shipped in casks, barrels and boxes marked 'Crockery' and 'Hardware' to avoid detection en route," wrote Rev. Edward Everett Hale. "We shipped 100 Sharps rifles as 'Bibles' and 'Books' that year. Beecher won the distinction of being called 'Sharps Rifle Beecher' and there was no name of which he was more proud." No one, however, was more active than Greeley; he even contributed a six-pound cannon, but, unlike the "Bibles," it disappeared mysteriously en route.

When the Brooklyn pastor was assailed for preferring rifles to Bibles, he replied, "We might just as well have read the Bible to buffaloes as to those folks out there. They understood rifles, however." The weapon was really a carbine. It had been patented in 1848 by a Swiss emigrant named Christian Sharps, who had a little firearms factory in Hartford, Connecticut. Buffalo hunters called it "Old Reliable"; they preferred it because of its short barrel and accuracy. When Kansas settlers were asked the kind of gun they wanted, only one answer came back: "Sharps." One of the original "Beecher's Bibles" is now in the Arthur L. Ulrich Museum in Colt's firearms plant at Hartford.

"If we win this election," wrote Greeley to correspondent Pike at Washington in August 1856, "it will demonstrate that a man need not be a 'dough-face' in order to have some show for office. ... It will mean that freedom can win in a pitched battle with slavery."

He greeted the Frémont ticket as enthusiastically as he had ever battled for Clay. It had the spirit of challenge; it meant a new grouping of younger minds taking the place of the old Whig politicians. As in the popular sovereignty fight in 1854, Greeley's *Tribune* was again "the drumbeat of the nation." Editorial after editorial tied the issue down to clear-cut anti–slavery-extension. Finally, in October, came Greeley's famous appeal: "Is there a North?"

"It is high time that this question was definitely answered," he insisted. "Year after year our public men have been giving up the ground under our feet and all the time protesting that there was a point beyond which they could not be driven. If that point is not now reached, it never can be. If the North quails now, it will be generally understood that the slave power may do its will and that the North will submit."

The campaign was a hard-fought contest between Republican John C. Frémont, Democrat James Buchanan and ex-President Millard Fillmore, the "Know-Nothing" candidate. When Greeley assured editor McClure of the Philadelphia *Times* that Frémont would have 50,000 plurality in New York state, the latter "thought that 'Uncle Horace' has lost his political cunning." Yet the actual figure was nearly 100,000. The Know-Nothing ticket, however, killed Frémont's chances for a national electoral majority. Still Greeley looked hopefully to the future: "We have lost a battle. The Bunker Hill of the new struggle for freedom is past; the Saratoga and Yorktown are yet to be achieved. A party born yesterday, without organization, without official power, without prestige, has not overcome the old party in this country. It is best to state the case fairly and in its broadest and worst aspects. Practically a majority of the American people have voted that it is not wrong to shoot and scalp men in Kansas for peacefully trying to keep theirs a Free Territory and make it a Free State.

"Meanwhile let us quietly preserve and perfect our Republican organization and this hour of darkness will prelude a glorious morning. The overthrow of the slave-breeders' rule is too great, too beneficent, a revolution to be effected in a year; with time, faith and energy victory must inure to the right. Let us never despair of the American Republic!"

But the Saratoga and the Yorktown so confidently prophesied might never have come to pass—certainly not with Lincoln as its chief—had editors Greeley, Raymond and Bowles, acting with several United States senators representing eastern states, succeeded in persuading Illinois Republicans to make unanimous the return of Little Giant Douglas to the Senate in 1858 for a third term. Douglas seemed to them to be, as Raymond said in the New York *Times*, "the man of the hour."

After forcing a constitution through a rump legislature at Lecompton, the slave power in Kansas had sent it to Congress for approval, without having submitted it to the people of the territory as all parties had agreed to do. In his annual message to Congress on December 8, 1857, President Buchanan justified this violation of the Douglas theory of "popular sovereignty" on the plea that he had merely "said" the constitution should be submitted but had never "instructed" that it should be. Douglas promptly denounced this evasion of a pledge.

"By God, I made James Buchanan," he exclaimed, "and now, by God, I'll unmake him!"

Soon rumor had it that Douglas was available as a Union candidate for the Senate, and later for the presidency. Even Indiana congressman Schuyler Colfax believed it possible to make over a hard-boiled Vermont-born Democrat such as Douglas into a leader of a sort of Constitutional and Union party that would command votes which a Republican candidate alone could not. "He is almost ready to be baptized a Republican," he advised Greeley.

But Greeley refused to believe it. "We are not going to say anything to repel proffered help," said the *Tribune* on December 2, "but we advise against cherishing delusive hopes that Douglas will assail the bogus convention." "We never saw reason to trust him," asserted the *Tribune* on the morning of the very day on which Douglas was arraigning President Buchanan for his attitude and declaring to him defiantly in the White House, "I have taken a through ticket and have checked all my baggage."

Despite his doubting mood, Greeley sensed that a real situation had developed at Washington, and he hastened there. The *Chicago Daily Times* correspondent met him "scrabbling down Pennsylvania Avenue looking like a Methodist exhorter, with his flapping white coat, broad-brimmed white hat and fringe of white hair, hurrying to give counsel to Douglas."

Of course, *Tribune* readers were amazed by Greeley's dispatch that the Douglas speeches in the Senate are "decisive of his secession from the Administration and southern radicals. If he confronts them boldly he has the whole North—the majority of the Nation—with him." Again Greeley telegraphs: "His speech is universally admitted to be the greatest he has ever made. It is admired by all sides. The struggle of Douglas with the slave power will be a magnificent spectacle."

Here was a most astonishing turnabout in American politics—Greeley for Douglas! Only three years before, the latter was denounced as "an executioner of liberty"; now he is greeted as its hope!

But Illinois Republicans warned Greeley's *Weekly Tribune* "to keep hands off Illinois politics." "No interference!"—"No dictation!" came the cry from there. They impolitely told editors Greeley, Raymond, Bowles and other eastern Republicans to "go to hell!"—they would run the politics of their state in their own way. In particular, they would nominate Lincoln.

Managing editor Charles H. Ray, of the Chicago *Tribune*, wrote Greeley: "I think I see Douglas' tracks all over the state. Not a single toe is turned toward the Republican party. Watch him, use him, but do not trust him—not an inch!"

Lincoln, of course, was worried. He was not in a pleasant mood when he said to partner William H. Herndon: "I think Greeley is not doing me right. His conduct savors of injustice. I am a true Republican and have been tried already in the hottest part of every fight, yet I find him taking up Douglas, a veritable dodger—once a tool of the South, now its enemy—and pushing him to the front. When he does that he pulls me down."

By letter Greeley denied to Herndon that he had ever "tried to instruct the Republicans of Illinois in their political duties," but when not long afterward Herndon called on him in the *Tribune* office, Greeley's conversation definitely indicated that he wanted Douglas sent back to the Senate as a Union nominee. He was not, however, added Herndon, hostile to Lincoln:

"'Greeley,' I asked him, 'do you want to see a third party organized and Douglas ride to power through the North which he has so much abused and betrayed?'

"'Let the future alone,' replied Greeley confidently, 'it will come out all right. Douglas is a brave man. Forget the past and sustain the righteous.'"

Lincoln did not share this view. He wrote to Senator Lyman Trumbull: "What does 'The Tribune' mean by its constant eulogizing and admiring and magnifying of Douglas? Does it, in this, speak the sentiments of Republicans at Washington? Have they concluded that the Republican cause, generally, can best be promoted by sacrificing us here in Illinois? If so, we would like to know it soon; it will save us a great deal of labor to surrender at once. No Republican here is going over to Douglas, but if 'The Tribune' continues to din his praises into the ears of its five or ten thousand subscribers in Illinois, it is more than can be hoped for that all will stand firm."

Fortunately, the wave of Republican enthusiasm for the "Little Giant" flattened to the smoothness of a mountain pond when on June 24, following his renomination by the Democrats of Illinois, the Republicans of that state met in convention at Springfield and defiantly declared that "Abraham Lincoln is our first and our only choice for United States Senator."

"Every man for Lincoln!" instantly headlined the Chicago *Tribune* exultingly.

But Greeley was never reconciled to the refusal to unite on Douglas. He wrote to Joseph Medill, who was chiefly responsible for insisting upon Lincoln: "You have repelled Douglas, who might have been attached to our cause, whatever he may now find it necessary to say or do. Now go ahead and fight it through. You are in for it. If Lincoln would fight up to the work, you may get through. You have got your elephant—you would have him—now shoulder him. He is not so very heavy after all."

Not until late August did Greeley declare that on the record of the debate "Lincoln has decidedly the advantage." Still, the "Weekly Try-bune" pursued a doubting cause. By October "there was a downward slide for Lincoln," according to partner Herndon, "due to Greeley's cowardly editorials."

When commenting on the Lincoln-Douglas result, Greeley gave no heed to the fact that Lincoln's battle had elected the entire Republican state ticket and that Republican legislative candidates had polled a substantial majority of the popular vote. He dealt kindly with Lincoln but had no word of a possible future for him. "Douglas has achieved a hard-won, brilliant and conclusive triumph," continued Greeley. "The Democrats must nominate him for President in 1860 or retire from the contest, surrendering the government to the Republicans. Yet, while the result gives Douglas an exalted rank among politicians" and "has probably paved his way to the Presidency," his speeches "lacked a quality of statesmanship." They were "volcanic and seething," lacking "the repose of conscious right."

No exulting feeling of triumph prevailed among the southern-dominated Democratic majority in the Senate, however, over the return of Douglas. Led by Jefferson Davis, they did all they could to bar his way to the presidential nomination. They stripped him of his chairmanships and of everything else but the senatorial title which the Illinois legislature had conferred upon him.

But they could not deprive Douglas of the keen interest accorded him by gallery visitors as he sat at his desk in the Senate. In a dispatch to his Cincinnati newspaper, editor Murat Halstead wrote this interesting story of the man:

> And here, coming from the cloak room on the Democratic side, is a queer little man, canine head and duck legs... everybody knows the "Little Giant"... he looks conscious of being looked at; he is pointed out by a hundred hands, as he makes pretentious strides of about eighteen inches each, toward his chair. Two or three admirers in the gallery are disposed to applaud, but you hear merely the rattle of a single boot-heel.... The "Little Giant" wears his black hair long, but it is getting thin and is not the great tangled mass we saw on his neck a few years ago. For O "Little Giant" it grows gray rapidly. Now he proceeds to twist himself down in his chair as far as possible, and places his feet on his desk; and thus his admirers in the gallery look upon the prodigious little man, squirming flat on his back.... He requires a large vest; large as he is about the chest, his waist is becoming still more expansive. But he has an immense head—in height, and breadth and depth—in indication of solidity and force; you cannot find its equal in Washington. There is great power under that massive brow, and resolution in that grim mouth; no doubt at all of that.

CHAPTER XVIII

Overland to the Pacific

IT WAS NOW time for another Greeley pilgrimage to distant places. Many northern states, including his own New York, had gone Democratic; the Senate and the House of Representatives at Washington were again under southern control. "Is there a North?" seemed to have been answered in 1858 in the negative. Greeley determined to find out for himself if there was a West—a Pacific coast West—and what that treasure house of limitless gold really looked like. It was a lure he could not resist. Besides, he had been one of the earliest advocates of building the Union Pacific Railroad. He now wanted to cross the deserts, mountains and rivers over which it would pass, and thus know their difficulties. Pessimists were saying that "constructing a railroad across fourteen hundred miles of such deserts and mountains would be like building a bridge to the moon or tunneling under an ocean." Greeley had more faith. So this fifty-year-old newspaper chieftain hazarded the discomforts and dangers of a stagecoach journey to the coast. "I want to learn what I can of that country with my own eyes," he explained, "and to study men in their cabins and at their work instead of reading about them in books."

If any traveler to the "Gold Coast" during the 1850 decade wrote of his experiences with more human interest than did Greeley in letters to the *Tribune* and in his book *An Overland Journey*, the story has yet to be read by this author.

Lugging the same old carpetbag with which he had twice toured Europe, Greeley left New York City on May 9, 1859, for St.

Joseph, Missouri—by the Erie Railroad. "Tried a sleeping car—not very successfully," said his first article. "We all retired at ten o'clock with a fair allowance of open window, but the rain poured in, the night was chill, and soon every orifice for the admission of external air was closed save the two humbug ventilators above." Barging down the Missouri River he reached Atchison, Kansas: "I have long been looking for the Far West and here it is! The color and consistence of the Missouri River are those of milk porridge; you could not discern an egg in a glass of it. A fly floating in a teacup of this dubious fluid an eighth of an inch below the surface would be quite invisible."

Across the prairie land of Kansas, and then to Denver, he traveled on by stagecoach. "Adieu to bed-rooms and wash-bowls, adieu to chairs, adieu to eggs and potatoes; I haven't slept in a bed in a month, nor with any floor under me but Mother Earth, traveling among Indians, buffaloes, wolves, antelope and a few white men. Yet I like Kansas. The twin curses of the state are one-horse politicians and land speculators with their paper cities and bogus corner lots. It takes three log houses to make a city in Kansas, but they call it a city as soon as they have staked it out. I asked how so many quarter sections were 'pre-empted.' 'How?' came the answer. 'Live a little on it and lie a lot!' And yet if the Garden of Eden exceeded this land in beauty and fertility I pity Adam for having to leave it."

As he left Kansas Greeley summarized the red man:

"The Indians are children. Their arts, wars, treaties, alliances, habitations, crafts, properties, commerce, comforts, all belong to the very lowest and rudest ages of human existence. I have learned to appreciate better than hitherto, and to make more allowance for, the dislike, aversion, contempt, wherewith Indians have been regarded since the days of the Puritans. It needs but little familiarity with the actual Aborigine to convince any one that the poetic Indian—the Indian of Fenimore Cooper and Longfellow—is only visible to the poet's eye. To the prosaic observer the average Indian of the woods and prairies is a being who does little credit to human nature—a slave of appetite and sloth, never emancipated from the tyranny of one animal passion save by the more ravenous demands of another. As I passed over those magnificent bottoms of Kansas which form the reservations of the Delawares, Potawatamies, etc., constituting the very best corn lands on earth, and saw their owners sitting round the doors of their lodges in the height of the planting season, and in as good, bright planting weather as sun and soil ever made, I could not help saying, 'These people must die out—there is no help for them. God has given this earth to those who will subdue and cultivate it, and it is vain to struggle against His righteous decree.' "

In Denver Greeley had his first experience with the real wild west of the cowboy. As he did not enjoy the unpleasant habit of gamblers and others of shooting up barrooms and hotels just for the fun of it, he remained there only until he could secure a seat in a stagecoach taking him farther west. "There is a fighting class among the settlers in the Rocky Mountains," he wrote to the *Tribune*. "This class is not numerous, but it is more influential than it should be in giving tone to the society of which its members form a part. Prone to deep thinking, soured in temper, always armed, bristling at a word, ready with the rifle, revolver, or bowie knife, they give law and set fashions which, in a country where the regular administration of justice is yet a matter of prophecy, it seems difficult to overrule or disregard. I apprehend that there have been, during my two weeks' sojourn, more brawls, more fights, more pistol shots with criminal intent, in this log city of one hundred and fifty dwellings, not three fourths completed nor two thirds inhabited, nor one third fit to be, than in any community of no greater numbers on earth."

Greeley reported on June 10: "I know that a million buffalo is a great many but I am certain that I saw that many yesterday. They darkened the earth around us all day like an army in battle array on the hills. Certainly all we saw could not have stood on ten square miles of ground. While there have been many shots fired at them by our party at point-blank distance I doubt that any buffalo has experienced any personal inconvenience therefrom.

"Of the seventeen bags on which I have ridden the last four

days, at least sixteen are filled with large bound volumes—mainly Patent Office reports franked by a California Congressman to his constituents."

At last, after more than a thousand miles of unbroken desert and poor country, "we rolled into the city of the many-wived 'Prophet' and the most conspicuous trophy of his genius and his power." Of course the journalist visitor had to seek a three-column interview with Brigham Young. Greeley-like, he was thus the first reporter ever to be accorded one. His talk with the Prophet, as published in the *Tribune*, was a frank discussion, but more interesting were his own observations. "No woman indicated by word or look her approval of polygamy," he wrote. "That women acquiesce in it as an ordinance of God I believe, but I am confident that there is not in all Utah a woman who does not wish that God had not ordained it. On the whole I conclude that as polygamy is a graft on the original stock of Mormonism it will be outlived by the root—that there will be a new Revelation ere many years whereby the Saints will be admonished not to marry more than one wife."

The Yosemite Valley excited Greeley's admiration. "It is the grandest marvel of the continent," he wrote back home. "Nothing else dwells in my memory that is at all comparable"—yet he paid for his sight of the wondrous cavern. "Fording brooks, stumbling over rocks, winding among trees, it seemed to me that the six miles from the point where we entered the Valley to the two cottages or huts near its centre would never end; but they *did* end at last, about 2 A.M.; and I dismounted, and lay down to a welcome, though unquiet, slumber. I was covered with boils (the penalty of drinking the alkaline waters of Colorado, Utah and Nevada), and had ridden in torture since noon, bearing my weight on my toes, barely stuck into Mexican stirrups far too small for me, whereby my feet had been so lamed that I could scarcely walk; hence, the prospect of soon rising to resume my travels was by no means alluring. I did rise, however; took breakfast; rode to the head of the Valley; examined with some care the famous fall; dined; and, at 2 P.M., started homeward; reaching Clark's ranche, on the South Merced, at 10 P.M."

Many anecdotes of Greeley's stagecoach experiences—some actual, all exaggerated and some that never were—were the talk of the mining regions for years following his visit; Mark Twain, in *Roughing It,* relates one of stage driver Hank Monk and Horace Greeley, of which he says, "Drivers always told it, conductors told it, chance passengers told it, in all the multitude of tongues that Babel bequeathed to earth flavored with whiskey, beer, tobacco, garlic, etc. I never smelt any anecdote so often as I smelt that during a period of six years in which I crossed the Sierras thirteen times. Just after we left Julesberg on the Platte River, on my first journey, I was sitting with the driver and he said: 'When Greeley was leaving Carson City he told Hank that he had an engagement that afternoon in Placerville and was anxious to go through quick. Hank cracked his whip and started off at an awful pace. The coach bounced up and down in such a terrific way that it jolted the buttons all off Greeley's coat and finally shot his head clear through the roof of the stage. He yelled at Hank to go easier—said he wasn't in as much of a hurry as he had thought. But Hank stuck to his first orders. 'Keep your seat, Horace,' he said assuringly, 'keep your seat and I'll get you there on time'—and you bet he did, too—what was left of him."

The Mark Twain story concludes: "Stage-coaching on the Overland is no more, and stage drivers are a defunct race, but the real grandeurs of the Pacific are not Yosemite or the big trees but the bald-headed anecdote of Hank Monk and his adventures with Horace Greeley."

In California, Greeley was hailed as a friend of labor, of enterprise and of the Union Pacific Railroad. At Folsom, his first stopping place, the welcoming committee watched him stumbling out of the high carriage "carrying a little old glazed traveling bag, a very rusty and well-worn white coat and still more worn and faded blue cotton umbrella, together with a roll of blankets tied so loosely that they were spreading."

Sacramento's welcome was greatest of all. The *Union* thus

described his busy day there as typical of all of his days in the state:

Greeley has come and gone. He was here a little short of thirteen hours, during which he held an informal levee, made a reception speech, partook of a special dinner, delivered an address, saw something of the city, opened and read his letters, partly arranged the programme of his journey through the state, and took sufficient night's rest to enable him to be up at five the next morning and take his seat in the stage which left the next hour for Grass Valley, a journey of between 60 and 70 miles over a wearisome mountain road. This despatch is characteristic of the man.

Greeley's touring did not end until he had found time for a visit to Jessie Frémont, the spirited wife of the Republican candidate in 1856. He found her living modestly in Mariposa, hoping for a turn of fortune for her restless husband. In late August the traveler started for home by way of what then was the Isthmus of Panama, with a new faith in the destined greatness of "my own green land forever," as he had hailed America's shores when returning from Europe in 1851. "Men and brethren," he wrote in his last letter to the *Tribune*, "let us resolve to have a railroad to the Pacific and to have it soon! It will add more to the strength and wealth of our country than would the acquisition of a dozen Cubas.

"I do grievously err if the historian of a future century does not instance the discovery of the Columbia River by a Yankee and the finding of gold in Upper California so soon after that country had fallen into our hands, as among the most memorable and fortunate incidents in the annals of our continent and, hence, of mankind.

"On gold per se I place no high estimate. If all the science and labor which have been devoted to the discovery and extraction of the precious metals had been as faithfully applied to the production of iron, copper, coal, lead, marble, slate, etc., I believe that our country would have been richer and our people wiser and happier. May the great-grandchildren of California's pioneers rejoice in the knowledge that her stormy, irregular youth has given place to a sober, respected, beneficent maturity! May her influence on the side of freedom, knowledge, righteousness be ever more greatly felt and greatly blessed throughout this awakening, wondering, plastic western world!"

A cheerful, refreshed, anecdotal Greeley rejoined his colleagues in the *Tribune* office that October. What wonders he had seen! What resolute men and women were building an amazing nation in itself beyond those lofty mountains! No longer did his "Go west, young man, go west!" mean the prairie states whose waters flow into the Mississippi; that call to a new life now meant the whole West. From the Atlantic to the Pacific, as he saw it, was to be the home and the hope of the man of industry as nowhere else in the world.

CHAPTER XIX

"Any Candidate but Seward"

I HOPE TO DO my part toward electing a Republican President this year. That done I intend to stop lecturing and running about. I shall limit my work, sit down and edit *The Tribune* and live out the residue of my life in peace."

Thus on January 6, 1860, Greeley repeated to his friend Mrs. Allen his frequent dream of a future that was never to be. The greatest triumph of his political career was less than five months distant in Chicago's Wigwam, and his severest trials were to follow it. He had returned home confirmed in his long-held opinion that the Democrats, if united on Douglas, were certain to elect him as Buchanan's successor in the White House. "I don't believe that the time has come when a Republican on a square issue can poll one hundred electoral votes," he wrote editor Baker of the *Independent*. Increasing hostility to the "Little Giant" among southern radicals afforded the strongest hope for Republican success, but Greeley saw no signs of Republican activity. He chose the last day of 1859 to arouse the party: "We must wrest the Federal Administration from the hands of slavery extensionists," he then declared, "and this, if ever, is to be done in 1860. At the risk of being denounced as croaking or faint-hearted we tell the Republicans of these United States that we believe they are to be beaten, and badly beaten, in the presidential campaign now opening unless they soon organize . . . and place their views and objects so clearly and fully before the great body of their fellow-citizens as to secure thousands of votes that will otherwise be cast against them."

Of one thing Greeley was certain—Seward could not be elected and should not be nominated. Dana was even more restless. "If we are to be beaten," Dana contended, "then Seward is the man to name, but I hope we are not to re-enact the old Whig tragedy of Henry Clay." He favored Chase. "Rely on it we are to have Douglas as our opponent, and a great fight throughout the Free States," wrote Greeley to Governor E. D. Morgan.

Late in March Greeley startled New York Republicans by publishing an editorial entitled "The Presidency," in which he summarized existing political conditions and candidates; from it the Seward boom got a puncture which its sponsors were never able to repair.

For Greeley to praise Seward as "our veteran leader," as "an able, patriotic statesman," and to point out his "honorable wounds" due to "prejudices and incessant misrepresentations," was not difficult, but at the same time to bury him as a candidate because of his too faithful party service called for all his finesse.

"Is the Republican party strong enough to elect a Seward or a Chase?" asked the editor. "Could either of them carry Pennsylvania, New Jersey, Indiana or Illinois? If yes, then the only question is which of the two foremost Republicans should be our standard-bearer. We have our own opinion, but we will leave decision to the convention and the delegates from the doubtful states to tell the convention what they can do with either man as the candidate. If the convention should decide that it cannot safely nominate Seward or Chase we hold with due submission that the man for the hour is Edward Bates, of Missouri, who, while essentially a Republican, has not been exposed to the unjust prejudices which incessant misrepresentation has excited against our veteran leader."

Having centered Seward's fate not upon the known wishes of New York but upon the decision of the "doubtful states," Greeley turned next to Pike, his Washington friend and correspondent, to inform him that he would not even attend the convention. He had published his opinion in the *Tribune* and he was through! "I don't care what is done at the convention," he added. "I know what ought to be done and, having set that forth, I am content. I stand in the position of the rich old fellow who, having built a church entirely out of his own funds, addressed his fellow-townsmen:

'I've built you a church
And bought you a bell,
Now go to meeting
Or else go to hell.'"

Oregon, remote Oregon, was to change that purpose and make Greeley the most active leader in the battle for the nomination of "any candidate but Seward."

Of the 465 delegates and thousands of spectators who crowded Chicago's Wigwam as the second Republican national convention began its work at noon on Wednesday, May 16, 1860, Horace Greeley and Thurlow Weed were more sought and discussed than were any other men in attendance. Greeley was seen everywhere in hotels and on the streets; Weed kept to his headquarters in the Tremont Hotel. Affable, cool, confident, he already sensed the powerful place he expected to hold as patronage distributor for the next national administration.

With New York's big delegation always under his control, Weed had been a substantial influence in nominating William Henry Harrison in 1840, General "Zach" Taylor in 1848, Scott in 1852 and Frémont in 1856. At Chicago this leadership broadened to his greatest ambition, for there he was endeavoring to nominate for President the man whose political career for thirty years he had fashioned to his pattern.

"I love my tyrant," Seward had written to Weed after his first election as governor in 1838. Now, twenty-two years later, his loyalty is as unwavering as ever. Why not? Weed had made him governor and then senator; why should not Weed now by the same skillful control of conventions, and despite Greeley, make him the Republican nominee for President? To Seward, at home in Auburn, it seemed a logical sequence. He left all to Weed, even permitting his neighbors to haul a cannon on his lawn to announce the expected triumph.

Over thirty thousand strangers crowded into Chicago—most of them without thought of bed and board so long as they could shout for their rail-splitter candidate. Seward had gaudily uniformed, beaver-hatted and epauletted marching bands parading the streets and stepping jauntily to loud brasses and rolling drums—but the Lincolnites had the sidewalks and the lungs. "Lincoln could have a parade, too, if like Seward we had $5,000 to spend on one," declared the Chicago *Tribune*'s editor Ray, "but we haven't $5,000 for all of our expenses!"

Weed headquarters were regarded as the seat of coming power and, therefore, of hope for aspiring politicians. There he warned an Iowa delegation inclined to Lincoln that in 1856 the Republicans had nominated a man who possessed not a single qualification for the presidency. That mistake should not be made again. In Seward the Republicans now had just the man equal to the place. To other delegations Weed boasted that Seward would be elected because he was the only candidate for whom campaign contributions could be secured from corporations, especially transit, water and gas corporations seeking franchises.

Doubtful October states? Yes, Weed admitted that Greeley and others were talking a lot about them, but a big campaign fund would easily take care of such states. Carl Schurz, who favored Seward, declared that he was "chilled" because Weed was "making commitments that Seward, if elected President, could not carry out without dishonor." William Cullen Bryant telegraphed the New York *Evening Post* that he was shocked by the freedom with which Weed boasted of a "barrel" of from $400,000 to $500,000 that only the Seward managers could raise. Others called the Weed tactics "a reproach" and "a by-word." To Weed it was all just as simple as that—dollars would elect his candidate, but they would be available to no one else.

Such a thing as a headquarters for Greeley was out of the question. To him headquarters would have been like a prison cell. He was content to share a room in the Tremont Hotel with two Oregon delegates.

He had reserved no hotel accommodations, for he had made up

his mind not to attend the convention. On March 25 he wrote to Pike accepting Pike's bet of $20 that Douglas would not be nominated by the Democrats and offering Pike one of $25 that Seward would not be named: "I can spare the money because I don't want to go to Chicago and mean to keep away if possible."

Less than three weeks before the convention date, however, he was surprised to receive formal notice by letter from Oregon that he had been substituted for one of its delegates. He was glad to respond to the call of a state then only one year in the Union and which was now to have representation for the first time in a national convention. Oregon and Minnesota were the two territories mentioned by Douglas during his conferences with Schuyler Colfax in December 1857 that should be promptly brought into the Union as states to strengthen it. And now Oregon was to respond with Greeley as its spokesman! It is strange that Republicans out in the farthest northwest, still largely wilderness, should have crossed the continent to New York City to secure a delegate for them in Chicago; strange that Greeley should have been selected—stranger still that this latest addition to statehood with "The Union" emblazoned on its seal and an American eagle poised atop of it should have thus brought to this convention the man who more than any other delegate influenced its choice of a candidate. Oregon—"pathless Oregon" as Webster had called it—certainly then wrote across the pages of history with a large and enduring hand, for had there been no Greeley in that convention there probably would have been no Lincoln as its nominee.

Tirelessly Greeley wandered day and night from one state headquarters to another seeking support for his candidate Bates, of Missouri, but particularly insisting that the nominee should be chosen on the basis of probable election and not on hope of Weed's corporation dollars. "Any candidate but Seward!" was his plea. To Addison Proctor, a Kansas delegate, Greeley "looked like a well-to-do dairy farmer fresh from his clover fields. He seemed to find a place in our hearts at once."

"To name Seward is to invite defeat," declared Greeley to the Kansas men.

"What do you think of Abraham Lincoln?" one of them asked him.

"Lincoln," replied Greeley, speaking earnestly and slowly, "has a host of friends out here who see in him something that the rest of us have not yet seen. The trouble with Lincoln is that he has had no experience in national affairs. Facing a crisis Lincoln is too risky an undertaking."

Thus Greeley moves from one group to another. "Mr. Greeley has made a great sensation here," reads a New York *Times* dispatch. "He is surrounded by a crowd wherever he goes, who besiege him for a speech."

Murat Halstead, editor of the Cincinnati *Commercial*, telegraphs his newspaper: "The principal lions are Horace Greeley and Francis P. Blair. The way Greeley is stared at as he shuttles about, looking as innocent as ever, is itself a sight. Wherever he appears there is a crowd gaping at him, and if he stops to talk a minute with someone who wishes to consult him as the oracle the crowd becomes as dense as possible; there is the most eager desire to hear the words of wisdom that are supposed to fall on such occasions."

On Tuesday night, the eve of assembling, Greeley had telegraphed the *Tribune* that the Seward forces were strengthening. The *Tribune* convention reporter did not agree with his chief; he prophesied an increasing undercurrent for Lincoln. Editor Raymond, despite his strong support of Seward, was "apprehensive." "The convention is perfectly willing to accept Mr. Seward's platform," he telegraphed his New York *Times*, "but it is not willing to accept Mr. Seward. In such a state of things it is idle to attempt to foresee the result." Editor Halstead foresaw no one but Seward, while the New York *Herald* correspondent put Seward in a lead difficult to maintain beyond two ballots.

So the two organizing sessions of the convention complete the first day with just enough uncertainty to bring New Jersey, Pennsylvania, and Indiana into the center of discussion. Plainly those states will have the decision as to the candidate. In his *Tribune* editorial of March, Greeley had shrewdly put responsibility upon them, but he now lacks confidence that they will respond favorably.

The second day of the convention is almost over when the Seward forces demand a ballot before adjournment. The platform has been adopted; there is no reason why candidates should not be formally put before the convention and at least one ballot taken. No reason but one—the clerks cannot find the tally sheets! Vainly they search. It is late afternoon. "Let's have supper!" cries one delegate. "Let's adjourn!" shouts another, and without further protest from the Sewardites the convention closes its session for the day. The fate of a presidential candidate may have been decided by that failure to find those tally sheets, for it is conceded that overnight the Lincoln managers traded Seward out of many votes.

"Make no contracts that bind me!" Lincoln had telegraphed them early.

"Hell!" exclaimed Norman Judd that night. "We're here to nominate him and he's in Springfield." At the close of the day's session the correspondent of the New York *Times* was one of the few men in Chicago who refused to regard Seward as nominated until uncertain Pennsylvania had been heard from. It was then that Greeley lost hope. Again his own correspondent differs with him. "'Old Abe,'" the latter telegraphs the *Tribune*, "seems to be the coming man."

In the Weed headquarters Seward was regarded as such a certainty that the night was one of confidence and enthusiasm, but it was a hectic night for Seward's opponents and for no one more than for Greeley. Toward eleven o'clock he canvassed the Ohio delegates and found them hopelessly split between Chase, Wade and McLean. Depressed, he finally sought comfort among the New Jersey men pledged to their own William L. Dayton but ready to move to a winner. He misunderstood their attitude as definitely set against joining any combination. Thereupon he sent to the *Tribune* his famous dispatch:

> Chicago, May 17, 11:40 P.M. My conclusion from all that I can gather to-night is that the opposition to Governor Seward cannot concentrate on any candidate and that he will be nominated.
>
> H.G.

In that message the instinct of a true reporter frankly to give the news as he interpreted it regardless of his personal prejudices came to the front in Greeley, for we may be sure that no words were ever more reluctantly written by him from a convention than the twenty-seven words he then used to advise *Tribune* readers of the situation as it probably existed at midnight—though, fortunately for Lincoln, not the situation that was to exist at sunup next morning. Poet Bourdillon's line, "the night has a thousand eyes," is truer of no night more than the night before a political convention is to call its roll for nominations. It was emphatically true of that night of May 17, 1860. All the conspicuous leaders except a few never-say-dies were confident that Seward would have a majority vote next day on either the first or second ballot.

Yet the eager, sleepless eyes of those few unbeatable men who searched through the night for a break here or a rift there in the Seward ranks demonstrated anew the lesson so familiar in politics that one can never tell what another day may bring forth.

In despair, Greeley after sending his telegram hurried to the Tremont Hotel room of David Dudley Field. By that time it was midnight.

"It's all over!" he exclaimed as he threw himself on a couch, exhausted and despairing. "We can't get together to stop Seward. All is lost!"

"No, Greeley, all is not lost!" shouted Field. "Let us up and at 'em! It isn't over! We can win! Let each of us visit every doubtful delegation. Judd and Davis are at this moment at work on Pennsylvania in this very hotel; Lane is bringing Indiana into line. Greeley, you get after your New England friends. There's to be no sleep for any of us; let's go to work!"

Instantly a new Greeley sprang up from the lounge. He looked as though a heavy strain had suddenly lessened. Eagerly he went in search of New England delegates. By morning Field and Francis Blair reported: "The work is done. Lincoln will win!" Even then Greeley did not share their confidence. He knew Weed too well.

At last the fateful morning session; candidacies are to be formally presented. William Maxwell Evarts, New York's great lawyer famous for his long sentences, makes this one-sentence speech that occupies only four lines of type in the official book of proceedings: "Mr. Chairman, I take the liberty, Sir, to name as a candidate to be nominated by this convention for the office of President, William H. Seward, of New York." In even fewer words Abraham Lincoln is named by Norman Judd of Illinois, Salmon P. Chase by Joseph Carter of Ohio, Edward Bates by Francis P. Blair of Missouri, William L. Dayton by Thomas Dudley of New Jersey, Senator Simon Cameron by Governor Andrew H. Reeder of Pennsylvania and Judge John McLean by Governor Tom Corwin of Ohio.

Of all seven announcements there is not one as long as the four lines by Evarts. Except for the applause that in turn greeted each nomination the entire presentation of candidates could have been completed in five minutes. But there was an unexpected development—just the kind that has so often turned the tide in our many conventions. Columbus Delano of Ohio asked attention. Standing on a chair, he shouted: "Mr. Chairman: On behalf of a portion of the delegates from Ohio, I rise to second the nomination of a man who can split rails and maul Democrats—Abraham Lincoln."

Even the rafters of the Wigwam seemed to join in the shouting as Delano took his seat. Then came the balloting. Seward led in votes, but that demonstration placed the heart of the convention surely with Lincoln. The three leading candidates stood:

	First Ballot	Second Ballot	Third Ballot
Seward	173	184	180
Lincoln	102	181	231
Bates	48	35	22

No formal announcement of the third ballot figures was ever made; before chairman George Ashmun could report the result, William M. Evarts withdrew the Seward candidacy and all opposition to Lincoln's nomination ceased. A big factor in that result was Greeley's plan of holding out a group of 48 Bates delegates. Had Seward on the second ballot been able to add any Bates votes to his column the influence of such a break, however small, would have made his candidacy look like a "band wagon" and enough delegates would probably have jumped on it to nominate him. But Greeley held his little band together except thirteen whom he was glad to release to Lincoln. The convention understood this strategy, and when Lincoln was declared nominated delegates crowded around and cheered Greeley as though he himself or his own candidate had been chosen. His face was described as one big, radiant sunburst of smiles; not a trace was left of the wear and tear of four nights and days of canvassing and pleading. Though Curtin of Pennsylvania and Lane of Indiana—both candidates for governor—had swung their "doubtful" states into line for Lincoln, the defeat of Seward was everywhere regarded as Greeley's personal triumph; Weed was quoted as declaring that defeat would have been easier to face it it had not come from one whom he "had taken out of an attic printing office in New York City and made prominent."

John D. de Freese, chairman of the Indiana delegation, wired word to Schuyler Colfax at South Bend: "Greeley has slaughtered Seward but has saved the Republican Party." George William Curtis telegraphed this editorial to *Harper's Weekly*: "We need hardly seek deeper than Greeley for the cause of Seward's rejection. 'The Tribune' was the creator of the Republican party and is still its great organ and censor."

"For the result Greeley labored harder and did tenfold more than the whole family of Blairs, together with the five gubernatorial candidates," telegraphed editor Raymond to the New York *Times*, lamenting the defeat of Seward. "Greeley's voice was most potential where Seward was strongest."

"I have done with Greeley!" declared Weed later.

"The past is dead" responded Greeley.

No man ever came out of a national convention more firmly endorsed by it as the guide and spokesman of his party than did the *Tribune* editor at Chicago. Other leaders had bargained and traded for and against rival candidates, but the notable feature of the three days' struggle was the earnestness with which Greeley talked to one group of delegates after another wherever he found them, and created a lack of confidence, even among Seward supporters, in Seward's election. Without patronage to give—or even to promise—without power to help or harm a single person in or out of public office, without one word of harsh criticism of any candidate and without promise of one dollar to match the boasted thousands offered by his opponents for the campaign or for other purposes, Greeley led in persuading the convention from a nominee who at first undoubtedly had a majority support.

Take from Greeley all credit for his leading part in the uprising that led to the Republican party, for his persistent advocacy of tariff protection and of homesteading the West, take from him credit for boldly outlining at the close of the Civil War the right attitude by the North toward those whom he called "our formerly erring countrymen"; question, if you will, his attitude toward Lincoln in the White House, or his wisdom in 1872 in accepting the Liberal and the Democratic nominations for President; even strip him of credit for all that he ever urged on behalf of the man of struggle—yet his courage as a substitute Oregon delegate to engage against an opponent vigilant, resourceful and presumably in control of the convention entitles him to a foremost place among those who in a crisis are the unwitting instruments of fate to bring to the world many of its greatest blessings.

"If ever in my life I discharged a public duty in utter disregard of personal considerations I did so at Chicago," declared Greeley. "I was no longer a devotee of Governor Seward, but I was equally independent of all others. If I had been swayed by feeling alone I should have preferred him to any of his competitors. But I did not, and I do not, believe it advisable that he should be the Republican candidate for President. Each day's subsequent developments tend to strengthen my confidence that what I did was not only well meant but well done."

Raymond could not wait until he had returned to New York City before assailing Greeley. In a dispatch to the *Times* from Seward's home at Auburn he called him a betrayer of friendships, charging that his course at Chicago was wholly malicious revenge on Seward for not having as governor twelve years earlier appointed him to office. "He could have had anything he desired if he had made his wishes known," remarked Weed—but as set forth in preceding pages, Greeley was not asking for recognition; unless it was voluntary it would be worthless to him.

A careful perusal of the newspapers of the time shows that substantially all the Republican press stood by Greeley; almost without exception they made light of the Raymond fusillade. By week end it was out of current discussion.

In a letter addressed late in 1860 to young men in politics, Greeley wrote: "The moral I would inculcate is a trite one but nonetheless important. It is summed up in the Scriptural injunction—'Put not your trust in princes'. Men even the best, are frail and mutable, while principle is sure and eternal. Be no man's man but Truth's and your country's. You will be sorely tempted at times to take this or that great man for your oracle and guide,—it is easy and tempting to lean, to follow, and to trust,—but it is safer and wiser to look ever through your own eyes, to tread your own path, to trust implicitly in God alone. The atmosphere is a little warmer inside some great man's castle, but the free air of Heaven is ever so much purer and much bracing."

Typical of Greeley's attitude toward all "Stop New York *Tribune*" communications was this correspondence with a disappointed Sewardite:

Aurora, N. Y., May 19, 1860

Editors "Tribune":

We have taken "The Tribune" daily from the morning of its first issue until now, through all its isms.

You will discontinue sending it to us. Our only regret is that we are under the necessity of losing a three-cent stamp in order to close our account.

Wishing you a good time for a few months to come.

We are truly yours,
Morgan & Mosher

New York, May 22, 1860

Gentlemen:

The painful regret expressed in yours of the 19th instant excites my sympathies. I enclose you a three-cent stamp to replace that whose loss you deplore, and remain,

Yours, placidly,
Horace Greeley

Messrs. Morgan & Mosher, Aurora, Cayuga Co., N. Y.

CHAPTER XX

"Hold Firm as Steel"

LINCOLN ELECTED—November 7, 1860! To many people it is a result that recalls Greeley's prophecy on January 5, 1854, of "the most gigantic, determined and overwhelming party the world has ever known.... Overcome it may be, but beaten it cannot be." Less than seven years later, here is the prophesied victory for that new party, and the *Tribune* jubilantly assures its readers that "the result may be to the highest good of the country will be the prayer of every patriot, every philanthropist and every Christian." Historian James Ford Rhodes wrote of the triumph: "I say emphatically that if you want to penetrate into the thoughts, feelings and grounds of decision of 1,866,000 men who voted for Lincoln, you should study the 'New York Weekly Tribune' through the campaign."

By supporting Lincoln, eighteen states north of the Mason and Dixon line had responded to the rousing editorial inquiry in the 1856 Frémont campaign, "Is There a North?" In the campaign just ended all four candidates for President—Lincoln, Douglas, Breckenridge and Bell—resided in states that were wildernesses when the Union was formed and that now remained in it. Lincoln was the second President not born in the previous century, Franklin Pierce being the first. Still more significant was the choice of a President, a Vice-President and an entire cabinet, with not one man among them who then owned a slave or even sympathized with slavery. It had taken eighty years to secure such a national administration. Greeley hailed it as the dawn of the awaited era of human freedom.

He called upon the slavery extensionists to accept their defeat and manfully abide by the result: "They are beaten now. They may triumph next time. In fact, they have generally had their own way; had they been subjected to the discipline of adversity as often as we have they could probably bear it more philosophically. We live to learn and one of the most difficult requirements is that of meeting defeat with graceful fortitude."

At the same time Greeley acknowledged the right of a state to secede—and this was reflected in the much-criticized editorial leader, "Let the Erring Sisters Depart in Peace." But the step must be taken deliberately after vote by its citizens. "We hold with Jefferson that governments are made for the people and not people for governments," he continued. "Let the people of the South be told just why they are asked to break from the Union. Let them have both sides of the question fully presented. Let them reflect, deliberate, and then vote; let the act of secession be the echo of an unmistakable fiat. When any portion of the Union large enough to form an independent nation shall show that, and say authentically, 'We want to get away from you,' regard for the principle of self-government will constrain the residue to say 'Go.' We shall willingly do nothing that looks like bribery or wheedling any state or section to remain in the Union. . . . The measures of the 'cotton' states now being inaugurated seem, however, to be destitute of gravity and legitimate force. They have the impress of haste, of passion and of distrust of popular judgment. They seem clearly intended to precipitate the South into rebellion." At once, Greeley's critics distorted this editorial into a willingness for the southern states to secede at the call of their disunion plotters, but not one word was ever printed in the *Tribune* acquiescing in secession in the way it was attempted.

"What will you do to save the Union?—was at once asked of us Republicans as if we had committed some enormity in voting for and electing Lincoln," wrote Greeley, "which we must atone for by proffering concessions. . . . On that issue, if there must be war, so be it!" A negotiated peace would mean just another period of troublesome peace such as the Clay compromise of 1820 and again of 1850 had proved to be. Against that attitude, however, was the timidity of the business interests of the North. Peace at any price seemed best to them, and an army of "fixers" in and out of Congress tried to make terms to escape the inescapable conflict.

From the first mention of such legislation Greeley's voice was heard in protest. "No compromise is the only true, the only loyal, the only safe doctrine," he declared. "Who ever heard of negotiation or compromise following a pro-slavery triumph on election day? Before any talk there must be clearly stipulated that Lincoln is the fairly chosen President of the whole Union."

To Lincoln, on December 22, he wrote one of his finest letters:

> I fear nothing, care for nothing but another disgraceful back-down of the free states. There is the real danger. Let the Union slide—it may be reconstructed; let Presidents be assassinated—we can elect more; let the Republicans be defeated and crushed—we will rise again. But another nasty compromise where everything is conceded and nothing secured will so thoroughly disgrace and humiliate us that we can never raise our heads. This country becomes a second edition of the Barbary States as they were sixty years ago. Take any form but that.

So far as known, the only indication of policy by the reticent Lincoln followed that letter. He advised William Kellogg, congressman from the Springfield district, "Entertain no proposition for concessions," and to Senator Trumbull, of Illinois, he sent word, "On that point hold firm as steel."

To Governor Morgan, on December 24, Greeley wrote:

> Dear Governor: Mr. Dana has suggested you would like to know what I think about national affairs. . . . I will say only briefly that I think no word should be uttered that encourages hope that we can ever accede or qualify our resistance to the extension of slavery. Let us be firm in purpose though kind in spirit, ready to consider but not to surrender.

In the Lincoln-Greeley record during the four years of war there were many opportunities to criticize and condemn Greeley for his insistence upon a war-conduct policy of his own. He is the poorer for that unwisdom. It is only fair to his record to keep in mind, however, that from election day to the "Forward to Richmond!" publication in July, Lincoln had no more loyal supporter than the *Tribune*. Indeed, among all the mud-slinging and unkind references to Lincoln there was never at any time from Greeley a single word that impeached the President's purpose or lacked in respect for him personally. There were even several "God bless Abraham Lincoln!" publications between his explosions of impatience. Through all the ages wisdom has had its sharp challengers until time has vindicated it. Lincoln shared that fate with a Congress that was continuously hostile almost to contempt, a cabinet that was a spider web of intrigue and a Horace Greeley insisting that "a Napoleon or an Andrew Jackson could reduce the rebellion in six months to a local riot."

During that first winter of tense uncertainties Greeley's *Tribune* led all the papers of the North in urging people to stand by the President, "with a task before him greater than that which devolved upon any other man since the days of Washington," to use Lincoln's own words. Greeley was in his element. He had always held that there could be no peace in the Union until freedom or slavery had definitely triumphed—and now freedom, finally in power, must not falter.

"Slavery is an evil to be restricted—not to be diffused," was his reply to the persistent compromisers. On January 20 he published the first of his series of "Stand Firm" editorials. Everywhere it was accepted as Lincoln's voice. Nevertheless it did not quiet the many who preferred concession to war. Greeley decided to call for unity against a solid South. On February 18 the *Tribune* published in large type, all capital letters, at the head of its editorial columns:

NO COMPROMISE!

No Concessions to Traitors!

The Constitution as It Is!

This was reprinted daily until the morning of Lincoln's inauguration, when the *Tribune* asked "for our new ruler the generous confidence and support of the American people. With a hearty good-will we bid Lincoln God Speed!"

Nor did Greeley extend his greetings only in print. At noon that day, among the thousands gathered to hear Lincoln there was not a more hopeful listener. He was seated close to Stephen A. Douglas, who, when he saw that the President could not find a place to rest his high stovepipe hat as he uncovered to take the oath of office, gallantly stepped forward and held it for him. Here was a real picture for history—the campaign rivals of 1858 and 1860 were now one in purpose—to save the Union! As Lincoln faced the crowd and began his address, everybody seemed to have but one thought anxiously in mind: Would he get through unharmed? Was an assailant lurking in that immense throng awaiting only opportunity to make a target of that tall form towering above all those around him? "I shared that feeling," wrote Greeley. "As he delivered his address I expected it would be arrested at any moment by the crack of a rifle shot aimed at his heart. . . . But it pleased God to postpone the deed, though there were forty times the reasons for shooting him in 1860 than there were in 1865, and there were then at least forty times as many intent upon killing him or having him killed. His hour, however, had not yet come."

Of that first inaugural speech the *Tribune* urged that "it should command the support of all good citizens. . . . To twenty million people it will carry the tidings, glad or not as the case may be, that the Federal Government is still in existence with a Man at the head of it." Few newspapers endorsed the address with as much confidence, nor in fact did Greeley deep in his own mind. Though disappointed by Lincoln's mildness, he was confident that he could be persuaded to a more vigorous policy. Before leaving Washington he sought him at the White House and there made the first of many vain efforts to influence him. Unhappily the "drumbeat of the nation" in 1854, the triumphant strategist of the 1860 convention, failed to realize that the people had since chosen a man to lead them in the effort to save the Union and that that man had his own ideas. During that first conference with the new President an astonished Greeley found "an obstinate calmness in his manner. He seemed to be controlled by a dogged resolution not to believe that our country was about to be drenched in fraternal blood. 'Do you realize,' I asked him, 'that you may have to fight for the place you now hold?' He could not, or would not. He clung to the delusion that forbearance, patience and soft words would yet obviate all necessity for deadly strife."

Still the *Tribune* remained a stanch supporter. Other newspapers began to question. On April 3 the *Times* declared that "the Administration thus far has not met expectations" and is giving no indication of any policy "beyond that of listless waiting for something to turn up. It allows everything to drift. We are in danger of losing everything—even honor. There is no policy so fatal as having no policy at all." On May 16 the *Times* asked: "Is the government in earnest? It is difficult to discover a distinct indication that Mr. Lincoln regards treason with any stronger sentiment of reprobation than did Mr. Buchanan."

These editorial extracts are used here as evidence that Greeley's criticism of the administration followed rather than led other newspapers. He was quick to evaluate the stirring influence of the attack on Fort Sumter on April 12: "Sumter is temporarily lost, but Freedom is saved! It is hard to lose Sumter, but in losing it we have gained a united people. Long live the Republic!"

On May 2 the *Tribune* again rose to Lincoln's support: "We admire the impatience of the public mind which demands so earnestly more swift and vigorous action, but let us conquer our impatience with justice." Again, on May 5: "We hold that the great office of the press is better executed in keeping the President informed of the state of public feeling in the North, and of the action it demands, and will sustain, rather than criticize too curiously each successive step he takes.... As long as he holds a firm hand on the plow we will not anticipate any danger of his looking backward.... No man ever held mightier issues in his hand than Lincoln or ever had a more illustrious career opening before him."

On May 23 the *Times* declared: "Lincoln must abandon personal administration or the ruin of the country will be the price of his presumption." To which Greeley responded next day: "We do not expect a great rebellion which has been thirty years ripening to be crushed in thirty days; even if a President and Cabinet should be momentarily bewildered and embarrassed by the rapid explosion of mine after mine of treason under their feet it would not prove them timorous or incapable, but simply human."

By June, however, Greeley could no longer ignore the rising temper of the people urging resistance to the rapidly arming South. He now joined the horde of critics in Congress and out who were demanding action. On June 26 came the memorable publication:

"The Nation's War Cry:

"Forward to Richmond!

"The Rebel Congress must not be allowed to meet there on July 20. By that date the place must be held by the National Army."

Loudly echoed in many newspapers the cry led to the disastrous battle of Bull Run; Greeley had to bear alone the blame for having hurried the Army into combat while unprepared. It did not matter that Lincoln's cabinet had agreed that the time had come for armed resistance, or that General Winfield Scott must have known that his troops were not conditioned for battle, or, finally that Greeley had had nothing to do with the publication. Editor Raymond seized upon the agitation following the battle to repeat his assertion after the Chicago convention that the *Tribune*'s attitude reflected Greeley's "unsatiated thirst for public office"—this attack coming from a fellow editor who had himself then served six years in public office while still conducting his newspaper and at the time was scheduled for a term in Congress! Raymond never corrected his charge, though it was at once made known that "Forward to Richmond" was written by Fitz-Henry Warren, then Washington correspondent of the *Tribune*. Managing editor Dana placed it at the top of a column on the editorial page and kept it there daily for the entire week before Congress assembled on July 4 in extra session. At the time Greeley was in the West;

upon his return he did not approve of Dana's daily iteration. Nevertheless, the *Tribune* had published it—and the *Tribune* was always Greeley. The first shock of war, the humiliating defeat, the charge that he had forced the battle, upset Greeley completely, and financially proved to be the heaviest blow the *Tribune* had ever recieved.

On July 25 was published the only explanation Greeley ever made for any editorial policy. It was entitled "Just Once." It was a frank, vigorous document and did much to moderate the storm. Summarized, he said:

"It is true that my ideas as to the general conduct of the war are those repeatedly expressed in 'The Tribune' and, of course, are not those on which the war has been based; that I have urged that it must be prosecuted with utmost vigor, energy and promptness or it will prove a failure; that every week's flying of the secession flag within a day's walk of Washington renders the suppression of the revolt more difficult, if not more doubtful. It is true also that I think that our obvious policy would have been to be courteous toward foreign powers but resolute and ready in our dealings with armed rebels; it seems to me that the opposite course has been pursued. But the watchword 'Forward to Richmond' was not mine nor anything like it, and I would have preferred not to iterate. And now if anyone imagines that I or anyone connected with 'The Tribune' ever commanded or imagined such strategy as the launching of barely thirty thousand of the one hundred thousand Union volunteers near Washington against ninety thousand rebels in strong entrenchments then demonstration would be wasted on closed ears. . . . 'The Tribune' does not approve and should not be held responsible for such madness."

The agitation led to an attack of brain fever that invalided Greeley for a few weeks. While in that condition he wrote to Lincoln "in the depths of bitterness" a remarkable letter that had an equally remarkable fate, revealing in Lincoln those qualities of humanity and gentleness that are now a priceless memory to the whole world.

The Greeley letter read substantially as follows:

New York, Monday, July 29, 1861

Dear Sir:

This is my seventh sleepless night. Yours, too, doubtless—yet I think I shall not die because I have no right to die. I must struggle to live, however bitterly. You are now considered a great man, and I am a hopelessly broken one. You are now undergoing a terrible ordeal. God has thrown the gravest responsibility upon you.

Can the Rebels be beaten after all that has occurred? . . . If they can—and it is your business to ascertain and decide—write me that such is your judgment, so that I may know and do my duty. And if they cannot be beaten, do not fear to sacrifice yourself to your country. Then every drop of blood henceforth shed in the quarrel will be wantonly, wickedly shed. If the Union is irrevocably gone, an armistice ought at once to be proposed. I do not consider myself at present a judge of anything but the public sentiment. That seems to be everywhere deepening against further prosecution of the war. . . .

You are at liberty to say to members of your Cabinet that I will second any move you may see fit to make. Send me word what to do. Do the thing that is the highest right and tell me how I am to second you.

Yours in the depth of bitterness,
Horace Greeley

Fortunately, Lincoln personally opened the letter. At once he recognized it as the product of an excited mind; very considerately he determined that no one else should know its contents. Adding it to other confidential papers, he wound a red tape around the bundle and placed it far back in his desk.

For a moment let us now move three years ahead—to midnight, April 30, 1864. Nicolay and Hay, the two presidential secretaries, are still busy in the White House study. Lincoln enters the room. His renomination for President is then being challenged by Republican leaders and conversation quickly turns to Greeley's opposition. Soon Lincoln begins searching through the drawers of his desk; at last he pulls out a red-taped bundle of papers from which he detaches one, and asks Hay if he can "decipher" it. This was the Greeley letter of July 29, 1861! Hay has some trouble but finally reads it aloud.

"That would be 'nuts' for 'The Herald,'" Nicolay exclaims. "Bennett would willingly give $10,000 for it."

To which Lincoln, while replacing the letter in the bundle with the others and slowly winding the red tape around the package, replies, "I need $10,000 very much, but Bennett cannot have it for many times that much." So the letter, now three years old, is once more filed where prying eyes cannot see it. It will not again have the light of day on it until twenty-five years later when the *Century Magazine* publishes it in a series of articles, the basis for the Nicolay-Hay *Life of Lincoln.*

The letter tells its own story of Greeley's unsettled mind in 1861 and justifies the pleas to him from many friends to take a rest. One of those friends was Samuel Wilkeson, then a Washington correspondent of the *Tribune*. To him Greeley wrote on August 24 this characteristic response:

New York Tribune
August 24, 1861

My dear Sam:

. . . I am amazed at your simplicity in asking me to go away at this time. Why don't you go to one of McClellan's sentinels over the river and tell him he will catch his death of cold if he doesn't quit his post and go into his tent? You know well that no one can manage a newspaper for another in such a crisis as this, and that I am peculiarly unfortunate in this respect. I must stay about "The Tribune" now or let everything go to destruction. . . .

Sam, I am done as a politician, but I tell you the first requisite in one who seeks the public confidence is a popular conviction that he is thoroughly sincere and earnest—that he lives for his principles, not by them. You will outlive me long enough to think of this.

H.G.

Still in the same mood Greeley wrote to Moncure Conway, then in London, on August 27: "My friend, the hour is dark but I have not lost my faith in God. If this people are worthy to fight and win a battle for liberty and law, that battle will be won; if they are not, I do not see that there is any more a place for so weak an instrument as I am. . . . In any case, and however the end may be postponed and obscured, this infernal rebellion seals the doom of slavery."

CHAPTER XXI

"The Prayer of Twenty Millions"

As 1862 opened, Greeley was not the only person seriously concerned about conditions. All the North seemed disturbed. The one bright spot in the Union war record was the capture of Fort Henry and Fort Donelson down on the Mississippi by the unknown Grant—"Unconditional Surrender" Grant. Recognition of the Confederate States by Great Britain was hanging in the balance; blockade of the Atlantic ports was ineffective; McClellan was getting nowhere; reverses for the administration in the coming spring and fall elections were generally forecast. No one realized the situation and the needs more keenly than did the worried Lincoln, but no one knew better than he that if he heeded Greeley and other critics he would be forming a new cabinet almost every week end and pursuing a different policy as frequently. To the hurry-up-and-win-the-war demands, especially as to General McClellan—"an auger that doesn't bore," commented Greeley—Lincoln replied that he knew of no general who could promise quicker results. "Anybody will do!" the hasty ones contended. "No," replied Lincoln to Senator Ben Wade of Ohio, "anybody will not do! I must have Somebody!" Greeley went further than the recall of McClellan. He charged that many high officers were also "augers that do not bore" and that it would "require as many of that type to put down the rebellion as snowballs to bring a tea kettle to boil."

By March, Lincoln had worked out his own plan for an approach to emancipation. On the seventh of that month he addressed a message to "his fellow citizens in the Senate and House of Representatives" recommending gradual abandonment of slavery by compensating "any State that will give freedom to its slaves," and declaring that "all means must be employed to crush the rebellion." Though generally it was doubted that Congress would endorse Lincoln's proposal or that any state would accept it, Greeley spiritedly applauded it: "We never printed a state paper with more satisfaction than we feel in giving to our readers the Special Message of President Lincoln to Congress yesterday. . . . The Message constitutes of itself an epoch in the history of our country. . . . It seals the fate of the rebellion in every Christian land. . . . No civilized nation will think of entering into an alliance with Jeff Davis in view of this glorious demonstration that 'Union and Liberty' are indeed 'one and inseparable.' Long live the American Republic!"

Next day, in an editorial entitled "The Message for Freedom," Greeley was even more enthusiastic: ". . . For our part, we thank God that Abraham Lincoln is President of the United States, and the whole country, we cannot doubt, will be thankful that we have at such a time so wise a ruler."

Greeley's enthusiasm led him to write Speaker Schuyler Colfax at Washington to say to Lincoln that he would support him in his emancipation effort if he would advise him what to do. To that suggestion Lincoln replied in one of the few letters he ever wrote directly to him:

Private

Executive Mansion
Washington, March 24, 1862

Hon. Horace Greeley—

My dear Sir:

Your very kind letter of the 16th to Mr. Colfax has been shown me by him. I am grateful for the generous sentiments and purposes expressed toward the Administration. Of course, I am anxious to see the policy proposed in the late Special Message go forward; but you have advocated it from the first, so that I need to say little to you on the subject.

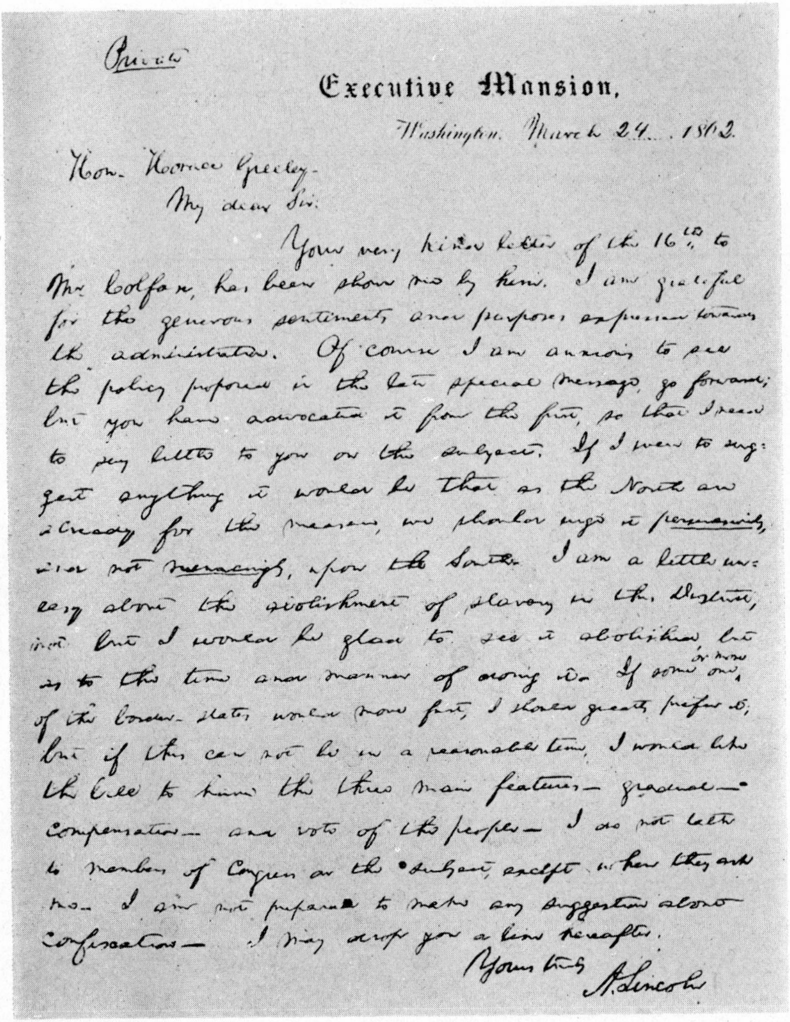

Private

Executive Mansion,

Washington, March 24, 1862.

Hon. Horace Greeley—

My dear Sir:

Your very kind letter of the 16th. to Mr. Colfax, has been shown me by him. I am grateful for the generous sentiments and purposes expressed towards the administration. Of course I am anxious to see the policy proposed in the late special message, go forward; but you have advocated it from the first, so that I need to say little to you on the subject. If I were to suggest anything it would be that as the North are already for the measure, we should urge it *persuasively*, and not *menacingly*, upon the South. I am a little uneasy about the abolishment of slavery in this District, not but I would be glad to see it abolished, but as to the time and manner of doing it. If some one or more of the border-states would move fast, I should greatly prefer it; but if this can not be in a reasonable time, I would like the bill to have the three main features—gradual—compensation—and vote of the people— I do not talk to members of Congress on the subject, except when they ask me. I am not prepared to make any suggestion about confiscation— I may drop you a line hereafter.

Yours truly

A. Lincoln

Lincoln's Reply to Greeley's Letter to Colfax

Courtesy of Herald Tribune

THE OLD ROOKERY

"The Old Rookery." The Tribune Office in Greeley's Day

If I were to suggest anything it would be that as the North is already for the measure, we should urge it persuasively, and not menacingly, upon the South. I am a little uneasy about the abolishment of slavery in the District, not but that I would be glad to see it abolished, but as to the time and manner of doing so. If some one or more of the border states would move first, I should greatly prefer it; but if this cannot be in a reasonable time, I would like the bill to have the three main features—gradual, compensation, and vote of the people. I do not talk to Members of Congress on the subject except when they ask me. I am not prepared to make any suggestion about confiscation. I may drop you a line later.

Yours truly,

A. Lincoln

But Congress refused to respond to the compensation idea, nor would any border state accept it. "Unpurchased and unpurchasable!"—was Maryland's curt response. Lincoln had to find another approach to emancipation. Finally, on July 22, he read to his cabinet a draft of the document soon to become historic. He frankly told his associates that he did not ask advice as to the proclamation itself, for his mind was firmly made up to issue it—it was a promise he had made himself. He sought suggestions only as to form and timeliness. It was on the latter point that Seward's advice prevailed. He contended that the document should be withheld until some substantial success by the Union Army would give it the character of a confidently advancing move. Lincoln accepted that view; he put aside the paper but not the purpose. "It was in my mind night and day," he told others.

Of course, such a cabinet discussion soon reached the whispering galleries of Washington in one garbled form or another, and reached Greeley, too. He learned also that Seward's policy of delay had prevailed. Already discouraged by the breakdown of the slave compensation idea, he wrongly assumed that silence from the White House meant another effort abandoned. At once he wrote to Senator Sumner: "Do you remember the old theological two-chapter text book?

"Chapter I—Hell.

"Chapter II—Hell, continued.

"Well, that is the way 'Old Abe' should be talked to.

"Still, I comprehend the wisdom of not breaking with the chief of the Republic in this hour of her fiery trial and shall respect it. Only you must do all his puffing, for I cannot help him. He's a poor stick."

But, with characteristic impatience, Greeley determined to do the talking himself. In the *Tribune* of August 19 came "The Prayer of Twenty Millions," in the form of an open letter to President Lincoln, signed by Greeley. Boldly he told the President that "all attempts to put down the rebellion and at the same time uphold its inciting cause [slavery] are preposterous and futile" and that "every hour of deference to slavery is an hour of added peril to the Union. . . . An immense majority of the loyal millions of your countrymen," he continued, "request you under the law to give freedom to slaves coming within our lines."

Again, as following the "Forward to Richmond" publication, Greeley was an object of attack. The *National Intelligencer* of Washington declared that he "needed a lesson in etiquette"—that he was "arrogant, dictatorial and acrimonious." Lincoln evidently thought so, too, but he did not delay a reply to the "Prayer" and took the unusual course of replying as he had been addressed—by newspaper publication. "Those who insist upon Presidential dignity are horrified at Lincoln's novel idea," read a Washington dispatch to the New York *Times*. The critics, however, did not know that Lincoln had been vainly seeking how to test public opinion before announcing his purpose; that he had sought suggestions from other editors with no result; Greeley alone had now provided him a method. But Lincoln did not want counsel through editorial demand. "If there be in it any statements or assumptions of fact which I may know to be erroneous, I do not now and here controvert them," he replied with much restraint. "If there be in it any inferences which I may believe to be falsely drawn, I do not now and here argue against them. If there be perceptible in it an impatient and dictatorial tone, I waive it in deference to an old friend whose heart I have always supposed to be right.

"As to the policy I 'seem to be pursuing,' as you say, I have not meant to leave anyone in doubt.

"My paramount object in this struggle is to save the Union and it is not either to save or destroy slavery. If I could save the Union without freeing any slaves I would do it, and if I could save it by freeing some and leaving others alone I would also do that. What I do about slavery and the colored race I do because I believe it helps to save the Union, and what I forbear I forbear because I do not believe it would help save the Union. I have here stated my purpose according to my view of official duty, and I intend no modification of my oft-repeated personal wish that all men, everywhere, could be free."

The reply, of course, did not reveal the particular step Lincoln had in mind. Greeley had made a dent, however. He knew Lincoln's real sentiments; he also knew that Seward and Postmaster-General Montgomery Blair were doing their utmost to hold the President in check. On August 23, he continued:

> It is an ostrich policy to close our eyes to the fact that slavery is at war with the American Union. . . . The man who opposes the Emancipation of the Slaves of Rebels favors the triumph of the traitors. . . . No Hannibal, no Caesar, no Napoleon, ever refused the ready support of a whole race because of their caste or color. No military consideration ever yet prompted a commander in a hostile country to regard and treat the millions who would gladly aid him as chattels of his deadly enemies. Only put this war on a strictly military footing—forget all bygone politics and irrational prejudices, and consider only how the Union arms may be made to triumph—and we shall have "good leadership"; now we are dying for want of same.

The great issue of freedom was a-borning. Greeley saw it dimly, many other editors not at all. As usual, the latter were not slow to criticize; also as usual Greeley was not slow to respond: "There are thirty or forty journals in different localities which seek to prolong their existence by disparaging and snarling at 'The Tribune.' Our counsel is—have some affirmative, positive, clearly defined purpose or policy and do not hope to live by merely carping and caviling at the views of your contemporaries."

There is no profit in arguing whether Greeley had craftily forced Lincoln's hand, as some critics charged, or how deeply Lincoln resented Greeley's effort publicly to anticipate a purpose he had already determined upon. It is enough that these two men realized the necessity for a bold step. Both were in character in their approach to action. Patient Lincoln was willing to wait opportunity; impatient Greeley was not. Lincoln shared Seward's fear that public opinion was not ready to sustain it. Greeley was confident that it was.

Later in the war there were many who believed that if all the Greeley criticisms were placed on one side of the beam of a scale as wholly unjustified and then that one Greeley "Prayer" placed on the other side of that beam, the good accomplished by intensifying the struggle for the Union would heavily outbalance all possible embarrassments caused Lincoln at other times by Greeley. The "Prayer" was Greeley to the bone. In every line was his "terrible candor"—the spirited note of challenge, the bold presumption that as editor he knew the temper of "an immense majority of your loyal countrymen" and could in their name point out to a President his duty. There was no need for anyone to perform that service for Lincoln, but there was need to provide opportunity for Lincoln to test public opinion for the greatest act of his career. The Greeley "Prayer" did that for him, as this Washington dispatch to the New York *Times* on August 23 attests:

> Several days ago the President read to a friend a rough draft of what appears this morning as a letter to Horace Greeley. He said that he had thought of getting before the public some such statement of his position on the slavery question in some manner and asked the opinion of his friend as to the propriety of such a course and the best way to do it. The appearance of Greeley's "Prayer" gave him the opportunity.

The value to Lincoln of that opportunity can be measured by its historic results. No date since the war's beginning marked so plainly new vigor for the Union cause as did September 22, 1862—thirty-four days after the Greeley editorial. On that day Lincoln announced that on January 1, 1863, he would, as President, proclaim freedom for all persons held in slavery in all states or parts of states then in rebellion.

Discussion of the subject had prepared the country for the act that later made Lincoln the Great Emancipator of history. The success of McClellan's army at Antietam on September 17 created an atmosphere of victory, mild though it was, which Lincoln believed necessary to give force to his proclamation.

Quickly to his support came Greeley. His next-day editorial was full of "God Bless Abraham Lincoln" enthusiasm and confidence. "It is the beginning of the end of the rebellion," he declared. "It is the beginning of the new life of the nation. God bless Abraham Lincoln! We are already separated by an age from the doubts and fears of one little week ago." Though the move was primarily a measure to persuade negroes in the secession states to join the Union army, and though technically it declared emancipation only in areas in which the national authority did not at the time prevail—for example, it did not apply in the border states—yet in effect it placed the war firmly on the basis of a struggle between freedom and slavery. It was no longer an effort merely to restore a political body called "the Union as it was." "It is now a war for abolition," commented General McClellan, still in command of the Army of the Potomac. On December 12, General Henry Wager Halleck declared, "The conflict is now a damned 'Tribune' abolition war."

On January 1, 1863, when Lincoln's promised proclamation was issued, the *Tribune* enthusiastically carried the flag of the nation first page at top of first column. Other newspapers and politicians, particularly Thurlow Weed, faltered and questioned, but Greeley acclaimed the document as the bravest ever written by a President, and a sure advance toward victory. "It's a step," William Lloyd Garrison commented grudgingly to Wendell Phillips, who promptly replied, "It's a stride!" Gettysburg and Vicksburg on July 4 confirmed it as a new era in American life.

Not once during 1863 did Greeley get back to his four-days-in-the-week support of the President. Particularly after Lincoln's letter to the Unconditional Union state convention in Illinois in

August he abandoned entirely the role of impatient critic. "It will be proven that among free men there can be no appeal from the ballot to the bullet," wrote Lincoln, "and they who take the appeal are sure to lose their case and pay the costs. I hope to stand firm enough not to go backward, and yet not go forward fast enough to wreck the country's cause."

"The President chooses a moment when doubts were arising in the minds of the people to speak words of wisdom," commented Greeley on September 3. "With the grasp of a statesman he appeals to the good sense and patriotism of the people. The most direct honesty of purpose and most vigorous common sense mark the letter. No compromise is possible save with the army of the rebels. Nor does he meet the Emancipation question less squarely and boldly. In that proclamation he did what, as commander-in-chief, he had a right to do and it was his duty to do. . . . Is that fighting for the negro? When the Union is saved, if then the President continues the war for the negro's sake it will be time enough to discover that fact and accuse him of it. In the meantime the negro, much like other men, is fighting with us for a motive. The motive we give him is the promise of freedom. And the promise, being made, must be kept. Again we say 'God Bless Abraham Lincoln!' The Promise must be kept!"

In the same mood that year Greeley wrote to Senator Charles Sumner:

My dear Sir:

In God's good time this is to be a land of real freedom, where equal rights and equal laws shall banish rebellion, treason and riot, and all manner of kindred diabolisms. I hardly hope to live to see that day, but hope that those who may remember me when I am gone will believe that I earnestly tried to hasten its coming.

Yours,

Horace Greeley

Nevertheless when, in 1864, the time approached for selecting a Union Republican nominee for President, the *Tribune* preferred almost anyone to Lincoln. "The history of his many good deeds will far outlive the memory of his mistakes and faults.

... Heartily agreeing that Mr. Lincoln has done well, we do not regard it as demonstrated that Chase, Frémont, General Butler or General Grant cannot do as well in their respective spheres; then we hold that the genius of our institutions, the salutary one-term principle, counsels the choice of another nominee."

Thereupon Greeley urged the postponement of the national convention until September, by which time he hoped that our army and navy would have scored success and a choice of candidate would be more clearly indicated. But here Greeley learned the oft-proven truth of politics: that you cannot defeat *somebody* with *nobody*. Neither he nor the many troublemakers in Congress were able to control a single state delegation against the President; no one urging the latter to withdraw could suggest a better candidate. "Perhaps some other man may do better than I," said Lincoln. "That is probable, but I am here and that other man is not." Early in March, Greeley realized the hopelessness of his effort when he wrote Mrs. Whipple at Westhaven: "As to the Presidency, I am not at all confident of making any change but I believe that I shall make things better by trying. There are those who go so far as they are pushed and Mr. Lincoln is one of them. He will be a better President, if re-elected, from the opposition he is now encountering."

"We cannot but feel that it would have been wiser to have nominated another," declared Greeley in the *Tribune* after the National Union convention in Baltimore had adjourned on June 7 with Lincoln as its candidate by unanimous vote. He deplored the probability of defeat. Unquestionably the Democratic national convention in August would nominate General McClellan on a platform urging that "the public welfare demands that immediate efforts be made for cessation of hostilities." Greeley dreaded that prospect; his political mind turned toward anticipating it; he would have the Lincoln administration show definitely that it was not resisting peace possibilities. "I wish to be known," he wrote New York's Senator Morgan, "as ready to support the justice and policy of compensation whenever the President desires support from the press.... No more slavery anywhere and all the States back in the Union at once. . . . The rebels are in their last gasp; let us not drive them to desperation."

It was while in such a mood that Greeley fell victim to the suggestion of four so-called Confederate commissioners gathered on the Canadian side of Niagara Falls that he secure for them a "safe conduct" to visit him in New York City and proceed thence to Washington to discuss peace terms with Lincoln. On July 7 he wrote the President, urging him to see these Confederate agents, and added: ". . . I venture to remind you that our bleeding, bankrupt, almost dying country longs for peace. . . . I fear you do not realize how intently the people desire any peace consistent with national integrity and honor. . . . I do not say that a just peace is now attainable, but I do say that a frank offer by you will at the worst prove of immense and sorely needed advantage to the national cause."

But again, as in the "Prayer" editorial of 1862, Lincoln had no relish for lectures from Greeley. More than all, he did not propose to undertake it as an administration move which, if it failed, would be deplored in a Greeley editorial. Here, Lincoln's keenness as a politician came into play—he placed responsibility for any Niagara Falls peace negotiation squarely upon Greeley. That was exactly what Greeley did not want; it was now his job—not Lincoln's. He was commissioned by the President to go to Niagara Falls, taking John Hay with him. "If you can find any person, anywhere," wrote the President to Greeley, "professing to have any proposition by Jefferson Davis in writing for peace embracing the restoration of the Union and the abandonment of slavery, whatever else it embraces, say to him he may come to me with you."

Greeley was still further outwitted in the correspondence when Lincoln wrote to him as he started for Niagara Falls: "I not only intend a sincere effort for peace, but I intend that you shall be a personal witness that it is made."

But the Niagara Falls group had no official standing; it abandoned even the pretense of one after Greeley arrived in Niagara Falls to meet them. Lincoln had pricked the bubble by that one requirement for credentials.

Prospects for Lincoln's re-election did not brighten. By August 18, Greeley was among those urging Lincoln to withdraw: "We must have another ticket, to save us from utter overthrow. If we had such a ticket as Grant, Butler or Sherman, with Admiral Farragut for Vice, we could make a fight yet." In this demand Greeley united with Thad Stevens, Ben Wade and even Senator Sumner—including Thurlow Weed who, on August 12, warned Lincoln personally that his re-election was impossible. Weed added that editor Raymond, who was then chairman of the Republican National Committee, believed that "unless some prompt and bold action is taken all is lost. The people are wild for peace. Raymond believes that commissioners should be sent to Richmond offering to treat for peace on the basis of the Union. Something should be done to give the Administration a chance for life." It was at this time—August 9—that Greeley reiterated his own prophecies of disaster in the following plea to Lincoln:

I know that nine-tenths of the American people, North and South, are anxious for peace—peace on almost any terms—and are utterly sick of human slaughter and devastation. I know that to the general eye it now seems that the rebels are anxious to negotiate and that we repulse their advances. I know that if this impression be not removed we shall be beaten out of sight next November. I firmly believe that if the election were to take place tomorrow the Democratic majority in New York and in Pennsylvania would be 100,000 and that we could be beaten in Connecticut, too.... Now I do not know that a tolerable peace could be had... at all events I know that an honest, sincere effort for it would have done us much good.

It was while Greeley, Weed and Raymond were prophesying defeat that Sherman was entering Atlanta to begin his march through Georgia to the sea, that Farragut was in Mobile Bay, that Phil Sheridan was scoring the first of his stirring victories in Virginia's Shenandoah Valley, and that Grant was slowly battering down Lee's army. The North began singing, in answer to the draft, "We're Coming, Father Abraham, 300,000 Strong." The political picture steadily brightened. The prophets of disaster became enthusiasts for victory—Greeley leading.

On September 1 the *Tribune* about-faced completely. It called everyone to stand by the administration. "We have come well-nigh to the overthrow of the rebellion—a little more energy, a little more courage, and we shall soon see the end of it even with such tools as we have. The choice is no longer ours whether we shall throw them aside and try new ones. We must work with such as we have, or not at all. 'Choose ye!' For our part, we have chosen. Henceforth we fly the banner of Abraham Lincoln. Mr. Lincoln has done seven-eighths of the work after his fashion; there must be vigor and virtue enough left in him to do the other fraction. We must re-elect him and, God helping us, we will!"

Six months were all of life remaining to Lincoln after his re-election, but in that brief period much was to happen in the nation, and "Uncle Horace" was "with us" all seven days of the week. This was the second "God Bless Abraham Lincoln" period in Greeley's relations with the President. With the war's end clearly in sight, he had found a permanent resting place cordially supporting Lincoln in his planning for the peace just ahead. Indeed, in the *Tribune* of February 23, 1865, Greeley stated that if it were put to a vote the country would place power wholly with Lincoln to continue the war or end it on any terms he would prescribe.

In March, Greeley paid his second visit to the White House. He saw in the President a tired, worn man anxiously awaiting the slow-coming word from Grant that finally Lee's retreating army had surrendered. He wrote of that visit:

"His face was haggard with care and seamed with thought and trouble. It looked care-plowed, tempest-tossed and weather-beaten, as if he were some tough old mariner who had for years been beating up against the wind and tide, unable to make his port or find safe anchorage. Judging from that scarred, rugged countenance, I do not believe that he could have lived out his second term had no felon's hand been lifted against his precious life. I had ceased to apprehend assassination—he had ceased to even think about it. Yet the sunset of life was plainly looking out of his kindly eyes."

CHAPTER XXII

"Magnanimity in Triumph"

LEE SURRENDERS! Jefferson Davis and his cabinet in flight! "The rebels are now our fellow countrymen!" declares Grant at Appomattox to his soldiers. Blessed April 11, 1865! Peace at last—but was it to be a peace of mutual understanding? Were the Confederate states to be held in subjection, or were North and South to be brought together as a reunited family? There was no doubt of Lincoln's purpose, but of all men not in public office no one was looked to so instantly for his opinion by so many people as was Horace Greeley. What policy would he urge in his *Tribune?* What attitude toward the surrendered rebels, individually and as a whole? Would he share the bitterness of many leaders of Congress and treat the Confederate states as a conquered province?

Before 1860 no man wrote more vigorously against slavery than did Greeley. For that reason, in the South he was the most hated of all northern men; but in 1865—following Lee's surrender—the plea that Greeley made was not for antagonism in peace but for the healing influence of fraternal unity. He did not hesitate. He knew that at the outset he would be under heavy attack, but he believed he was right—and that belief was all that Greeley ever needed for action. With Lincoln leading the people toward reconciliation, Greeley saw an opportunity to take war's hatred out of the nation's future and thus strengthen it to resume its interrupted progress toward a great destiny. In the hearts of many bereaved people there would be a hostile feeling to be subdued; in Congress, stubborn irreconcilables would make savage resistance. But to be battling at first in a minority was to Greeley no new experience; all his struggles had such a beginning. To him, it meant hard fighting. Should he undertake it?

There was just one factor to which no one but Greeley could give consideration—he wanted to be out of all strife. He had had enough of conflict. He really longed for more opportunity to do literary work and, in addition, for the repose of farm life at Chappaqua. That prospect was a mirage that had buoyed him for a long time, but the need to reconcile wartime enmities among his countrymen was to Greeley a call of the nation in new peril from a chaotic peace; at that call the seasoned warrior for many causes went into action. Two days after Lee's surrender he published an editorial which at once became the subject of national controversy. It was entitled "Magnanimity in Triumph," and urged Lincoln not to delay making known his policy of peace. "In behalf of our country," he then declared, "burdened with a war which is still costing her three millions of dollars per day, and which has carried mourning to every fireside—in behalf of all downtrodden, suffering humanity, we entreat the President promptly to do and dare in the cause of magnanimity. What we ask is that the President say, in effect, 'Slavery having, through rebellion, committed suicide, let the North and the South unite to bury its carcass and then clasp hands across the grave.' . . . A new era has begun! A new world is born, and the sun of peace rises in splendor to send abroad over the land its rays of warmth and light!"

In even clearer tones Greeley expressed his convictions in a letter to Mrs. Rebekah M. Whipple, neighbor of his boyhood home at Westhaven, Vermont:

April 13, 1865

My Friend of Other Days:

Our great triumph is God's answer to the prayer of the colored people; it is not our victory, and the result will show it. Whatever may now appear, the fruits of this great success will inure to the blacks chiefly.

I am becoming still more alienated from the religion which passes among us as orthodox and Christian. Its teachers and leading professors are loudest in the cry for bloodshed and vengeance against the beaten rebels. They all want to erect a gallows over the South and hang all the baffled traitors whom we have not killed in battle. I am sure Jesus of Nazareth is not truly represented in this spirit.

As for me, I want as many rebels as possible to live to see the South rejuvenated and transformed by the influence of free labor. I shall deem it a calamity to have Davis die these ten years. I see great trouble in the future growing out of tardy, enforced conversion of the Gospel of Equal Rights. I fear more calamity is needed to convert us to the true faith that wrong done to the humblest, most despised is an injury and hurt to all.

Yours,
Horace Greeley

"Magnanimity in Triumph" aroused both praise and criticism in the North, but a sullen, defiant South was not interested in "magnanimity"—especially magnanimity by grace of Horace Greeley. Pleading against reprisals and for unity under such conditions was certainly an upstream job. It meant a campaign of education by Greeley—not one like the spirited movement he had led through the 1850's; this time it was an appeal for amnesty, for universal suffrage, and for a genuine resumption of national citizenship—an appeal to both sections, as he finally phrased it in 1872, to "clasp hands across the bloody chasm." In 1865 that chasm certainly was wide and bloody—much too bloody for any hands to stretch across it, from either side, unstained and unchallenged. Lincoln might possibly have done so. Greeley vainly tried; and for that patriotic effort he paid the heavy price that every pleader against victory's instant passion born of war always has to pay. The storm he aroused meant sacrifice of personal fortune, of the *Weekly Tribune*'s popularity, and of sales of *The American Conflict*.

Two opposing currents of opinion flowed through the North even during the few days between Lee's surrender and the assassination of Lincoln; as usual, Greeley and Raymond were their clashing spokesmen. Medill in the Chicago *Tribune*, and Bowles in the Springfield *Republican*, stood with Greeley. Taking the country as a whole, the (N.Y.) *Tribune* and the *Times* voiced the differences between the contending factions. For that reason brief extracts from their editorials are set down here side by side for reader judgment:

NEW YORK *TRIBUNE*
April 11, 1865

MAGNANIMITY IN TRIUMPH

...We hear men say—"Yes forgive the great mass of those who have been misled into rebellion, but punish the leaders as they deserve."

Where is your touchstone of leadership? We know none....

...A single Confederate led out to execution would be evermore enshrined in a million hearts as a conspicuous hero and martyr. We cannot realize that it would be wholesome or safe—we are sure it would not be magnanimous—to give the overpowered disloyalty of the South such a shrine....

We plead against passions certain at this moment to be fierce and intolerant, but on our side are the ages and the voices of History. We plead for the restoration of the Union, against a policy which would afford a momentary gratification at the cost of years of perilous hate and bitterness.

NEW YORK *TIMES*
April 12, 1865

WHAT SHALL BE DONE WITH JEFF DAVIS?

...We beg pardon of "The Tribune"—we shall speak of it. All this talk of "Magnanimity in Triumph" is excellent in its place, but when it comes to include the pardon of every rebel leader, of Jeff Davis himself, we demur, we protest....But if he is caught, he should be hung. If we let him go unhung, we must in decency abolish hanging altogether....Whatever may be done to his accomplices, or to the accessories after the fact, he at least should suffer the extreme penalty of the law.

NEW YORK *TIMES*
April 14, 1865

...If "The Tribune" will pardon us, we will say that the hanging of Jeff Davis is called for to correct just such lax notions of governmental authority as "The

NEW YORK *TRIBUNE*
April 13, 1865
TO WHAT END?

...The New York "Times," doing injustice to its own sagacity in a characteristic attempt to sail between wind and water, says, "Let us hang Jeff Davis and spare the rest." We do not concur in the advice. Davis did not devise nor instigate the rebellion....

NEW YORK ***TIMES*** **(cont'd)**

Tribune" itself sometimes inculcates.

...To let Jeff Davis and his confederates go unpunished would not be so much an amnesty for the past as a plenary indulgence for future treason; for a precedent so mighty this, once set, must stand forever.

But the bullet from John Wilkes Booth's pistol that on April 15 put an end to Lincoln's life also ended instantly all temperate discussion—especially of the fate of Davis. Said the *Tribune* on April 17:

We have labored long and earnestly to produce a feeling favorable to conciliation and kindness toward the defeated rebels, which a miscreant's murderous hand has in one moment overthrown. We have not hesitated to brave misapprehension and alienation if we might restore peace and amity to this stricken land—and now all is lost but the good intention, which is never entirely fruitless. We have before us the slow and difficult task of treading out the embers of a dying but desperate rebellion.

A cry went up from the North that the assassination was actually a conspiracy of rebel chieftains, with Davis as principal plotter. A reward of $100,000 was offered by President Johnson for his arrest. "They'll hang Jeff Davis to a sour apple tree, as they go marching on," had been two lines of a Union soldiers' war song entitled "John Brown's Body." Now, again, in deadly earnest the whole North chorused the words of the old song, demanding life for life—demanding in particular that Davis be placed on trial for treason or for murder, whichever was certain to result in a penalty of death. Stories, whether true or false, of a futile effort by Davis to elude Union pickets in Georgia by disguising himself under his wife's raincoat added to the intensity of northern indignation. Davis was securely lodged in Fortress Monroe, his legs fettered with ball and chain to prevent possible escape. However, they were taken off after some weeks. For many years General Nelson A. Miles, then in command, had to bear censure in military silence because it was generally believed that in shackling Davis he had acted on his own authority. The truth is that he had the following order from Charles A. Dana, former *Tribune* editorialist, then assistant secretary of war and personally at Fortress Monroe representing Secretary of War Stanton:

Fortress Monroe
May 22, 1865

Major-General Miles is hereby authorized and directed to place manacles and fetters upon the hands and feet of Jefferson Davis and Clement C. Clay, Jr., whenever he may think it advisable, in order to render their imprisonment more secure.

By Order of the Secretary of War.

C. A. Dana
Asst. Secretary of War

"For the sake of the country," urged Greeley, "it may be hoped that this crime of crimes will not be fixed on men who have worn all but the highest honors of the Republic, and who before the war had borne fair personal reputation. Let us have an orderly trial of the accused, let us get the facts, and let punishment be meted out in accord with a just verdict."

Said editor Raymond in the *Times*: "Davis is the veritable exponent of inherent wickedness. His deliverance to the gallows will only help consign the rebellion itself to infamy."

And so on and on, as to Davis, through two years of deliberate deception of the people by U. S. attorney-generals Speed and Stanbury, each of whom in turn persistently dodged the issue by hiding behind William M. Evarts and Richard H. Dana (author of *Two Years Before the Mast*), engaged as special counsel. It was always conceded that Davis could not go on trial for treason without bringing to court all other Confederate leaders, including

Lee. That meant a new chaos, new hatreds, endless bitterness—a prospect that Greeley contended was inescapable.

Evarts and Dana never sought to have an indictment either for treason or for murder even noticed for trial. Both men were always agreed that the case could not be won. They were paid $20,000 in fees for finding a way to keep it out of court but to keep Davis in jail.

Meanwhile the injustice of imprisoning Davis, or any other man, for two years without according him his day in court aroused suspicion of the government's sincerity. Greeley led in the demand for trial or release. "By and by the farce will become too glaring and then he will be let go," he declared in the *Tribune* of January 22, 1866. "What is the use of persisting in a cheat whereby nobody is cheated? Davis is not to be tried—at all events not with the intent or expectation of convicting him. Let us have an end of the sham!" Abolitionist Gerrit Smith wrote President Johnson August 24, 1866: "Davis' long confinement without trial is an insult to the South and a dishonor to our government. There are many men who opposed slavery as strenuously as he upheld it who would eagerly go his bail. I am one of them."

Finally, on May 13, 1867, Evarts, recently appointed attorney-general in Johnson's cabinet, made only a formal protest against the release of Davis on bail. Associate Justice John C. Underwood, of the U. S. Circuit Court sitting in Richmond, agreed to accept a bond of $100,000, guaranteed by twenty men to the amount of $5,000 each, provided it was not furnished exclusively by Southerners. Underwood was a Herkimer County, New York, man. He insisted that at least five northern men of known antislavery opinions should go on the bond, mentioning Gerrit Smith, William Lloyd Garrison and Horace Greeley as types. Underwood's plan was communicated to Greeley by Davis' counsel, and he agreed with him to go on the bond. Garrison refused, but Smith agreed; they were joined by Cornelius Vanderbilt, Augustus Schell, chairman of the Democratic National Committee, and Horace F. Clark, a New York City lawyer. Garrison declared that Davis should be hanged. He wrote of Greeley: "The editor of 'The Tribune' is the worst of all compromisers in times of great public emergency."

Those who prefer a more detailed description of the real Greeley spirit at that time will find it in managing editor Young's story of a *Tribune* office scene the night before Greeley's departure for Richmond. In his *Reminiscences* Young wrote: "He came into my room impatient with friends who had dissented from his course, for it was not in his nature to endure dissent once he had made up his mind. 'Gentlemen,' he said, 'I know all about the things that may happen to me, but what I am to do is right and I'll do it!' There was a duty to perform; the seas might rise or the mountains fall but he was going to Richmond! And he went! He went his way as Luther of old, smiling and brave. Those of us behind the scenes saw the sublimity of this self-renunciation; it was the act of a patriot who felt that the dearest of his life were as nothing when the country could be served."

Greeley and Davis had their only meeting in the courtroom as Greeley turned from signing the bond. While they stood in brief conversation, Davis faced a federal jury box in which sat five negroes who, if the trial had proceeded, would have had a voice in deciding his fate.

Instantly a nation-wide cry went up against only one of the five northern bondsmen—Greeley. There was no protest against the other four men. "At last we have a man in this country more unpopular than Jeff Davis," exultingly wrote John Bigelow, formerly associate editor of the New York *Evening Post,* "and he is Horace Greeley."

The uproar stopped temporarily the sale of the second volume of Greeley's *American Conflict,* but the *Weekly Tribune* never regained its former circulation and profits.

One of the sensational incidents of the Davis agitation was a special meeting of the Union League Club in New York City on May 17, called by request of thirty-six members for the purpose of disciplining their fellow member. To President Jay's notice that he could fix any evening he desired on which to meet the charges, Greeley replied that he would attend no meeting nor make any defense. His letter to the committee is one of the most powerful arraignments of radical Republicanism ever written, and soon the whole country was debating it. It is an historic example of postwar literature. In part, he told the Union Leaguers:

> I do not recognize you as capable of judging or even fully apprehending me. You evidently regard me as a weak sentimentalist, misled by a maudlin philosophy. I arraign you as narrow-minded blockheads who would like to be useful in a great cause but don't know how. Your attempt to base a great enduring party on the hate and wrath necessarily engendered by a bloody civil war is as though you should plant a colony on an iceberg which had somehow drifted into a tropical sea. I will tell you here, out of a life devoted to the good of mankind, that your children will select my going to Richmond and signing that bail bond as the wisest act and will feel that it did more for freedom and humanity than all of you were competent to do.
>
> All I ask of you is a square stand-up fight by yeas and nays. I care not how few vote with me, nor how many against me, for I know that the latter will repent in dust and ashes before three years have passed. Understand once for all that I dare you and defy you. So long as any man was working to overthrow our government he was my enemy; from the hour in which he threw down his arms he was my formerly erring countryman.

The club held its special meeting but concluded that Greeley had done nothing calling for action by his fellow members.

Greeley published the correspondence with the club but otherwise met the storm in silence. In August he wrote Mrs. Whipple at Westhaven:

"I am going to Vermont but not to speak. Nothing I could say on the Davis subject would be regarded as otherwise than a vindication of myself, and I need none. I go to see friends. . . . Do not trouble to answer those who think ill of me for bailing Jefferson Davis, or for anything else. I never write a word defending myself and feel confident that all will come out right. I do not care who is to be President [1868] but he must uphold the new loyal governors of southern states, or we lose most that has been gained by the overthrow of the Rebellion. I trust there is to be no such word as fail. At all events I must not fail.—H.G."

CHAPTER XXIII

Reid as "First Writing Editor"

HOW THE HEATHEN ROAR!" Greeley had exclaimed to Colfax of the Davis agitation. "I am used to it! Bless their souls, it doesn't annoy me, and if it does them any good that is all clear gain."

But it really did annoy him. To Mrs. Whipple, back home, he confessed: "To work as hard and bear up under anxieties as I do, and be cussed for it every day—feeling that I am losing money and ground, too—it is discouraging. I cannot stand it always." By that time, out of his own experiences, Greeley had learned how truly he had been prophesying to his lecture audiences on the lyceum circuit when he assured them, "Fame is a vapor, popularity an accident and riches take wings." The sharp antagonism of his party to his reconciliation policy, the sudden sweeping away of income by the Davis storm, made him a discouraged man, though he would never admit it. "At all events," said Greeley when discussing his affairs, "the public has learned that I act upon my own convictions; hence any future paroxysm of popular rage against me is likely to be less virulent in view of the fact that this one proved so plainly ineffective. I don't know how much the second volume of 'The American Conflict' will bring me," he said, "but I am sure of $10,000 from my first volume, for I have had it and have paid it out to settle some of my debts." He had turned to writing *Recollections of a Busy Life*, in the hope of more royalties to settle another batch of debts. Fortunately, they did.

Though during the two years after the war the *Tribune*'s gross and net revenue was the largest since he founded it, little of the output from that newspaper gold mine then went to Greeley; even his few shares of stock were heavily mortgaged. Whitelaw Reid, in commenting on Greeley's life, in the *Century Magazine*, stated that "in a period of twenty-four years 'The Tribune' had distributed $1,240,000 in dividends, besides appropriating $381,939 to purchase the corner of Nassau and Spruce Streets and much new equipment. The average annual dividend for each share had been $516.66. By January 1, 1849, Greeley had parted with eighteen of his fifty shares; by July 2, 1860, he owned only fifteen shares, and by 1868 only nine shares." Reid thus explained this waste of fortune: "He bought wild lands destined never to be anything else, copper mining shares, desiccated egg companies, patent looms, photolithograph companies; gave money away profusely, loaned to plausible rascals, and was the prey of every inventor who chanced to find him with money or with collateral that he could readily convert into money." Reid estimated these losses at one million dollars.

Greeley himself had given evidence supporting this Reid version in many letters to borrowers, but particularly in one written to his friend Bowe back in 1850: "Won't you have some money? I earn a good deal and two-thirds of it goes every way to all manner of loafers—why not you? I would rather send you $50 than not if you will let me—say so and I will do it. I long ago quit wanting to be rich—I never did want to live extravagantly. I own a house; some mining stocks, which mean to be good sometime; and a quarter of 'The Tribune' which PAYS, not to speak of any number of I.O.U.'s that DON'T pay and won't—they'd see me in Heaven first. Let me send you $50, to be paid when perfectly convenient."

While Greeley was thus ruining himself, Raymond, his former employee, became rich as owner of *Times* stock given him by George Jones in 1851 to assume editorial direction; Bennett, who was Greeley's "one-man-in-a-cellar-against-the-whole-world" rival, became a millionaire several times over as a result of *Herald* prosperity; William Cullen Bryant, editor and part owner of the *Evening Post*, was always financially comfortable. These three veterans of the *New Yorker* era were now all remaining in the field. Greeley, founder of the second most prosperous newspaper, though still its active head and still the hardest worker, was financially the poorest. A checkup of his assets and income in the last of the years during which his *Tribune* was earning a total of $1,240,000 profits would unquestionably have revealed as a bankrupt the man whose genius had made it all. At Chappaqua, however, he had a farm he loved, and he had won a foremost place for himself with the people. He was their "Uncle Horace"—a title that meant more to him than would a heavy bank account without it. Besides, no matter who owned the stock of the *Tribune* company or who received its dividends, was not the *Tribune* read because it was Greeley's *Tribune?* It was his pride, though no longer his property.

He was keen enough to know, however, that after a quarter of a century of trial and labor he would not fit in with postwar times. Peace had brought new problems and new ways to newspapers; the whole nation was responding to new effort. He planned to meet such a future by organizing a *Tribune* staff that would need less of him—perhaps none of him. His first move was to replace Sydney Howard Gay—Dana's successor in 1862 as managing editor—with John Russell Young, just over in New York City from Forney's *Philadelphia Press.* Young's training for the position was to Greeley ideal. He was born of poor parents in Tyrone, Ireland, and had come up "from the case" as a printer. He wielded a pen that wasted no words in saying exactly what he thought; at twenty-five, in full flower of physical strength, he was a glutton for work, and the staff responded. More than satisfied with his new managing editor, Greeley next turned his thoughts toward securing "a first writing editor."

On several occasions he had met Whitelaw Reid in Washington; he had even discussed with Schuyler Colfax, then speaker of the House of Representatives, Reid's possible connection with the *Tribune.* Finally he wrote Reid:

Greeley and Reid in Conference

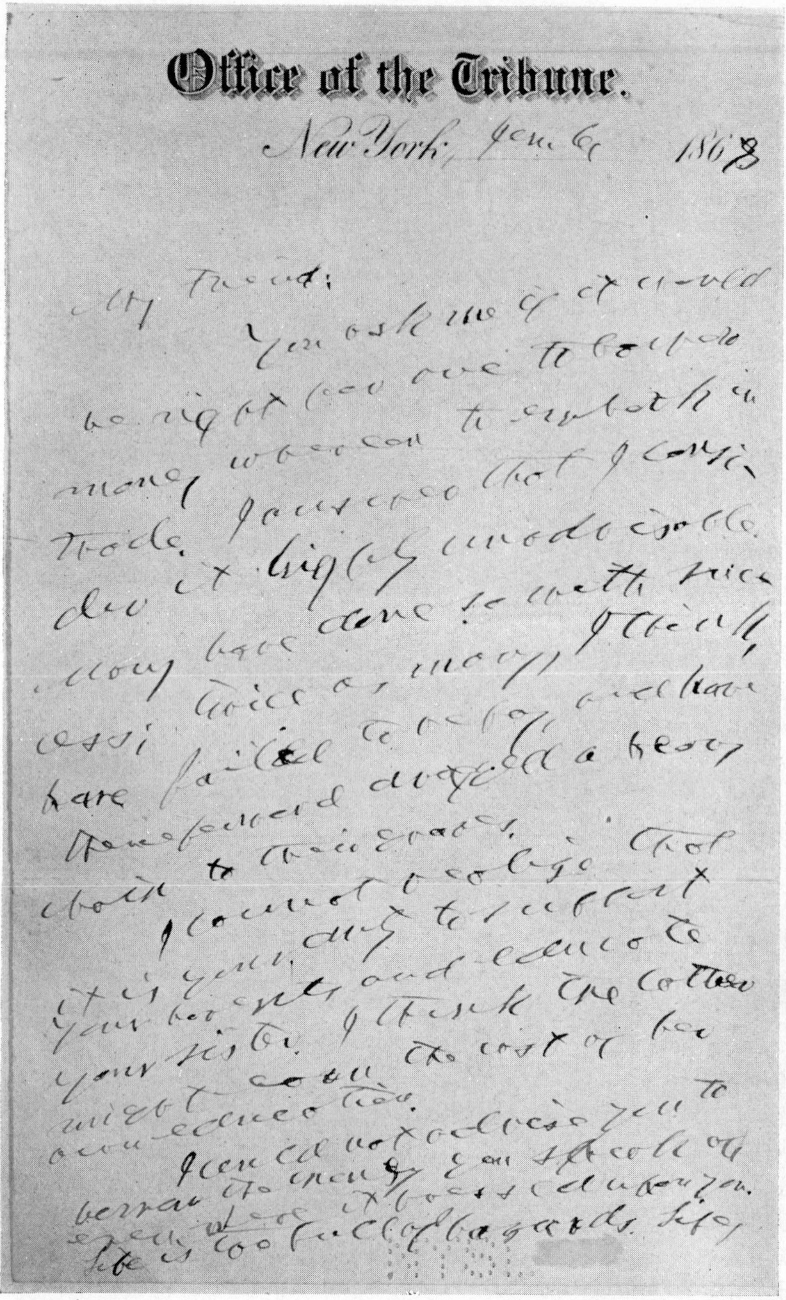

Office of the Tribune.

New York, Jan. 6 1868

Courtesy New York State Library

Extract from a Letter to Helen R. Marshall Dated January 6, 1868; a Good Example of Greeley's "Worm Fence" Handwriting

New York Tribune
January 19, 1866

Friend Reid:

Supposing you should have a good chance to come to this city on "The Tribune," would you do so? And how much would you think a fair compensation? And would you be willing to spend the sessions in Washington if that should be deemed desirable?

I write this apropos to nothing in particular, but with a view to possibilities you will answer as tardily and as you please—or even not at all.

Is Sam Wilkeson still in Washington? If so, what doing?

Yours,
Horace Greeley

In response to this first link in a seventy-five-years' family control of the *Tribune,* Reid met Greeley in New York City at the Gramercy Park home of their mutual friend, my uncle Henry Luther Stuart; but Reid's work on his book, *Ohio in the War,* and other undertakings prevented prompt acceptance. Greeley, however, persisted. He wrote Colfax at Washington, "If you ever get a letter from Whitelaw Reid that you can spare a body, please enclose to yours, Horace Greeley." In 1867, still after Reid, he wrote to him in Cincinnati:

"I would not have you weaken your hold on 'The Gazette' [Cincinnati] until you are wholly sure of something better, for I know that yours is a strong concern whose dividends of late beat 'The Tribune.' I infer that nothing can definitely be done presently, but when you have the money that you don't borrow I hope you will authorize me to buy one or two shares in 'The Tribune' for you. I believe you are mistaken as to my withdrawing from active direction of 'The Tribune' in 1869. I guess I shall be able to do it. At all events, I hope to try." Again in 1867, he wrote to Reid in Louisiana: "I will be in Cincinnati during the winter. Will you try to be there when I am? If the mountain will not come to Mahomet, etc." But the mountain and Mahomet did not meet that winter, nor until September, 1868, when the office bulletin board announced that Whitelaw Reid had joined the *Tribune* staff as "first writing editor subject only to Mr. Greeley and John Russell Young."

For years that bulletin board in the *Tribune* newsroom had been the talk and gibe of Printing House Square. It often criticized the use of words and of phrases, listed other mistakes or imposed fines for minor offenses, and assigned topics to different writers. Managing editor Young, having been in the army, fell into the bulletin board habit, even going so far as to number each order. The board reached its high point of fame in newspaper circles when in 1867 Young issued the following orders:

Order No. 56—There is too much profanity in this office.
Order No. 57—Hereafter the political editor must have his copy in at 10:30 P.M.

Both of these orders were directed at Amos J. Cummings, Ireland-born like Young and, like him, former printer and soldier. He took up the challenge at once and posted the following:

Order No. 1234567—
Everybody knows ——— well that I get most of the political news out of the Albany "Journal," and everybody knows ——— ——— well that the "Journal" doesn't get here until eleven o'clock at night, and anybody who knows anything knows ——— ——— well that asking me to get my stuff up at half past ten is like asking a man to sit on a window-sill and dance on the roof at the same time.

Cummings

Cummings bulletined himself out of a job.

Next day he called at the *Sun* office and asked Dana for one.

"Why are you leaving the *Tribune?*" inquired the *Sun*'s editor.

"They say I swear too much," replied Cummings.

He got the job he sought, and made his first hit with Dana when, as copyreader of a young reporter's news story, he ran across a French phrase in the body of it. "What does that mean?" he asked, and was told. "Then why in hell didn't you write it that way?" yelled Cummings. "This paper is published for people who read English!"

Thus, Cummings established himself as one of those men who, under Dana, made the *Sun* famous as a newspaper "published for people who read English."

Though Greeley failed in his first approach to Reid, his eagerness for newspaper development was never timed closer to big events than when in May 1866 he had managing editor Young post a notice in the usual formal way, assigning George Washburn Smalley to be European correspondent of the *Tribune*, resident in London. War clouds were hanging low and dense over both Austria and Prussia, and Greeley determined to have one of his own staff report the expected conflict. American newspapers were then wholly dependent upon foreign correspondents for their European news and views, but seeing Europe through foreign eyes had never suited the intensely American Greeley. Dana, George Ripley, Bayard Taylor and Margaret Fuller had been abroad for the *Tribune* on brief assignments; Greeley now wanted one of his home staff resident there. In Smalley he had a true blue-blooded New Englander, Harvard of course included, a bachelor and fond of roving. He was at his desk in the reporters' room one Monday morning when Young made straight for him. "Smalley," he said, as calmly as though he were assigning him to a local story, "we want you to get the first possible steamer for Europe. War has broken out and you are to report it."

The first steamer Queenstown-bound was to sail from Boston Wednesday noon. Smalley was the correspondent who, after a thirty-mile horseback ride from the battlefield through the night, had telegraphed Lincoln the news of Lee's defeat at Antietam. He was as prompt to get that Boston boat, and thus became the first American correspondent to establish a bureau in London. Though his notice to go abroad was unusually short, his stay there was unusually long, for he remained in London as the *Tribune* correspondent until, in 1905, Whitelaw Reid was appointed ambassador to Great Britain. For obvious State Department reasons, Smalley, after forty years' service abroad, returned to this country and became Washington correspondent of the *Times* of London.

From London, on July 30, 1866, Smalley cabled the news that

decision had been made by diplomats at a peace table in Berlin and not by the armies of Prussia and Austria on a battlefield. He condensed it into few words because of the tolls of five dollars a word: "Peace certain. Prussia carries all her points. Liberals support Bismarck's foreign policy." This was the first news beat to cross the Atlantic by cable; Greeley eagerly told the world of the *Tribune*'s enterprise and of its own resident correspondent.

But the Smalley cablegram, historic as it was as a newspaper feature, was not the first message to cross the ocean from the other side. That message, of course, came from Cyrus W. Field in London by way of Heart's Content, Cape Breton, Newfoundland, notifying President Johnson of the installation there of the shore ends of the 2,000 miles of undersea cable. The entire first page of the *Tribune* was given over to the story of Field's ten years of discouraging struggle and final triumph. Across the top of the center columns there was printed the first dispatch to appear in American newspapers announcing the landing and operation of the cable on American shores. Other newspapers were not so confident.

The *Times* was skeptical about the *Tribune*'s cables, especially from Smalley. "There is a vast deal of humbug about this matter," it remarked; to which Greeley responded: "'The Times' finds comfort in speaking of our dispatches as 'bogus' and 'hocus-pocus.' If that newspaper wants to experience a sensation in the way of journalism, we shall be happy to show it our bills. 'The Times' also does not believe in the Atlantic cable. It's a way these third-rate journals have."

"The cable is another step in the onward march of civilization," prophesied Greeley, "for it will unquestionably prove a powerful agency in promoting international amity. The world will soon be girdled with this instrument for the transmission of thought with the lightning's speed; and thus 'the ends of the earth will be brought together' in fulfillment of ancient prophecy. 'Peace hath its victories,' and the success of the Atlantic cable will ever be regarded as one of the most glorious of them all."

As a high tariff advocate Greeley rejoiced to make known the fact that the cable had been manufactured in the Cooper-Hewitt plant at Trenton, New Jersey, and that two Americans—Cyrus Field and Peter Cooper—were firm believers in it through all of its uncertainties. Five years after the first cablegram Peter Cooper sold his cable stock at a profit which he devoted wholly to building and endowing Cooper Union, still at the junction of Third and Fourth Avenues, Seventh to Eighth Streets, New York City.

CHAPTER XXIV

Johnson in the White House

THROUGH FOUR LONG YEARS following Lincoln's death Greeley had more than Jefferson Davis and "magnanimity" to worry about politically and so had the country—in the person of North Carolina-born Andrew Johnson, of Tennessee, former governor, congressman, and United States senator. He is our only Vice-President whose inaugural speech, because of liquor, was too incoherent ever to be made public; and our only President to face an impeachment trial. Whatever opinion you may have formed of the Johnson of the White House from 1865 to 1869, it is not to be forgotten that he was Lincoln's choice, and only Lincoln's, on the National Union ticket of 1864; remember, too, that he was the Union part of it—not the Republican part—for he never ceased to be a Democrat and a Southerner. He was the only senator who did not follow his seceding state out of the Union in 1861. He refused to resign his seat when Tennessee took that step, declaring: "Run away from here because Lincoln enters? I worked against him in the campaign, I talked against him and I voted against him, but Lincoln is now the only man who can save the Union, and by God I will stand with him! I still love my country; I love the Constitution. I intend to insist upon its guaranties, with the confident hope that if the Union remains together in less than four years the triumphant party of today will be overthrown."

At Lincoln's request in 1862 Johnson became military governor of Tennessee; he held that position when, two years later, Lincoln, to strengthen his own re-election, called Johnson to his side. He believed it better campaign politics to have a Union Democrat from borderline Tennessee with him on the national ticket than a Republican from sure-Republican Maine. That is why Vice-President Hannibal Hamlin was retired.

Besides, there was a background of struggle to "Andy" Johnson that suited the people. Like Lincoln—and like Greeley, too—he was from the grass roots, and not deep roots at that. When eighteen years old he worked and tramped, barefoot and ragged, over the mountains to Greeneville, Greene County, Tennessee, where he found a job as journeyman tailor; there, too, he met a young woman who during evenings as he worked in his tailor shop gave him his first lessons in spelling and writing, for Johnson never saw the inside even of a village schoolhouse. Later he married that girl and she became mistress of the White House for four years, with her children and grandchildren about her to give it the needed atmosphere of a home. In Greeneville young Johnson emerged early in politics as an Andrew Jackson Democrat. Five successive elections to Congress (1843-1853), followed by election as governor, and in 1857 as United States senator, afford a test of popularity that few men survive.

This, in brief, is the career of the man who made such a spectacle in the Senate Chamber on March 4, 1865. He was never to preside over the Senate, for Congress was not to meet until December. Lincoln, confident of Grant's early victory, was enjoying his first relief from four years of anxieties, and Johnson, restless to return to Greeneville, had made a White House parting call. Not quite six weeks had elapsed since inauguration when came the assassin's shot, the midnight news to Johnson asleep in his hotel, his hurried trip alone to the dying Lincoln's bedside through Washington's darkened streets with their excited crowds, despite warnings of his own danger; at dawn came the realization that he was to be President—but President of a nation in the still-burning embers of sectional war, with bitterness and confusion sure to be intensified by this act.

As he took the oath of office at noon on April 15 he turned

from Chief Justice Chase to face a group of senators and congressmen impatient to question him whether he would pursue a policy of "conquered provinces" toward the defeated rebel states, or attempt, in the words of General Benjamin F. Butler, "to administer the political estate of Abraham Lincoln." Here were the problems and vexations of this new President's four years in office plumped at him in the first hours of his administration. Some visitors left him sure that they had won him to the conquered-province reconstruction plan of Congress. They recalled that during his campaign in Tennessee, not a year back, he had declared that "the American people should be taught that treason is a crime and must be punished." "I'll put old Greeley on the warpath for it," declared *Tribune* correspondent Wilkeson, with more enthusiasm than ability to perform.

Others who crowded in on Johnson that first day as President came away with a very different opinion. He had "reconstructed" his own state in 1864, electing a Union governor, legislature and Congress delegation, besides ratifying emancipation. Why, then, they argued, should he not follow that pattern in other rebel states? So rumor ran—even with Lincoln's body still lying in the White House. Nor did discussion stop with policies. How about his cabinet? the radicals asked. Why not get rid of some of Lincoln's men—not, of course, of Stanton in the War Department; but of Seward and others. Major Benjamin Truman, who was Johnson's secretary, published in the *Century* of January 1913 a letter he had received from the President, after his retirement, in which he wrote that Montgomery Blair urged him to put Oliver P. Morton of Indiana, John A. Andrews of Massachusetts, and Horace Greeley of New York in his cabinet at once to strengthen it. "I told Blair that I would not have Greeley on any account. I always considered him a good enough editor before the war, although I never agreed with him; but in all other matters he seemed to me like a whale ashore. He nearly bothered the life out of Lincoln and it was difficult to tell whether he wanted union or separation, war or peace. Greeley is all heart and no head. He is the most vacillating man in the country. He runs to goodness of heart so much as to produce infirmity of mind. Blair reasoned with me as a friend but I could not see his point. I told him that Greeley was a sublime old child but would be of no service to me."

Nevertheless, Greeley's *Tribune* started out with Johnson more cordially than did most Republican papers. He took that attitude at once and held it for more than a year. The day after correspondent Wilkeson undertook to "put old Greeley on the warpath" for the conquered-province policy, the *Tribune* had this to say of the new President:

> Johnson is emphatically a self-made man, with the energy, self-reliance and courage befitting that character. He believes in the Republic, venerates the Union, and has learned to hate slavery and the Rebellion with his whole soul.... He has decided ability, earnest patriotism, and undoubting faith in our national destiny. If any Rebel ever thought it would be well for the clan to have Andrew Johnson in the White House rather than Abraham Lincoln he is bitterly mistaken.

Johnson was the third Vice-President in Greeley's time to succeed to the presidency because of death of his chief. But with John Tyler (1841) following "Tippecanoe" Harrison and with Millard Fillmore (1850) following Zach Taylor the succession had not the significance of Johnson in Lincoln's place. His short, burly body, broad shoulders, topped by a well-rounded head, with intensely black hair and eyes, a firm, square chin, not a care ever permitted to furrow his ruddy cheeks—all were in sharp contrast with Lincoln physically; so were his ways. The one was pugnacious, hasty, and dogmatic; the other tolerant, slow, and farseeing. The one was likely to aggravate old enmities; the other was fitted to heal them. Only two weeks before the assassination Greeley had said in the *Tribune* that the country would approve of Lincoln's policy whatever it might be; that they would trust reconstruction to him. Senator Simon Cameron of Pennsylvania, who had been Lincoln's first Secretary of War, also made a true analysis of the future, had not tragedy intervened. While visiting Lincoln about the same time he said to him: "You will be elected for a third term in 1868. No one can clear up the belongings of this war in four years, and the people will not permit any other man as President to handle it and make a mess of it."

And now, less than two weeks later, that "other man" is handling it; the mess that the veteran Pennsylvania politician apprehended is in the making. Chaos looms ahead. A war-weary nation, its citizens eager for immediate development of its factories, farms, and mines, has a Chief Executive certain to be in conflict with a politically hostile Congress. War had its trials and anxieties through four long years; but here are the serious problems of peace demanding instant solution—how to rebuild a government that has been close to disintegration for so long. Though war has ceased, two sections of the country glare at each other in sullen mood. The fact that bullets do not change opinion is again being demonstrated to the world. Defeat has not proven to such stanch Confederates as Jefferson Davis that slavery was wrong, nor has it led the southern white man to accept his former chattel as his equal in citizenship. Even an amendment added to the national Constitution, commanding as Holy Writ though its words might be, could not and did not do that.

From Clay's Missouri Compromise of 1820 until Greeley's call for "magnanimity" while the rebel army was putting aside its swords and guns, there had been no rest for the nation for almost half a century from intense agitation, physical encounters in Congress, "Uncle Tom's Cabin," fugitive slave hunts through a defiant North, Dred Scott decisions, and the Douglas popular sovereignty foment over Kansas. For those who had lived through such a racking period followed by war there could be no vision of national brotherhood unblurred, if not wholly blinded, by recollections. A glib counsel to the South to raise less hell and more cotton as a way to cool its passions fell on unheeding ears so long as a soldier in blue on duty everywhere in Dixie was plain evidence of a conqueror's purpose to enforce his will. Greeley insisted that that soldier should be brought north to other duties.

The new President had eight months in which to develop what he called "My Policies" before Congress would convene in December. Not many weeks had elapsed, however, before he realized that any purpose by him short of capitulation to the radicals would be resisted. "Congress is the people!" declared these constitutionalists who were thus defying the Constitution. Only a year before, in a published arraignment of Lincoln, Thaddeus Stevens, Senator Ben Wade, and Senator Charles Sumner, speaking for a Republican caucus, had declared: "If he [Lincoln] wants our support, he must confine himself to his executive duties and leave political reorganization to Congress. . . . Though the President is Commander-in-Chief of the Army, Congress is his commander and, God willing, he shall obey."

Such was the mood in which those men greeted Lincoln's successor when Congress met in December 1865 to receive his message detailing his acts to date and his purposes.

That first message was a record of progress toward reconstruction of which Johnson was proud. Regardless of the policy of it, he had done a thorough job. Three governors appointed by Lincoln and seven by Johnson were now functioning in hitherto rebel states; complete delegations of senators and congressmen awaited admission at Washington. Responsibility for reconstruction had been placed upon Southerners themselves. Their salvation was in their own hands. "Let military rule be ended. Let us have patience for a fair experiment," urged Johnson, "—one that will make us once more a united people, bound more than ever to mutual affection and support. . . ."

"Weak words," sneered Stevens, now master of Congress though seventy-five years old and so infirm that he often had to be carried to his seat. "Rebels have no rights. They are at the will of their conquerors." The House cheered him.

The conservative tone of the message disappointed the radicals. They had prepared by caucus action a reply in kind to a challenging, defiant document. Instead they listened to pacific counsels so unlike Johnson that they led to inquiries as to the mind that had prompted them. Gossip settled on Secretary of State Seward.

Generally the country liked the Johnson document—none more so than the *Tribune*. Promptly that newspaper declared:

. . . We doubt whether any message of a former President has, on the whole, contained so much that will be generally and justly approved, with so little that will or should provoke dissent. It is a State paper of signal ability and of unusual frankness, dealing unreservedly with every great question of internal or internationl policy and calculated to increase the hold of the author in the regard and confidence of the people.

To Washington, and to the White House "not uninvited," hurried Greeley as the storm broke, with the result that the *Tribune* endeavored to pour oil upon the troubled waters. "The first interest of this as of every other people is justice," wrote Greeley, "the next is peace—peace based on justice, peace between North and South, rich and poor, white and black. Such is our pressing necessity. We only need to go to work—generally, heartily, trustingly—to put everything right very speedily. There is not the shadow of valid reason for any differences between Congress and the President. They were called to responsibility by the same fiat. Their obligations—even to the southern blacks—are identical. If they stand together and triumph they will share the plaudits of well done. If they should be estranged a common fate awaits them."

But the immediate response of the Republican Congress was to appoint a Committee of Fifteen—six senators and nine congressmen—to take over the whole problem of the rebel states. The governments already established were to be set aside; soldiers were to stand at every ballot box to see that negroes voted. With Republican Ben Wade presiding over the Senate, with Republican Schuyler Colfax as speaker of the House, both backed by Republican majorities, Stevens insisted that the Lincoln National Union party of 1864 had been dissolved, and that the Republican party of 1856 and 1860 had been restored to ascendancy. It must be kept there. It had a mission "to keep the war won." A Jackson Democrat in the White House could have no part in such work; there could be no co-operation with a President who was bringing traitors to the front. Thus the Republicans in Congress created an issue that led finally to the desperate effort in 1868, by impeachment, to supplant Johnson with Ben Wade, next in line. In so doing they wrote a chapter in our national politics that historians unite in deploring. Not closer together but further and further apart moved the people of the two sections. Unyielding antagonism to the black Republican party, as Stephen Douglas was the first to christen it in 1854, was an inheritance that every southern voter prized. A Solid South became political history—not yet wholly written.

Only one important Republican newspaper united with Greeley in his early support of Johnson. That one was the New York *Times* which reflected the views of its editor, Henry J. Raymond, then a member of Congress. Naturally Greeley was not happy in lonely association with his old opponent, especially as his friends—Sam Bowles of the Springfield *Republican* and Joe Medill of the Chicago *Tribune*—were strongly with the radicals. Little by little the Greeley warmth for Johnson cooled. Late in February came the President's veto of the Freedmen's Bureau bill passed by the Republican majority. "It looks as though the President had made up his mind to go whole hog with those who predicted that 'the blacks cannot live among us except as slaves' and are striving to make good their prophecy," declared Greeley. It was his first open break with the White House—though not unexpected there. In July followed the veto of the reconstruction bill establishing military control of the South, and doing away with Johnson's governors. When passed over the veto, its enactment had Greeley's approval. The man who had "so much goodness of heart as to cause infirmity of mind" was now "on the warpath," where correspondent Wilkeson had failed to lure him months before. Yet Greeley had to admit that he did not relish the proposed military rule. "The President's dislike of military tribunals has a certain amount of our sympathy," he wrote. "We are anxious to see the swords of our army turned into plowshares."

But he was now even more anxious to have Johnson's policies in the South jettisoned and to unite with a Republican Congress behind measures of complete domination over the secession states. He was not yet ready, as Sumner was, to impeach Johnson or to regard him as "an obstacle to be removed," as Wendell Phillips insisted, but he had become the ally of Thad Stevens and Ben Wade. The President soon found himself a President without a party—without even an organized following. He was stripped of power and defied by Republicans; he was disowned by Democrats. The political firm of Weed, Seward & Raymond, successors since 1854 to Weed, Seward & Greeley, was now openly in command of Johnson's fortunes. Seward dominated the cabinet, Raymond was spokesman in Congress, Weed was the strategist. Here was a combination that directly challenged Greeley. His old partners were out to make good for their overthrow in the Chicago Wigwam in 1860. They proposed to take over the National Union organization of 1864, and forget that there had ever been a Republican party.

When a call was published late in June by the National Union Club of Washington, D. C., for a convention to be held at Philadelphia on August 13 to "boost" Johnson, everyone knew that the three New York men who in 1854 were too thoroughly Whig to join the new Republican party were the real planners of this effort to start another one in 1866. With no right whatever to it, they appropriated the title of Lincoln's convention of 1864—National Union. In its name they called for delegates "who sustain the administration in maintaining unbroken the Union of the States under the Constitution . . . indissoluble and perpetual. . . . There is no right anywhere," it continued, "to dissolve the Union, or separate the States either by voluntary withdrawal, by force of arms, or by Congressional action, or by the national government in any form. . . . Every patriot should frown upon such acts that rekindle the animosities of war. . . . We call upon the people to elect to Congress none but men who agree that all the States of the Union have an equal right to a voice and a vote, and who will restore to their seats therein the representatives from every state in allegiance to the United States."

The move brought out the old Greeley spirit like sparks from an anvil. *Tribune* editorials and Washington dispatches by their vigor reminded readers of the fight on Douglas in 1854. "It's a fraud," he cried, "to impudently, brazenly represent this bolters' meeting as a convention of the National Union Party of 1864. Not ten of the 180 members of Congress elected on that ticket will have anything to do with this gathering, while their adversaries in that contest will make haste to indorse it. . . . It is to be made respectable in the members represented by a general attendance of supporters of George B. McClellan and Jefferson Davis."

"Who will be there!" asked the *Tribune*. "New York will have her most illustrious sons. Secretary of State Seward will write a letter in the loftiest boarding-school style and say something about Tammany Hall." Following humorous references to George Francis Train, John A. Dix and Horatio Seymour, the *Tribune* added: "Above all things, we shall send the venerable and illustrious Thurlow Weed with his wagon load of rich men, and Henry Raymond as rider. T. W. has driven many wagons in his day and Raymond has done his share of riding in all sorts of vehicles, but never such a wagon as this! Vanderbilt and A. T. Stewart, Roberts and Daniel Drew and Leonard W. Jerome—comfortably jammed and packed, and going all the way to Philadelphia this sultry weather, to stand by the Union, the Constitution, and Andrew Johnson. In fine, the convention will be a meeting of marvelous odds and ends, the reconstructed shreds and patches of rebellion; free-booters in politics."

Just before the meeting date Greeley made this final thrust: "The convention is likely to be a melancholy and miscellaneous gathering kept together, if at all, by some law of coherence as yet unpublished by political philosophers. It will exhibit both the variety and the vivacity of a menagerie at the precise moment when the attendants are bringing in the baskets of beef; but it will diminish the pleasure of the spectators and the safety of the performers if strong cages are not provided for the hottest and hungriest of the animals. Mr. Weed, who will have charge of the pole, will no doubt select a long one for stirring up the beasts; but even with every precaution he may be lacerated by the tigers, or crunched by the hyenas, or out-chattered by the monkeys."

After deploring the possible fate of Vanderbilt and Stewart, the *Tribune* added: "What, O ye gods!, if Mr. Thurlow Weed himself, while engaged in oiling the waters, should fall in heels over head, flask in hand, and never come up again? This is a catastrophe which we will not permit ourselves to contemplate."

Then follow sarcastic references to the "down-trodden and negro-trodden" whites of the South. "But we do not expect Mr. Weed to give them any money. We can fancy him exclaiming in the language of Canning's 'Friend of Humanity,' 'I give you six pence? I'll see you d——d first!' Calm yourself, sage of Albany. We ask no more of you than a sheaf of resolutions—every resolution a plaster, a poultice and a persuader."

Greeley surely was himself again with all his early fierceness of pen, but he was not permitted to occupy the field of comment alone. The New York *Times* had plenty to say about his present course as well as about his complainings of Lincoln during the war. Nor was that newspaper sparing of its language: "There is not in the whole Union, if indeed there is in the whole wide world, a prominent individual with a record so inconsistent and so contradictory (we use no milder terms) as that of Horace Greeley.... He is master of the sharpest blackguardism and billingsgate. He uses every epithet that malignity can coin—the double-distilled venom of disappointed ambition and toothless rage."

The *Times* hailed the convention as a gathering of "patriotic, thoughtful people to whom it has become evident that the state of political anarchy at Washington" should not be tolerated longer. Their purpose was to destroy the Republican majority in Congress at the November elections and to have that body controlled by a National Union majority responsive to President Johnson. They built a hall in Philadelphia facing Girard College and called it a Wigwam—a name as appropriate in that city as it would have been for Chicago, in 1860, to have called the hall it built for the Lincoln convention on the borderline of Indian country a Quaker meeting house.

There was plenty of enthusiasm from start to finish. Thirty-six states were represented. As the Massachusetts and South Carolina delegates marched two by two, arm in arm, to their seats, the band played "Rally Around the Flag." Cheers rang through the hall, but rain dripped heavily through the unfinished roof; the whole scene recalled Noah's Ark to cartoonists. The high point of the convention came when General John A. Dix, a Democrat who was to be elected governor of New York in 1874, introduced as keynoter of the convention Henry J. Raymond, chairman of the Republican National Committee, capable editor of the *Times* since its founding a quarter of a century earlier, a member of Congress and of the Republican party caucus there. All that Greeley ever said of the miscellaneous character of the gathering came to mind when Raymond's forceful indictment of the Republican Congress and his eulogy of Johnson's policies were enthusiastically applauded by Samuel J. Tilden and Horatio Seymour, who were to be Democratic candidates for President; Thomas A. Hendricks of Indiana, who was to be Vice-President during Grover Cleveland's first term; Clement L. Vallandigham, the chief Copperhead during the war; ex-Mayor Fernando Wood of New York City and Ben Wood, who led the Copperheads of that city, as well as others of the same way of thinking during the war days. They had been elected as delegates but were entreated not to sit as such.

It was a strange picture—Republican national chairman Raymond exhorting a convention overwhelmingly Democratic, and the veteran Republican leader, Thurlow Weed, directing its organization; despite efforts to conceal its make-up, not one-third of the delegates had voted for Lincoln in 1864 and not that many, two years later, supported Grant.

They had come together to place Johnson's cause before the people in what they called the true light; they certainly made the best possible job of it, with speeches, resolutions and enthusiasm lasting through three days on a single theme—Johnson. "The finger of Providence points unerringly," telegraphed the President to them, "and will guide you safely through." No doubt the convention aided the Democratic vote in several states and defeated some Republican candidates for Congress, but its most immediate and decisive result was to throw into political bankruptcy the firm of Weed, Seward and Raymond. Two partners were formally expelled from the Republican organization, while Seward thereafter was ignored in party councils. Greeley, the former unheeded and restless junior partner, alone survived as a political force twenty-eight years after Weed persuaded him out of a printing office and cast him, as he said, "on the boiling sea of politics."

The final chapter in the effort to "boost Johnson" began a week after adjournment of the convention, when the President started his disastrous "swing around the circle." It was a tour from Washington to New York, Buffalo, Chicago, St. Louis, Cincinnati, Pittsburgh, and Washington. It marked the end of all hope for Johnson as a national figure. Crowds everywhere taunted him into defiance; his speeches became merely angry rejoinders to the heckling. By the time he had "swung" back into the White House the helpful influence of the Philadelphia convention had been largely dissipated, and the Republicans in Congress were more determined than ever to resort to impeachment.

Greeley had no sympathy with that purpose, but chiefly the inability of the Republicans to develop a national leader depressed him. The bullet that had killed Lincoln also penetrated the vitals of Lincoln's party. No Republican emerged other than one rooted in sectional prejudices. "Magnanimity" was an unspoken word. In Congress one heard only the voices of the old crowd and the urge to "vote as you shot." Even younger congressmen like those soon-to-be leaders James G. Blaine of Maine, Roscoe Conkling of New York and James A. Garfield believed that their popularity rested upon waving what was then called "the bloody shirt."

Greeley was alarmed at the conflict between Congress and the President. On February 5, 1867, he wrote Senator E. D. Morgan:

Dear Senator:

Of course you see what is going on around you and know that we are within thirty days of a fresh civil war—one likely to rage on the Hudson and the Delaware as well as on the Potomac and the Mississippi. Do you propose to let us drift to the inevitable catastrophe? or what?

For my part I feel that I have done my best—earnestly and unselfishly, however unwisely—first, to get the country out of civil war; next, to secure a real, thorough adjustment that would keep her out. If I have any influence, any power, I have used them freely—used them up. Henceforth, I stand in the background and wait.

I have a little property; you have much; and I can't realize that I care less about living a few years longer than you do. So I guess I can stand whatever is in store for us as well as you can. So, if you say let her drift, so be it!

It happens that you are on terms of personal intimacy and accord with Sumner and Conkling on one hand and with Seward, Beverly Johnson, on the other; so that you can at least make an earnest effort to avert the impending tornado if you choose. And if it is to be averted you with others in like position will have to work very hard, beginning at once and sacrificing much. It is barely possible that the clash may be averted. I would like to hear that you propose to do, or not do, what is needed.

As for me, if worst comes to worst, I shall probably go with the party of Progress rather than that of Reaction; but I see nothing to be gained by courage in War which may not as surely be achieved by wisdom and effort in Peace.

I shall probably visit Washington the last days of this month—not sooner. I can do no good there now.

Still deeply impressed by the growing intensity and realizing his own inability to lessen it, Greeley went lecturing as far west as Minnesota, publishing before his departure a warning to Republican leaders against the peril of having Congress unmake a President at will. "We must go slowly," he said of the threatened impeachment. "It is the last recourse and then only when the honor of the country is involved. It would be a deplorable necessity."

In another editorial he declared against transferring "the crazy French practices in government" to this country. Nevertheless the *Tribune* blazed away at Johnson with managing editor Young's most vigorous language until Greeley, after returning home, finally asked him: "Why hang a man who is already bent on hanging himself? All that Andy wants is rope enough and he will save us the trouble. Why should Thad Stevens insist upon transforming a case of desirable suicide into one of undesirable martyrdom?" But Greeley soon fell in line with the anti-Johnson crusaders and eventually stood with the most insistent.

On February 21, 1868, came the President's ouster of Secretary of War Stanton, appointing General Lorenzo Thomas to his place. This move was a deliberate defiance of the Tenure of Office law recently passed by the radicals to curb him. Johnson really expected the issue to be taken to the Supreme Court for test. At once the Republican Congress accepted the challenge, however, and endorsed its Reconstruction Committee's recommendation that "Andrew Johnson, President of the United States, be arraigned before the Senate and impeached of high crimes and misdemeanors." "Who dares to hope that the Senate will betray its trust?—will disgrace itself in the face of the nation?—who will dare the infamy of posterity?" shouted Thad Stevens as he prophesied impeachment. In the House only the forty-seven Democratic members dared.

"It is not perhaps a wise precedent," commented Greeley. "It gives power to a temptation which passion cannot always resist—only to be used when absolutely necessary for the salvation of the country. The only alternative now is impeachment or infamy."

Came March 30—the first day of trial. The Senate Chamber, bare of ornament save the flag of the nation at either end of the presiding officer's dais, is crowded to its very walls, the diplomatic section filled with representatives of foreign governments in brilliant uniforms or formal dress, congressmen and department chiefs in the reserved galleries—but not a soldier of our nation there to suggest by his presence that the military has any voice in the proceedings. Three branches of our government are the sole participants—the accusing House of Representatives, the Senate as a court of decision, and the Chief Justice of the Supreme Court as presiding officer. Seated in the well are the six members of the House of Representatives impeachment committee—John A. Bingham of Ohio, George S. Boutwell of Massachusetts, General John A. Logan of Illinois, General Benjamin F. Butler of Massachusetts, Thomas Williams of Pennsylvania and Thaddeus Stevens.

Fifty-four Senators from the twenty-seven states then recognized as qualified to act sit in the semicircle of desks. They are to be the arbiters of the future of the nation's chief executive; among them Henry B. Anthony of Rhode Island, John Sherman and Benjamin Wade of Ohio, Zachariah Chandler of Michigan, Simon Cameron of Pennsylvania, George F. Edmunds of Vermont, Roscoe Conkling of New York, Charles Sumner of Massachusetts, Frederick

T. Frelinghuysen of New Jersey, William Pitt Fessenden of Maine, Thomas F. Bayard and Willard Saulsbury of Delaware, Thomas A. Hendricks and Oliver P. Morton of Indiana—all memorable national figures! But history for which the nation is everlastingly thankful was to be made during this trial by a Senator in the back row who never before or afterward attracted particular attention in public life—Edward G. Ross, in early years a roving printer over Wisconsin, Iowa and Nebraska—now owner of a weekly newspaper at Lawrence, Kansas, and by appointment a United States Senator from that state. Keeper of his own opinions while the battle rages around him, he is to be the central figure in its closing moments.

Promptly at high noon the court crier calls for order. A silence that has dramatic intensity prevails. Chief Justice Chase, robed in court gown, enters and is escorted to his chair with much formality. At once he directs the sergeant-at-arms to read the proclamation. That deep-throated official responds in sonorous tones:

> Hear ye! Hear ye! Hear ye! All persons are commanded to keep silence on pain of imprisonment while the Senate of the United States is sitting for the trial of the articles of impeachment against Andrew Johnson, President of the United States.

Such words had never before been uttered in this country, nor, declared General Butler, counsel for the prosecution, in the whole world had the removal of the head of a nation ever been attempted through the pacific means provided by our Constitution and now to be employed. At other times and in other lands, he said, despotism was fought only by overturning government itself. This court of fair trial is a triumph of our Constitution over rump parliaments, scaffolds and guillotines. It is the American way of determining whether the nation's chief executive has wrongly used the powers of his office.

No event in our history save war ever stirred the people so deeply as this final effort of the radicals to get rid of Johnson. It was praised and denounced with equal fervor, Greeley's chief comment being that the proceeding was too slow, the lawyers too boring, dragging day by day through legal red tape. He was in a drum-head court-martial mood. "It is a nightmare!" He left Washington and in the *Tribune* deplored that the court was enmeshed in technicalities and long speeches. Nevertheless people everywhere followed with increasing interest the battle of oratory between William M. Evarts and Attorney-General Harry Stanberry for President Johnson and Butler as prosecutor.

It is a tense moment on May 16 as Chief Justice Chase directs the clerk to call the roll for votes on the eleventh article dealing with the removal of Secretary Stanton. That article is taken first because it is the heart of the accusation. Its fate is the fate of the whole proceeding. Even Greeley hurries from New York, for he expects to rejoice over the impeachment and to congratulate Ben Wade on the floor of the Senate as the new President. The accusing committee of the House of Representatives is told of the purpose to vote that day, and all its members are present. Chief Justice Chase advises the senators that their names will be called in alphabetical order; each one in turn is to rise and his response must be limited to "Guilty" or "Not guilty"; no explanation and no debate.

"Mr. Anthony," calls the Senate Clerk.

Chief Justice Chase—"Mr. Senator Anthony, how say you? Is the respondent, Andrew Johnson, President of the United States, guilty or not guilty as charged?"

Mr. Anthony—"Guilty."

Grimes of Iowa, ill and weak, is told that he may remain seated in his chair, but he insists upon rising to declare "Not guilty" in the loudest voice of all.

So the call continues until after Senator Alexander Ramsay of Minnesota has voted "Guilty"—making twenty-four votes of guilty, fourteen not guilty. Among the latter are four Republicans —James Dixon of Connecticut, James R. Doolittle of Wisconsin, William Pitt Fessenden of Maine, James W. Grimes of Iowa. Two more Republicans—Lyman Trumbull of Illinois, Peter Van Winkle of West Virginia—known to be against impeachment are among the sixteen senators to follow Ramsey. Six "Not guilty" Republican votes are thus assured. Will Ross furnish the needed seventh?

Every eye is on this silent man from Kansas. It is known that he dislikes Johnson; he has always voted with his Republican colleagues to override the President's vetoes; he has been deluged with threatening letters and telegrams should he now sustain Johnson. But never a word has come from him to indicate how he will vote. It is now realized that his response will mean success or failure of the prosecution. "Guilty" from him will mean thirty-six senators—the necessary two-thirds—for impeachment; "Not guilty" will mean only thirty-five senators—one less than the needed number.

Ross rises in his place as the clerk calls his name. He knows as the whole crowded chamber knows the importance of his vote.

Chief Justice Chase—"Mr. Senator Ross, how say you? Is the respondent guilty or not guilty?"

Mr. Ross—"Not guilty!"

There had been repeated admonitions against demonstrations during the roll call, but as Ross takes his seat it is impossible to stop the outbursts for and against the Kansas senator—most of them against. The end of our most serious rivalry for control of the national government had come.

That afternoon the trains for Chicago carried most of the disheartened Republican senators out of Washington to that city, where the Republican national convention was scheduled to meet four days later to nominate the Great Captain of the Age, as Grant was then popularly known; as Greeley said in his *Tribune*, "to call the people to the polls by beating on a drum."

Grant! Grant!—Unconditional Surrender Grant! No other man was ever the man of the hour more than he as the Republican national convention began its sessions on May 20, 1868. One observer of public opinion declared that to the crowd the ashes of this soldier's cigar, even the wreaths of smoke that arose from it, were evidences of statesmanship, and his silence was the wisdom of Socrates. "The sashed and girdled Sphinx," as John Russell Young called him in the *Tribune*, had only to nod his assent to be nominated chief magistrate of the nation he had done so much to save.

A bankrupt Republican party was "making a mess" of "clearing up the belongings of this war," as Senator Cameron had told Lincoln that it would; it turned prayerfully to the only man who could surely save it from defeat. "Ask no questions. Answer none. Just hurrah!" was the order of the day to delegates. The candidate they were to nominate had been a Know-Nothing and a Democrat, but never a Republican. He had voted only in 1856—was not to vote again until 1876. When his name was first mentioned as a possible candidate for President, he really believed that he would be more content to remain as the nation's military chieftain. He was definitely not interested in politics. "The best policy is to make friends of our former enemies," he wrote only a year after he had patriotically declared at Appomattox, "The rebels are now our fellow-countrymen"; but as a candidate for President he accepted a party platform that had none of that spirit. The stolid Grant could not be persuaded to announce his course if elected. "I do not even know my own status with the new Administration." Yet this man of few words gave to the campaign its most inspiring slogan, "Let us have peace!" and Miles O'Reilly contributed heavily to its enthusiasm when he wrote:

If asked what State he hails from,
Our sole reply shall be
He hails from Appomattox
And its famous Apple Tree!

Despite this national enthusiasm, it was not easy for Greeley to yield to Grant's nomination. He was his fifth soldier candidate —Harrison, Taylor, Scott and Frémont preceding—quite a list for support by one who did not believe in soldiers in politics. "What use is it," he asked, "to shower attention on a military man who is so extremely afraid of damaging his chances for the Presidency that he never permits himself to go beyond 'much obliged'? When is a man to express his opinion if not when he is talked about as the nominee of a great party for President?" Again he wrote: "Future generations will read as the final evidence of the serene patience, the dogged endurance which history will attribute to General Grant, that he was the undismayed hero of a thousand receptions and banquets."

But there was no other man in the whole Republican party who had an even chance of election, and Greeley knew it. Chief Justice Chase was the one man he openly suggested as an alternative—Chase who was then basing his only hopes on the Democratic convention. Greeley had really wanted Chase nominated in 1864, and so wrote him in October 1863. They had an interesting correspondence, with superlatives on both sides—the Chase letter especially so. It read in part:

"I am proud of your approval and your preference. It is a great reward for the little I have done. No man has so powerfully promoted the increase of just sentiments concerning political rights and duties as you have done. Postage reform, the Homestead Act, liberality toward emigrants, freedom of the Territories, constitutional emancipation and kindred movements have found in you a constant advocate, animated by genuine principles. The immense audiences which have heard your voice through 'The Tribune' have been constantly inspired by your generous and progressive sentiments."

Greeley was not the man to forget such a letter when he had an opportunity to respond. Though he knew that Chase had no chance for nomination against Grant, he continued to refer to him as a possibility until, as he said, one Republican state convention after another—particularly Chase's own state, Ohio—ignored him. The *Tribune* then swung out for "the taciturn, reticent First Soldier of the Republic—Grant and Victory!"

"Men are of small account in comparison with principles," Greeley explained to Charles B. Stoer. "We must establish the principle that this is an all-man's government, not one of whites only. Of that principle Grant is the standard-bearer." . . . "The country needs a Chief Executive who will mind his own business energetically and faithfully, and a Congress that will attend to theirs."

CHAPTER XXV

"The Mighty Dollar"

PEOPLE PROMPTLY TURNED to other things than politics. "Andy" Johnson could remain in the White House unchallenged until the expiration of his term, March 4, 1869, and Grant would be elected his successor—it made little difference to men and women living in a dream of wealth and great achievement. Not yet the giant corporation—the Man still counted in the life of the nation, but the restlessness for conquest in new fields made him a receding figure. Thousands of miles of new railroad tracks linking the two oceans and gridironing the whole country, busy cotton and woolen mills in New England, rich oil, coal and iron in Pennsylvania, steel plows in the West, the venturesome greenback dollars of New York City financiers—all meant new activities and riches. "There's millions in it!" was the incentive and temptation for ambitions dammed up by four years of war. Even Greeley dreamed of an ideal city to be called "Greeley," in Boulder County, Colorado, and planned its development with no fences between neighbors and no rum sold within its borders. It was one of the "isms" for which he was assailed. After many initial hardships the community prospered under the leadership of its editor-founder, Nathan Cook Meeker.

In Cleveland, in 1867, twenty-six-year-old John D. Rockefeller was making his first venture in oil; in Pittsburgh, Andrew Carnegie at twenty-eight was investing his savings of eight thousand dollars in a little steel mill as his first cautious approach to fortune, and employing young Henry Clay Frick as his office boy; Connecticut

Yankee Collis P. Huntington was pushing the Central Pacific Railroad east to bring the Union Pacific from Utah to the coast. When a gold spike was driven into the rail that joined the two roads, and a train passed over it, the chimes of old Trinity in New York City rang out the long-awaited news, while in Philadelphia the historic bell of Independence Hall was heard. Henry Villard was planning a Northern Pacific that some day Jim Hill would head; Cornelius Vanderbilt, graduated from the captaincy of a Staten Island ferryboat, was now consolidating the many sections of the New York Central Railroad into a single corporation, and also racing palatial night boats to and from Albany in rivalry with Daniel Drew's fleets. Jay Gould, Jay Cooke and Jim Fisk were wagering fortunes in daily battles on the Stock Exchange. Cattle crowded into Chicago from 50,000-acre ranges in the Southwest and made that city the stockyard center of the world; wheat, corn and oats from former prairie land and wilderness were finding a central sales market there. Its most significant development was the McCormick reaper which, with the Deere steel-rimmed moldboard for plows, gave to the world its first relief from centuries of farming dependent wholly on man's muscle. Thus that brawling, confident city was responding vigorously to its civic motto, "I will!" Indeed from Atlantic to Pacific that same spirit gripped everybody. America was on the march! "Easy come, easy go!" during those gilded days—yet the gains were nation-building.

Of course, just as all roads once led to Rome so all flowed to a center in New York City, with its lending banks, its shrewd directing heads, its solid rows of Astor brownstone dwellings that bore their proprietor's hallmark, its society queens who finally limited their number to the famous "Four Hundred," of whom Ward McAllister named 399 plus himself. The Fifth Avenue Hotel, facing Madison Square at Broadway and Twenty-third Street, was the uptown gathering place for notables—the Astor House on Broadway, Barclay to Vesey Street, the downtown center. Not to be seen at either place meant that you were out of town. As you neared the old Western Union building at Dey Street about noon, you were a stranger if you did not halt, take your watch in hand, open-faced, and observe the red ball slide down the high pole on the rooftop at twelve o'clock to the second. From office windows and sidewalks that crimson ball regulated hundreds of timepieces.

Printing House Square—then the greatest center of newspaper-making in the world—always had a kindly nod and word for its most picturesque and best-known figure, as he trudged through it with his awkward gait. Nearly forty years had passed since he had first been seen here, attired in his Eton jacket with its open shirt collar, his cotton pants, worn shoes and straw hat of many summers. Then he walked the streets in awe, but now he moved along welcoming greetings whose cordial tone attested their sincerity. But if Greeley had grown to conscious greatness, so, too, had the city for which he had abandoned wilderness life. Its residences now extended as far uptown as Fifty-ninth Street, where the new and rocky Central Park was getting cart-loads of soil year after year to form its grassy mounds. To the east of it street gaslights extended to Seventy-ninth Street—but no paving and only narrow sidewalks.

Colorful stagecoaches that had for years started at the ferries and ended their tour at Twenty-third Street were giving way to streetcars running on hourly schedule on Third, Fourth, Sixth and Eighth Avenues. Only the present Madison Avenue line ran above Fifty-ninth Street—usually drawn by one horse above Twenty-third Street. The city was zoned, and fares varied with each zone. So did the color of the thin little slip punched as the fare was paid. A schedule of fares and colors was posted in every car. Isaac H. Bromley, of the *Tribune* editorial staff, satirized the punched ticket in this verse that had nation-wide popularity:

Conductor, when you receive a fare,
Punch in the presence of the passenjare!
A blue trip slip for an eight-cent fare,
A buff trip slip for a six-cent fare,
A pink trip slip for a three-cent fare,
Punch in the presence of the passenjare!

Chorus

Punch, brothers, punch! Punch with care!
Punch in the presence of the passenjare!

"The jingle took instant and entire possession of me," wrote Mark Twain later in the *Atlantic Monthly*. "I tried to write but all that came to my pen was 'punch in the presence of the passenjare.' I rolled, tossed and jingled right along; my mind was full of blue, buff and pink trip slips, and of that conductor punching them. . . . It was a nightmare."

A capacious Croton reservoir occupied the site of the present New York Public Library; Union Square had Tiffany's as its center of fashionable shops; the Union League Club built its first home on the north side of it, with the Century Club on the east. The Union Club fringed the eastern side of Madison Square. Farther down a society of its own exclusive Knickerbocker type had circled Washington Square with spacious homes of red brick with white trim—even restricted Gramercy Park or Stuyvesant Square over on Second Avenue, from Fifteenth Street to Seventeenth, could not equal its social austerity. Columbia College had moved far uptown from its Park Place site to East Forty-ninth Street overlooking the New York Central car yards and fronting on a dirt road now called Park Avenue; the College of the City of New York was a big red brick building on Lexington Avenue at Twenty-third Street. Lester Wallack's Theatre, at Broadway and Thirteenth Street, was the fashionable uptown playhouse, with the Union Square Theatre as its rival around the corner.

And of course at Fourteenth Street and Irving Place was the memorable Academy of Music, forever rich in recollection of the men and women artists who then graced the opera stage—Adelina Patti in particular. Perhaps the "diamond horseshoe" of the present Metropolitan Opera House in its heyday twenty years ago reflected more dazzling wealth than the old Academy in its time of glory—but its appeal, social and lyric, broke down even Greeley's early antagonism to opera. He was a frequent attendant. So was everyone who counted in the life of the community.

Nevertheless, with all its marvelous advance in trade and finance, its leadership of the nation, tight little Manhattan Island was still all that constituted the city of New York. Its area had not extended beyond the original Knickerbocker twelve and a half miles from the Battery to Spuyten Duyvil and only two and a half miles across at its widest—a little more than thirty square miles in all. Ferries from Catherine, Fulton and Wall Streets crossed the East River to the thriving city of Brooklyn, one to Long Island City and nine across the Hudson to the Jersey shore; a bridge at Third Avenue spanned the Harlem River to the rural Bronx. Even then the cry was for a Greater New York—one befitting its future. It took thirty years, however, to convince Brooklyn, Queens, Staten Island and the Bronx to unite with Manhattan as one municipality of 5,000,000 citizens, many millions of annual expenditures and a great many millions of bonded indebtedness.

When Whitelaw Reid joined the *Tribune* staff in those days—1868—with youth and the confident spirit of the times, he was destined soon to rank with New York City's four great editors whose careers for nearly half a century, beginning with Bennett in 1835, were the top ambition of newspapermen everywhere. Dana had just bought the *Sun;* Bennett's *Herald* was at the peak of its marvelous prosperity; Raymond was out of politics and deep in the editorial work he did so well. Of these men who occupied such a foremost place in their profession three were of *Tribune* origin—Greeley, Raymond and Dana. It was of Raymond that Greeley had written to Rufus Griswold in 1839: "I decided to keep him because I believe that I can train him in the way he should go."

Of course there were other men of reputation then in New York City journalism—William Cullen Bryant was rounding out a half-century as editor of the *Evening Post;* Manton Marble was making the *World* the "best-written but least-read" newspaper in the morning field; Thurlow Weed, now, like Raymond, out of politics, had bought the *Commercial Advertiser* and was back to his original job as an editor; Erastus Brooks had the *Evening*

Express, and David Hale, who in 1831 had chased young Greeley out of the *Journal of Commerce* office as a runaway apprentice, was still its presiding head and Greeley's intimate friend.

Newspapers, like all else in the country, were responding to the enterprising spirit of the postwar days—the cable, the telegraph, the special correspondent reporting from the battlefields of Europe or, like Henry Stanley, finding the lost Livingston in "darkest Africa" for the New York *Herald*. No editor then thought of the cost of gathering news or of the heavy investment in faster and faster presses that whirled increasing thousands of printed pages speedily to more and more readers. "The whole, the boundless, world" was now a scene of intensive daily search for all that could be put in a newspaper column to inform, instruct or astound —and in the effort dollars did not count. Greeley told for all the story of advance in newspaper-making when on April 10, 1871, he wrote of the *Tribune*'s thirty years:

"Originally 'The Tribune' was a small folio sheet, employing about twenty persons in its production; it is now one of the largest journals in the world, containing ten to fifteen times as much as at first and employing on each issue four to five hundred persons. The total cost of its production for the first week was $525; it is now over $20,000 per week. Other journals have been established by a large outlay of capital and many years of faithful, patient effort; the 'Tribune' started on a very small capital, to which nothing has been added except through the abundance and liberality of its patrons. They enabled it to pay its way almost from the outset. Taking the average of these thirty years our efforts have been amply rewarded . . . from regular receipts. We have rendered an earnest and zealous, though by no means indiscriminate, support in the earlier half of 'The Tribune's' existence to the Whig party; and through the latter half to the Republican party—but we have asked no favor of either and no odds of any man but that he should pay for whatever he chose to order."

"Asked no odds of any man"—what a touchstone of power! Yet that spirit did not abide in Greeley alone. An editorial roll of honor in those far-off times was made up of men throughout the country who today are but dim figures as seen through the deepening shadows of so many yesterdays. They boldly followed policies of character building for their newspapers that ever since have been, and must ever be, an encouragement to all editors who believe in integrity, independence and usefulness to their community.

Among them were Samuel Bowles of the Springfield *Republican*, George D. Prentice of the Louisville *Journal*, Arunah S. Abell of the Baltimore *Sun*, Henry Watterson of the Louisville *Commercial*, Murat Halstead of the Cincinnati *Commercial*, Joseph Medill of the Chicago *Tribune*, Joseph R. Hawley of the Hartford *Courant*, Gideon Welles of the Hartford *Times*, Henry Anthony of the Providence *Journal*, Nathan Hale (father of Edward Everett Hale) of the Boston *Advertiser*, Cassius M. Clay of the Lexington, Kentucky, *True American*, Tom Ritchie of the Richmond *Enquirer*, George W. Childs of the Philadelphia *Public Ledger*, Joseph W. Gray of the Cleveland *Plain Dealer*.

Those men won distinction in an era of what is called personal journalism—the last of its type. The title of a newspaper did not then mean so much to the reading public as did the name of its editor. It was "Greeley's *Tribune*," "Bowles's *Republican*," "Abell's *Sun*," "Bennett's *Herald*," "Joe Medill's *Tribune*," "Ritchie's *Enquirer*," "Blair's Washington *Globe*," "Hawley's *Courant*," and so on.

Naturally there were many stories of Bennett, of Raymond and of Greeley—the whys and wherefores of their rise to prominence. The truth is, of course, that each man had it in himself. Of Greeley it was said that Dana was really responsible for broadening the *Tribune* during the 1850's; that managing editor Sidney Howard Gay had held Greeley in check during the war years; that John Russell Young had really forced him into the fight on Johnson; and, finally, that Reid had come into commanding influence at just the right time for a tired and worried Greeley.

These four men, with Raymond, were grouped in the newspaper talk of the day as Greeley's "brilliant managing editors"—as they undoubtedly were. Undoubtedly, too, they had weight in editorial councils, but if any record of a newspaper's direction is crystal clear it is that of Greeley with his *Tribune*. "On the nail! On the nail!" was his familiar urge to his associates for promptness and vigor in news and opinion. There was just one mind, and only one, as definitely when the policies were attacked as when applauded. Dana always frankly said so. In 1870 Reid wrote to his chief: "I am always sorry when you leave and delighted when you get within consulting distance. I feel more comfortable when once in twenty-four or forty-eight hours I can get to you for advice or counsel."

Of the four New York City editors, Raymond, in 1869, was the first to pass on; Bennett followed in March 1872, and Greeley in November. Dana was the sole survivor when I began work on the *Tribune*. I recall seeing him on several occasions later on in the old red-brick *Sun* building still standing at the Frankfort Street base of Printing House Square, in a room not much larger than a spacious clothes closet; it opened out on the reporters' room through a door that was never closed. Through one window he had a broad view of City Hall Park. A faded rug covered less than half the floor space. An old iron hat-and-coat rack, a newspaper file and two cane-bottom chairs, beside his own, completed the furnishings. At a small table with a single row of reference books and above it an autographed photograph of his old chief Greeley looking down on him from the wall, Dana sat reading or writing—skull-capped, spectacled and gray-bearded—proud of his sharp, concise phrases and content as he crossed sixty years of age to move placidly along on the ebbing tide of life. Quite a contrast he was in appearance and opinion with the Dana of Brook Farm in 1841, then more eager than Greeley to arraign capital for its selfishness, and not yet planning a newspaper career.

A century has passed since he, with Greeley, Bennett and Raymond, made Printing House Square an historic newspaper center; there remain today as the only evidence that it ever existed two bronze statues, one of Benjamin Franklin and one of Horace Greeley—both like lonely, wind-and-rain-battered memorial panels bearing fading inscriptions that remind you of so much that once was but is no more.

Dana gathered around him such a notable staff of men—there were no women on the *Sun* in those days—that to have been one of "Dana's young men" assured a welcome on every other newspaper.

Eugene Field, brilliant columnist of the Chicago *Tribune*, wrote of the "Noo York Sun" and Dana and the man who worked there in these popular verses:

Thar showed up out'n Denver in the spring uv '81
A man who'd worked with Dana on the Noo York Sun.
His name wuz Cantell Whoppers, 'nd he wuz a sight ter view
Ez he walked inter the orfice 'nd inquired fer work ter do.
There warn't no places vacant then,—fer be it understood,
That wuz the time when talent flourished at that altitood;
But thar the stranger lingered, tellin' Raymond 'nd the rest
Uv what perdigious wonders he could do when at his best,
Till finally he stated (quite by chance) that he hed done
A heap uv work with Dana on the Noo York Sun.

Wall, that wuz quite another thing; we owned that ary cuss
Who'd worked f'r Mr. Dana must *be good enough fer* us!
And so we tuk the stranger's word 'nd nipped him while we could,
For if we didn't *take him we knew John Arkins would;*
But we *set back and cackled, 'nd hed a power uv fun*
With our man who'd worked with Dana on the Noo York Sun.

This feller, Cantell Whoppers, never brought an item in,—
He spent his time at Perrin's shakin' poker dice f'r gin.
Whatever the assignment, he wuz allus sure to shirk,
He wuz very long on likker and all-fired short on work!
If any other cuss had played the tricks he dared ter play,
The daisies would be bloomin' over his remains to-day;
But somehow folks respected him and stood him to the last,
Considerin' his superior connections in the past.
So, when he bilked at poker, not a sucker drew a gun
On the man who'd worked with Dana on the Noo York Sun.

But when Dana came to Denver in that fall uv '83,
His old friend Cantell Whoppers disappeared upon a spree;
The very thought uv seein' Dana worked upon him so
(They hadn't been together fer a year or two, you know),
That he borrered all the stuff he could and started on a bat,
And, strange as it may seem, we didn't see him after that.
So, when ol' Dana hove in sight, we couldn't understand
Why he didn't seem to notice that his crony wa'n't on hand;
No casual allusion, not a question, no, not one,
For the man who'd "worked with Dana on the Noo York Sun."

We dropped the matter quietly 'nd never made no fuss,—
When we get played for suckers, why, that's a horse on us!—
But, as for us, in future we'll be very apt to shun
The man who "worked with Dana on the Noo York Sun."

But the era of personal journalism is now over. Newspapers have become great enterprises which only in exceptional instances may one man guide. Charles Dickens was closest to the truth when, in 1868, he said to Greeley: "Your newspapers will not reach their greatest power until they cease to be the personal opinions of an individual and become great institutions like the London 'Times'."

CHAPTER XXVI

"To Write Nobly is Better Than to Rule"

YOU HAVE ONLY to read Greeley's lecture "Literature as a Vocation" to query whether a reputation as great as that which he won in journalism did not await him in the world of letters had he persisted in his earliest ambition. Certainly he had a deep love for literature. As a boy he had turned from farming and at twenty-three had no thought of a newspaper career when as his first venture he established the *New Yorker*. He slaved for it—to make it "the magazine I have in my mind's eye"—even after Thurlow Weed had tempted him into "the boiling sea of politics." On his sixtieth and last Christmas, Greeley confessed that his life had been too hurried to make many friends. That did not annoy him greatly, but, he said, "I most regret the lack of time for reading books." In politics he had alliances with prominent men but they were never counted as friendships; in literary circles, however, he had many prized associations and in such company he passed his only unharried moments.

Greeley's mastery of newspaper publication, his keenness for the detection of public opinion, his industry and his spirit are well-known features of his unique career; but few are equally aware of his intimacy with the masters of world literature—an intimacy that meant countless hours of thoughtful reading. In his own day there were some observers who regarded the education of Horace Greeley by Horace Greeley as a marvel of achievement, for it resulted in a purity, conciseness and vigor of expression that few writers equaled. Yet he could see to read but dimly, his early years were a desperate struggle to advance, and his mature life a period of sharp conflict and constant wandering around the country. Who can say how this man of wilderness choppers found the time and had the grit thus to seek and absorb the literary treasures of the centuries?

Unquestionably Greeley's failure to secure a permanent place for himself in literature was the unsatisfied ambition of his life. It was always in his mind to seek it; particularly after 1865 he planned and planned to devote himself to it, but unfortunately politics still had its strangle hold of him. Yet it was in those years that Edwin Lawrence Godkin, the erudite editor of *The Nation*, and later of the New York *Evening Post*, said of him, "He has an enthusiasm that never flags and an English style which for vigorous tenseness, clearness and simplicity has never been surpassed except by William Cobbett." Cobbett, though he ranks close to the top of England's essayists, never had any schooling; and Greeley in his last years said, "From the bottom of my heart I thank my parents for their wise decision not to send me to college when opportunity was offered by our neighbors. Much as I have needed a fuller, better education I rejoice that I am indebted to no one for my schooling." Nevertheless, both Greeley and Cobbett, who, according to Godkin, "scraped knowledge together by fits and starts" out of the book of life, used it with surpassing skill. It has been asked whether Yale, or Harvard, or Princeton, or Oxford would have explored the minds of these two men and better fitted them for expression of thought than their own eager, tireless, search did. On that score Greeley wrote:

Of our country's great men, beginning with Ben Franklin, I estimate that a majority had little if anything more than a common-school education, while many had less. Washington, Jefferson and Madison had rather more; Clay and Jackson somewhat less; Van Buren perhaps a little more; Lincoln decidedly less. How great was his consequent loss? I raise the question; let others decide it. How far Lincoln's two flatboat voyages down the Mississippi to New Orleans are to be classed as educational exercises above or below a freshman's years in college, I will not say; doubtless some freshmen learn more, others less, than those journeys taught him.

Yet Greeley never undervalued the work of a teacher, and in his lecture "Teaching and Teachers" he gave that profession first place among the influences which would someday rule the world. "Not the warrior nor the statesman," he declared, "nor yet the master worker as such, but the teacher in our day leads the vanguard of Humanity. Whether in the seminary or by the wayside, by uttered word or printed page, our true King is not he who best directs the siege or sets the squadrons on the battlefield, or heads the charge, but he who can and will instruct and enlighten."

"Heed not the croaker's warning that the world overflows with books and authors," urged Greeley. "So it did in Solomon's time—yet how many very good books that mankind could hardly spare have been written since! Truly the universe is full of light and has been these thousands of years, yet for all that we would not dispense with the sunshine of to-morrow! . . . Consider how . . . men of thought can still instruct the wisest and delight the most critical among us and you will conclude that to write nobly, excellently, is a far better achievement than to rule, to conquer or to kill—it is to look down from an eminence which monarchs can feebly emulate and the ages can scarcely wear away. . . . The world could not spare Cicero's Orations, but what recks it of his Consulate!"

In 1864 Greeley began work on *The American Conflict*. Those two large volumes are the earliest exhaustive analysis of the Civil War era. "I proffer it," wrote Greeley, "as my contribution toward a fuller and more vivid realization of the truth that God governs the world by moral laws as active, immutable and all-pervading as can be operative in any other."

In an office in Bible House, owned by the American Bible Society and still standing at Fourth Avenue, Eighth to Ninth Streets, he hid himself from all callers for at least half of each day. For the first time in his life he employed a secretary; to the joy of his publishers he also dictated instead of writing. It was then that he referred to himself despairingly as "the slave of a newspaper" and assured Whitelaw Reid that he intended to free himself for literary projects such as his *Recollections of a Busy Life*—a volume which in 1869 had a large sale, for by that time the Jefferson Davis bail-bond furor had died away.

In the late months of 1867 the *Tribune* published a series of letters "from all points" between Paris and Cairo and then to Jerusalem, written by a touring correspondent who signed himself Mark Twain. In book form those letters were destined to delight generations even unto this day under the title *The Innocents Abroad*. Greeley thus gave to that famous writer what the latter frankly termed in his autobiography "my first notoriety"—just as thirty years earlier Greeley had given Dickens his first recognition in America by publishing in the *New Yorker* a story entitled "Delicate Attentions," by "Boz." He had scissored it from the London *Monthly*, a magazine as obscure as was Dickens himself at the time. To both Dickens and Twain the publications by Greeley were introductions to fortune for which both showed appreciation in a lasting friendship. In May 1843 Greeley chanced to get a copy of Carlyle's *Past and Present* before it was on sale in this country; at once he reported over his own initials to *Tribune* readers: "This is a great book, a noble book. There has been no new work of equal value in a century. . . . Beg or borrow it. . . . There has been no work containing so much Gospel since the days of John the Baptist. I have read it all but will go without sleep until I have one or two more readings. It does tell folks more truth than they have ever yet known."

While tutoring on Staten Island in 1843, Henry David Thoreau formed a friendship with Greeley—"very much in earnest" and "as hale and hearty New Hampshire boy as one would wish to meet." Greeley advised him "now be a little neighborly," and helped him by placing his manuscript with *Graham's* and other magazines. "This is the best kind of advertisement for you," he assured him. "Though you may write with an angel's pen yet your work will have no mercantile value unless you are known as an author. Emerson would be twice as well known if he had written for the magazines a little just to let common people know of his existence." During the next twenty years Thoreau visited "my old friend Greeley" on several occasions, the two men going over to Brooklyn on a Sunday morning to hear Henry Ward Beecher at Plymouth Church. While Mrs. Greeley was abroad they bachelored two week ends at the Chappaqua farm.

In a letter dated May 19,1848, Thoreau showed his appreciation of Greeley's kindness:

My Friend Greeley—

I have to-day received from you fifty dollars. It is five years that I have been maintaining myself entirely by manual labor—not getting a cent from any other quarter or employment. Now this toil has occupied so few days—perhaps a single month, spring and fall each—that I must have had more leisure than any of my brethren for study and literature. I have done rude work of all kinds. From July 1845, to September 1847, I lived by myself in the forest, in a fairly good cabin, plastered and warmly covered, which I built myself. There I earned all I needed, and kept to my own affairs.

My Friend, how can I thank you for your kindness? Perhaps there is a better way—I will convince you that it is felt and appreciated. Here have I been sitting idle, as it were, while you have been busy in my cause, and have done so much for me. I wish you had had a better subject; but good deeds are no less good because their object is unworthy.

The Katahdan paper can be put in the guise of letters, if it runs best so; dating each part on the day it describes. Twenty-five dollars more for it will satisfy me; I expected no more, and do not hold you to pay that—for you asked for something else, and there was delay in sending. So, if you use it, send me twenty-five dollars now or after you sell it, as is most convenient; but take out the expenses that I see you must have had. In such cases carriers generally get the most; but you, as carrier here, get no money but risk losing some, besides much of your time; while I go away, as I must, giving you unprofitable thanks. Yet trust me, my pleasure in your letter is now wholly a selfish one. May my good genius still watch over me and my added wealth!

How helpful for several years Greeley was to Thoreau is told in this letter to him under date of November 23, 1852:

My dear Thoreau:

I have made no bargain—none whatever—with G. P. Putnam concerning your mss. I have indicated no price to him. I handed over the mss. because I wish it published, and presumed that was in accordance both with your interest and your wishes.

And now I say to you that if he will pay you $3 per printed page I think that will be very well. I have promised to write something for him myself, and shall be well satisfied with that price. Your 'Canada' is not so fresh and acceptable as if it had just been written on the strength of a last summer's trip, and I hope you will have it printed in Putnam's Monthly. But I have said nothing to his folks as to price and will not till I hear from you again.

Very probably, there was some misapprehension on the part of George Curtis. I presume the price now offered you is that paid to writers generally for the "Monthly."

As to Sartain, I know his magazine has broken down, but I guess he will pay you. I have not seen but one of your articles printed by him, and I think the other may be reclaimed. Please address him at once. I have been very busy the past season, and had to let everything wait that could till after Nov. 2d.

Yours,

Horace Greeley

H. D. Thoreau, Esq.

The kindly relation with Thoreau was not uncommon for Greeley. Every striver for literary fame had in him an encouraging ally. Edgar Allan Poe in February 1847 got a loan of $50 to help save his *Broadway Journal;* at the same time Greeley gave "The Raven" its first publication in a daily newspaper. "When I began my career as a poet I remember that you took some notice of me, for which I am grateful," wrote Buchanan Read from Florence, Italy, to Greeley on November 27, 1854. "Knowing your interest in whatever touches or advocates the welfare of humanity I am bold to address you on the subject of a poem I have composed entitled 'The New Pastoral.' It is written to exalt the commonest sphere of labor, to teach the man at the plow to feel as proud of his profession as the banker or lawyer. I believe that it is the first attempt at a poem purely American." So help went, too, to

Phoebe and Alice Cary, living poorly in Cincinnati when Phoebe's famous poem "One Sweetly Solemn Thought" stirred the country. Greeley persuaded the sisters to move to New York City and there achieve a national reputation.

Thus one can follow Greeley's love for literature from the days of Mrs. Felicia Dorothea Hemans' *Casabianca*, and Mrs. Lydia Huntly Sigourney's poems in the *New Yorker* to the historic banquet to Charles Dickens in New York City April 18, 1868, nearly thirty years later. Greeley was chosen to preside in tribute not only to the publication of "Delicate Attentions" in his magazine but also to his discovery of the merits of *The Old Curiosity Shop*. He published it serially in the *Weekly Tribune*. He was orator, too, at the centennial celebration of the birthday of Robert Burns on January 25, 1869.

In 1870 came the Greeley book entitled *Essays Designed to Elucidate the Science of Political Economy*. It was in fact a defense of a protective tariff. More interesting than the book, however, on the subject was this letter written to Schuyler Colfax as early as July 29, 1845:

> Let me give you, in my own loose way, my ideas of our political economists. Alexander Hamilton was the first of them in more ways than one, as indeed he was the first in a good many things. Hamilton essentially founded our government. Marshall cemented and preserved it. Jefferson has written some very strong, shrewd things on this as on other questions, but he always wrote what the exigencies of the moment (that is, his interests or his prejudices) required, and he is consequently glaringly inconsistent. Madison has written ably and luminously on this subject and some things he has said have a permanent value. Old John Adams wrote nothing on the subject worth speaking of and John Quincy does not well understand it. Monroe knew very little as we all know, Jackson ditto with respect to Jefferson. Clay has discussed it with consistency and lucid ability. Webster has spoken eloquently on both sides of this question (tariff). Calhoun takes a deeper view of the subject than any of the public speakers of our time.

On February 3, 1871, his sixtieth birthday, Greeley published his last work, *What I Know About Farming*. This completed a seven years' record of literary output difficult for many authors at any age to equal. Only he himself realized how worn down he was. In his diary he summed up what all his activities meant as he stood on the line of three-score years and sensed at last the emptiness of constant strife. "My sixtieth Christmas is going soberly, and with an abundance of work," he wrote from his wifeless home to Mrs. Allen. "I am not richer, unless in friends. After ten years of hard work I begin to long for peace and rest—have hardly known what home has meant for years, and am too busy to enjoy anything. I hope I shall not die as ignorant as I now am. I most regret the lack of time for reading books."

Despite his heavy literary efforts and lecture tours, Greeley never neglected his work in the *Tribune* office. His associates marveled more than ever at his endurance, for he never missed an appointment and never failed to do his daily quota of "brevier," as editorial writing was then called. More to the point he never failed to show by his comments that he had read the *Tribune* thoroughly every morning.

In 1869 John Hay joined the *Tribune* group. Greeley and Hay, of course, had not got on well together during the Lincoln period, but Greeley waived those incidents when Reid engaged Hay, and soon paid him tribute as being "the most brilliant writer ever on the staff." In that year Hay's famous "Little Breeches" and "Jim Bludso" verses were published in the *Tribune,* followed by others of his "Pike County Ballads."

Edwin Lawrence Godkin in his studies of things American after more than forty years in this country, wrote in his *Life and Letters*:

The Tribune in particular excited my warm admiration. The writers were all, as it were, partners in a common enterprise, and Greeley, though all-powerful, was simply looked upon as a primus inter pares. The influence of such a journal was deservedly high. Greeley from the outset had supplied the spirit which made the paper an authority in the land, for he sacrificed everything—advertisers, subscribers, and all else—to what he considered principle. . . . During the three or four years before the war, to get admission to the columns of "The Tribune," almost gave the young writer a patent of literary nobility, and Greeley in those years welcomed talent, male and female, from any quarter and in every field.

Tyler Dennett, former president of Williams College, in his recent *Life of John Hay* carries this distinction beyond the war years, for he declares that "in 1870 'The Tribune' had the ablest set of writers that any newspaper of the day could boast."

It was in that same year that Joseph Bucklin Bishop found that the *Tribune* office "harbored a moral and intellectual spirit that I met nowhere else during thirty-five years of journalistic experiences. . . . Every word 'The Tribune' printed was believed implicitly because Greeley was the man behind it." Just graduated from Brown University, Bishop persuaded Greeley to give him an opportunity. He remained thirteen years with the *Tribune*, to be followed by eighteen years as associate editor of the *Evening Post* and, following Godkin, as editor of that newspaper.

After his retirement Bishop wrote *Notes and Anecdotes of Many Years*, and in that book he gave this fascinating description of life in the *Tribune* office the year he joined the staff:

> In those days the editorial office of the "The Tribune" was a thoroughly democratic place. It was situated in the fourth story of an old ramshackled five-story building, and consisted of the most thoroughly ill-furnished and ill-kept suite of rooms imaginable. There was scarcely a desk in any one of them that had not been for many years in a state of well-nigh hopeless decrepitude, and scarcely a chair with a full complement of its original legs, the piece of board nailed to the side. There were only about half enough chairs and desks to go round. Reporters and even editors were obliged to take turns in writing their copy, and each man secured a share of a desk only after a considerable period of service. One of my earliest recollections of the editorial room is hearing Isaac H. Bromley say to Clarence Cook, who was the most merciless of art critics: "Cook, are you through with that desk? If you are, scrape off the blood and feathers and let me come."

The editorial room fronted on Printing House Square and was entered through the reporters' room. A half-partition of wood and glass, the latter very dirty and never washed, separated the two. It was only eight feet in height, but, low as it was, to the minds of the reporters it was the most formidable of barriers. They regarded the front room as the very heaven of their aspirations. They looked with admiration and envy upon the men—George Ripley, Whitelaw Reid, Bayard Taylor, William Winter and John Hay—who walked daily through the city room into it. For, ill-furnished and ill-kept as "The Tribune" office was in those days, it harbored a moral and intellectual spirit that I met nowhere else during my thirty-five years of journalistic experiences.

Every member of the force, from reporter to editor, regarded it a great privilege to be on "The Tribune" and to write for its columns, and that there could be no higher ambition than to write for the same page as that for which Horace Greeley wrote. All the reporters who were ambitious studied that page with care daily seeking to imbibe the spirit and to fit themselves to write ultimately for it.

The quaintest figure in the place was that of the great editor, Horace Greeley, careless and dishevelled in dress as if he had put his clothes on in the dark, with the round and rosy face of a child and a cherubic expression of simplicity and gentleness. At the time of which I am speaking he occupied a small room on the second floor of the building, access to which was by means of an iron stairway from the counting room.

"The Tribune" was a tremendous force in the country because of the personal faith of the plain people in the honesty of its editor. Every word "The Tribune" printed was believed implicitly because he was the man behind it.

The power that he wielded was not equaled by any editor of his time—neither has it been equaled by any editor since.

There could have been no more fitting close to the literary career of an editor responsible for such a newspaper as Godkin, Dennett and Bishop outlined than the dinner given to Greeley on his sixty-first birthday—on February 3, 1872—by his publisher friend Alvin Jewett Johnson at the latter's home at 323 West Fifty-seventh Street. It was attended by leading men and women in the literary world, and described as "the most memorable event in literary circles since the Dickens banquet." Three months later at Cincinnati, Greeley was to be nominated for President, and soon thereafter was not to know from the abuse heaped upon him whether he "was running for a penitentiary or the Presidency"; but while celebrating his birthday that night he was surrounded by friends not one of whom had other than kindly feelings.

After Greeley and editor Bowles, of the Springfield *Republican*, had greeted each other with "Hello Sam" and "Hello Horace," there was a round of applause for this tribute by Bowles:

We hail the present evidences of his more thorough emancipation from party and complete uplifting into the realms of independence. What to others seem to be treason, what to others appears and represents a mass of confusions and inconsistencies stands to us a new and firmer effort to lift himself and his great journal wholly out of the arena of purely personal and partisan politics and to place him and it where they belong—in the front rank of independent journalism.

Edward Eggleston, editor of the *Independent* and brother of George Cary Eggleston, could not be present, but this interesting letter sentimentally addressed to "H.G." was read in place of a speech he had expected to deliver:

February 3, 1872

There are certain letters and combinations of letters of the alphabet, if I remember rightly, that are used in algebra to signify unknown quantities. H.G. is not of that sort. If there is any well-known quantity in the ever-changing quadratic equation of American politics, that quantity is represented by H.G.

Some men like H.G., some men hate H.G., but nobody yet suspected H.G. of being a negative quantity. All there is of him is plus, and it is all multiplied by itself—squared and cubed. There the figures break down.

But people have very various ideas of what H.G. means. To the staunch old farmer fed on "The Tribune" from childhood, the letters stand for a white-headed philosopher who pulls his own turnips and milks his own cows. To such a man H.G. is pre-eminently the symbol of sub-soil plowing. To those who laugh at temperate habits, H.G. is hominy and gruel; to friends of the Administration H.G. means Hard on Grant. To free traders, Protection and Pig Iron begin with H.G. To cartoonist Tom Nast H.G. means a white coat.

I am hardly a follower of H.G. I differ with him on five points where I agree with him on one. But I have an unstinted admiration for his sincerity. Mr. Greeley is the most representative man in America. The source of his ascendancy is not in his opinions but in his attachment to them. And the belief that "Old Horace" is in earnest is at the bottom of his wonderful influence.

CHAPTER XXVII

Greeley's "Itch For Office"

WHY CRITICIZE Greeley for the "itch for office" that his opponents talked so much about?

He certainly never used the *Tribune* as a personal campaigning ground; no person ever charged that Greeley sought his support. Charles A. Dana had this to say of Greeley and of editors generally in public life:

When I hear that commonplace criticism, which in many quarters is so freely launched against the memory of Horace Greeley and which deplores, either with sincerity or with sham, the ambition which led him, as we are told, out of his proper sphere into the paths of political aspiration, and made him dream that he could sit in the seat of George Washington—when I hear that criticism I hear it without sympathy and without respect.

When I hear also that there is too much ambition in the minds of intellectual men, gifted with power by nature, trained for public duty by practice and by familiarity with public affairs—when I hear that I feel that the evil that we suffer from, on the contrary, is that there is too little of such ambition; too little of that high aspiration which aims boldly and freely at the noblest rewards which the people have to give; too little of that readiness to submit one's self to the most grave and serious duties which the people can impose.

Of all of Greeley's experiences in life none could possibly have equaled in unhappiness for himself the trials he surely would have had in public office. No one knew this better than he did, yet like the moth fluttering around a candle flame he ignored the peril and in 1872 paid the penalty of death.

The first suggestion of Greeley's name in connection with public office was early in the winter of 1840-41 while he was in a "blessed if I know" puzzle as to what to do. His friend Griswold upbraided him for not demanding a job. Greeley replied: "You are displeased that I am not an applicant for office. I can't help it. That road is too muddy and cut up with throngs of hungry travellers. I do not believe that even you would have respected me, and I would not respect myself. I do not regard either money or office as the supreme goal. Though I have never had either I have been so near to both to see what they are worth. I regard principle and self-respect as more important."

In 1846, Greeley was mentioned for governor by his friend Sanford, of Amsterdam. He promptly informed Weed, "I wrote Sanford that there are forty different reasons why it would be the maddest foolery ever started and why it would not only expose me to needless ridicule but would be certain to prove the worst kind of a joke. All I bother you about this nonsense is this: If Sanford should succeed in getting my name in some newspaper or other, say to John Young that I am as at present advised for him for Governor against any other man and I am for any other man but myself. Don't mention this absurd business to anyone."

Just one public office fell to Greeley's lot—that of member of Congress for a ninety-day unexpired term from December 5, 1848, to March 4, 1849. His course there may be taken as a pattern of his activities in any office he might hold. He was in his seat promptly at eleven o'clock every morning to begin the day's work. There were seldom more than twenty other members present. He did not believe in empty desks doing the nation's business, and his demand for a roll call forced a majority of members to reluctant attendance. Seward wrote to Weed: "Greeley is doing himself ungracious service in trying to reform the House all at once. I am sorry—but who can reason with him?"

But the sensational thing that Greeley did was to expose the twenty-cents-a-mile swindle by which many Congressmen charged for circuitous routes from home to Washington, though actually traveling by direct road. Thousands of dollars were thus illegally taken. The truth of his revelations was never challenged, but had he not been editor of the *Tribune* the results to him while in Congress would certainly have been more unpleasant than they were. "I have divided the House into two parties," he wrote Griswold, "one that would like to see me extinguished, and the other is one that couldn't be satisfied without a hand in doing it."

To Margaret Fuller, then in Rome, in a letter dated January 29, he wrote this interesting review of his experiences: "I have only been home once since Congress assembled, and then for two days only—the last two of 1848. I am very much engrossed here with woes and duties, to say nothing of quarrels, with which I am completely environed. Elected to the House by accident, and a successor already chosen, I resolved to do what good I might in these brief months, being my first and quite likely my last of official life. So I commenced resisting abuses and prodigal expenditures, and soon had a whole swarm of hornets about my ears. It is delightful to see with what avidity those who profit by every abuse rush to the rescue when one is assailed. Thus, in four months, I made myself the most thoroughly detested man who ever sat in Congress, enveloped by a crowd who long and pray for a chance to extirpate me. They have had three or four rushes at me, but have not thrown me yet. They mean to expel me or disgrace me somehow if they can. We shall see. I shall be very glad to see the last of the session and go home. March 4 is the happy day!"

Nevertheless, Greeley later wrote: "I look back upon those three months in Congress as among the most profitably employed of any in the course of my life. I saw things from a novel point of view and if I came away from the Capitol no wiser than I went there the fault was entirely my own." Yet, if Greeley had done nothing while in Congress but make his fight for homesteading he would have scored a much needed public service. He rooted that issue deep in the minds of the people and never failed through the next fourteen years consistently to insist upon its enactment.

"If I had my way there would never be another auction of public land," declared Greeley. "Secure to all as far as possible a chance to earn a living on the soil; then if they will run away from it and shiver and starve in cities, why, there is no help for them. But shame on the laws that send an able, willing man to the almshouse or to any form of beggary when soil on which he would gladly work is barred against him and awarded by this government of freedom to those who have the money to pay for it." If any one law ever peopled a wilderness the Homestead Act of 1862 did, and no name has right to a higher place of credit for it than that of Congressman Greeley.

When, in January 1861, the news came from Springfield that Seward was to be Lincoln's secretary of state, the legislature, then in session at Albany, had to choose another man for the new term of senator. Though the Weed machine had been badly crippled by events at Chicago, it had a governor in Edward D. Morgan. As in the Seward days, Weed made headquarters openly in the Governor's room; the Republican legislature, however, was not such a cordial atmosphere for him as in other years. The Weed candidate was William M. Evarts, who had led the New York delegation at Chicago and whose reputation seemed to assure his election.

But there was another and larger issue than any man—the Weed machine. It was still dazed and hanging over the ropes as a result of Seward's defeat at Chicago, and many Republicans were determined to give it a knockout blow. Who could most surely deliver it? Obviously Greeley, and in Greeley they found a willing candidate. "I would like to go to the Senate," he wrote Beman Brockway, "and would not like to go into the Cabinet. I don't like official routine, with great big dull dinners. I do like my little farm. Besides, I belong to 'The Tribune.' As a Senator I could continue to write for it. I am sure I can do nothing to make myself Senator, and I am even more sure I would not try very hard if certain of success."

With a candidate such as Evarts the way seemed clear to Weed; but the first ballot showed Evarts 42, Greeley 40, Ira Harris

25; next ballot—Greeley 42, Evarts 39, Harris 22. Dana and Brockway were Greeley's spokesmen. Evarts had plainly run his course, but Greeley advanced to 43, then to 47, and finally to 49. Weed realized that another ballot would nominate Greeley. Forgetting that he had a lighted cigar in his mouth, he pulled another from his pocket, lighted it and, with increasing loudness until it became a frenzied shriek, declared: "Tell the Evarts men to go to *Harris!* TO HARRIS! *TO HARRIS!*"—whom he disliked only less than he now disliked Greeley. Weed's consolation was that at least he did not surrender, as at Chicago, to his discarded partner; but he never again had power to nominate a candidate of his own choice.

Few men knew Greeley more intimately than did Whitelaw Reid or were more aware of Greeley's real attitude toward public office. He gave this opinion in an article in the *Century Magazine* in 1913:

"With my intimate knowledge of Greeley at that period I should hardly have said he had a passion for office. What I did think was that he had a passion for recognition and was very sore at being treated not as an equal and comrade but as a convenience to the machine by Weed and Seward. It was less office that he sought than an opportunity to teach those gentlemen their places and his."

CHAPTER XXVIII

"The Dream of Rest is Over"

WITH Reid in full charge of the *Tribune*, up to Montreal went Greeley in December 1868 to diagnose to Canadians the disease that may be identified on this page as "presidentitis" as he saw it in others, though not then any symptoms of it in himself. He described it in this way:

> Daniel Webster was not only a gentleman but he had the elements of moral greatness. He failed in only one respect and in this respect I differ with him—he wanted to be President and I don't. We have seen one of our greatest men (Chief Justice Salmon P. Chase) making the same blunder. I have seen men who had the disease early and died of it at a very old age. General Lewis Cass died at about 82 and up to the day of his death he wanted to be President. No one escapes who once catches the disease; he lives and dies in the delusion. Being a reader and an observer, at an early age I saw how it poisoned and paralyzed the very best of our public men, and I have carefully avoided it. We at least in our day have a President-elect (Grant) who did not try to be President. He was elected mainly on that account.

But Grant had not been a year in office before he had a second term definitely in mind and acted accordingly. He abandoned himself to the "good hater" radicals of the Republican party with whom as a soldier he had never sympathized. Independent newspapers like the Springfield *Republican*, Cincinnati *Commercial* and Chicago *Tribune* became "ungenerous and unjust," according to Greeley. "We have had greater Presidents than Grant," he wrote on May 6, 1871, "but scarcely one who deserved the running fire of invidious carping and fault-finding to which he has been subjected by these 'independent' oracles.... They treat Grant harshly, captiously, unjustly. We would fain induce its conductors to reconsider and modify their course. They may fancy that they are only disparaging and weakening President Grant, but they are in fact undermining the Republican party." To which Sam Bowles replied in his Springfield newspaper: "If Grant is re-elected he will owe it more to the criticisms he has received—truculent, and possibly unjust sometimes—than he will to the favoring sycophancy of the Philadelphia 'Press' or the hesitating, concealed unfriendliness of the New York 'Tribune'."

Greeley, of course, had to respond to that charge; he lost no time in doing so. "Since we are charged with 'concealed unfriendliness' to President Grant it is clear that we need not defend 'The Tribune' from any possible imputation of servility or sycophancy. And it is certainly true that we are not seeking the re-election of General Grant. Should he be the Republican candidate we shall, of course, support him to the best of our ability; but pending the nomination we may be fairly charged with 'unfriendliness' to running him or any other man for President while he wields the vast patronage of that high office. We ardently desire to see the principle established that a President shall have no aspirations except to serve the country eminently and win thereby a lasting and enviable renown.... Be it understood, then, now, and evermore, that what the *Republican* terms our 'unfriendliness' to General Grant is at all events not 'concealed.'"

There was a basis for editor Bowles's contention that Greeley's *Tribune* was not revealing Greeley's personal opinion, for he had been showing signs of unrest even in 1870. The administration was ready to nominate him for governor that year. "I am a sort of traitor in the camp," wrote Reid to Joseph Medill in Chicago in July 1870. "As I told Greeley last night, I don't want him nominated for Governor. The business of naming him to lead a forlorn hope ought to be over." When Stewart L. Woodford was nominated and defeated, Greeley wrote to Reid: "And now if Grant will only let me alone there is no more trouble ahead for two years at least. At any rate if he should ask me to go to England I shall decline and no one will know anything about the matter. But I guess he won't bother." But Grant did bother and Reid was sounded as to whether Greeley would want that mission. He used only eight words in his emphatic response: "All we want is to be let alone."

Nevertheless Grant persisted. He used John Russell Young, who was still Greeley's close friend, as his connecting link. In a letter dated November 15, 1870, the President wrote to Young: "Greeley is an honest, firm, untiring supporter of the Republican party. He means its welfare at all times. But he is a freethinker, jumps at conclusions, does not get the views of others who are just as sincere as himself in the interest of the party that saved the country and that now wants to pay its honest debts, protect its industries and make progress to a prosperous future. I have long desired a full, free talk with Mr. Greeley because I have confidence in his intentions. I have thought at times of inviting him to Washington for that purpose but I have been afraid that the object might be misinterpreted. If he ever does come to Washington I certainly will try to see him."

How far Young went in his conferences with Greeley is not known, but Reid's words held good. Never were eight truer words spoken—"All we want is to be let alone!" In the *Tribune* office everybody knew it; there the shrill voice of old had lost its sharpness, complaints were few and in kindlier spirit, headaches and fever much too frequent. Early in 1869, Greeley's wife had gone to England, taking their two daughters with her; a deserted house offered him cheerless welcome at Chappaqua when he went up there week ends to wander over the farm. Work and travel were his refuge from loneliness. "I have hardly known what home has meant for many years," he wrote. In his city house on East Nineteenth Street he kept busy on the concluding chapters of *What I Know About Farming*, and also on his treatise on a protective tariff as a national policy. "The dream of rest is over"; "Work crowds me on every side"; "I have not many friends";

"My life is a fevered march"; "One must be in the world or out of it, so I keep on"—are sentences in his correspondence that tell their own story. He was adrift on the world.

How far adrift Greeley really was during those last two years of his life is clearly revealed in letters to Mrs. Margaret Allen at Jamestown, New York. Their correspondence began in 1864 with his revealing letter to her from the little cottage at Chappaqua outlining his religious creed. It ended eight years later with a letter written from the Choate Sanitarium at Pleasantville, "out of the depths," "before night closes on me forever." It was the last he ever wrote to anyone.

No man ever was close enough to Greeley to have his deeper thoughts. They were reserved for three women to whom he wrote frankly: Mrs. Rebekah Whipple, who grew up with him at Westhaven, Margaret Fuller in Rome, to whom he told the pathetic story of Pickie and of Castle Doleful at Turtle Bay, and Mrs. Allen. They were his only confidantes. Joel Benton, the custodian of the Allen letters, declared that "they constitute the most unreserved correspondence that Greeley ever indited. . . . It furnished for him the most welcome communion and relation he ever had." There a Horace Greeley whom the public never knew is reflected—a Greeley who might have been strong enough to abandon politics and seek repose and comfort had there been for him a home in which, using his own words, "anybody ever lived." Read all the letters, and you will find that for eight years they place her high among the influences of his life. The correspondence would never have had publicity had not her loyalty to her friend stirred her resentment of the charge that he schemed to secure the Liberal nomination for President, and that his death was due primarily to his defeat for election. Greeley's correspondence with her contradicted his enemies, and she felt strongly that she should do her part.

On the advice of P. T. Barnum and Charles A. Dana the letters were given to Joel Benton, with authority to publish those that would accomplish Mrs. Allen's purpose. Her name and her home city were withheld, but assurance was given of her one desire to bear testimony for her friend now that it was impossible for him to speak for himself. Long after her death her identity became known.

The letters having to do with the approaching presidential campaign form a group by themselves and are so presented in that chapter. Several have already been used in appropriate places, but others are summarized or reproduced in full. They begin with one dated September 24, 1870, in which he regrets that he cannot join the pilgrimage to the Good Luck Conference of Universalists as he is going to St. Louis. "I did not see you yesterday," he adds, "or rather you did not find me, because I was obliged to visit my farm and that took all day. But I received your friend's note and beg you to receive this as my response. Tell her that it is the only letter among at least thirty received together that I have yet found time to answer. That health may bless and happiness crown your days and that these may be long in the land, is the fervent prayer of—Yours, Horace Greeley."

Then follows this correspondence:

New York, April 5, 1871

My Friend:

I cannot attend the annual Universalist convention in September, since I must be in the West. Next month I go to Texas. So, you see, my life is all a fevered march, and I now seem unlikely ever to sit down and have a quiet talk with you.

. . . I regret to find you inclined to disparage yourself. There are but two kinds of people on this planet—those who try in some humble way to do good and the other sort. The former are all equals and should so regard themselves, as well as each other. I have no friends who would not be happy and proud of your acquaintance.

I hope to have a long bright day at Chappaqua. And so, dear friend, adieu.

April 20, 1871

My Friend:

I go to Texas reluctantly. There seems no choice but to be in the world or out of it. I am not sufficiently broken down to refuse to bear my part among men, so I keep on. It will be just the same a hundred years hence.

You judge that men will not suffer forever. If to suffer implies pain, I agree with you; in the sense of loss I think that suffering will endure. That is, I believe that the very wicked here will never be quite so well off as though they had been good—that they will never make up the leeway they lost while serving the enemy here. I judge that Mary Magdalene is now and ever will be in a lower grade than Mary, the Mother of Jesus. As to the Scriptures, please consider Daniel XII 5. I do not insist that this refers especially to the future life—I only urge that it indicates the general principles on which the divine government rests. So all that speaks of "rendering to every man according to his works," in these passages, may not especially apply to the future life, but their spirit pervades all God's dealings with man.

I hope that you will yet visit your friends in this city and never fail to count me among them.

Off to Texas—"reluctantly," he insisted—went Greeley early in May, but before leaving he wrote Mrs. Allen:

New York, May 9, 1871

My Friend:

I dropped in at Mr. Barnum's this morning to bring away some things I had left there and inquired if they had heard from you. He gave me your letter and I learned that I also had one. I had hoped that you would write, but I did not request it, wishing it to be your own unprompted act.

On Saturday I went up to say goodbye to Chappaqua. It was cloudy. Everything was drowned in rain and all was rendered gloomy by contrast with the sunshine and your presence on the previous Saturday. On the whole my last day at Chappaqua was not a success.... Mr. Barnum has asked Mrs. R. to visit him at Bridgeport this summer with you and I have promised to spend part of the time there.

My Friend, I charge you not to disparage yourself and especially not to regret that you do not, when I have the pleasure of seeing you, talk mainly philosophy or epigrams. I have a large acquaintance with those who are regarded as brilliant men. They appal and fatigue me, while you charm and cheer me. I pray you not to be like unto them!

New York, August 28, 1871

My Friend:

I want you to assure the P———s that I usually behave better than I did last Thursday. I absolutely needed to go away and rest when I found that there was no use for me till dinner.

Those dripping woods at New Egypt had given me a chill, whereof the net result was neuralgia in my teeth and I was not fit to be around. So I seemed selfish and rude when I was really sick and suffering. Then I had to ride to Bordentown and to lecture there in an open wood at night—and, of course, not one-tenth of the vast crowd could hear a word. After lecturing in this absurd way, we drove up to Trenton and my night's rest was lost.

Dubuque, Iowa, Sept. 24, 1871

My Friend:

Do you care to hear further about these poor old teeth? I think I wrote you that I was leaving New York an invalid, with my face bound up in cotton bandage, neuralgia rampant and generally out of repair. I had to ride all the next three nights and did not gain much. After that I soon wore out my torment by the help of dentists and their severe but transitory affliction.

But for riding nights and speaking outdoors at fairs I should almost enjoy this vagabond life, but I get so weary sometimes that I can hardly stand up. Then I feel the weight of years as I do not when fairly treated.

Yours,
Horace Greeley

On October 7, he "rode straight to Chappaqua" after returning that morning from his western trip. "Lonely as it is, it looks like home after five weeks of travel." He was in no happy mood when later he wrote the two letters that follow:

My Friend:

I have not many friends. My life has been too hurried, and too much absorbed in pressing duties and anxious cares. Of my few friends most are women and these I am proud of. Some of them were schoolmates and know all that may be said in my dispraise. I wish to hold you permanently enrolled among them because hardly one of my older friends is in full religious sympathy with me. Even ——— has gone to the Catholics, as has ———, the only one with whom I am in intellectual rapport; and so I grow old and weary. I need you as the one woman who can understand and appreciate my reveries concerning the Unseen World.

I am right glad that you were here to hear Parepa, though I did not meet you. I am not regularly at the office, though frequently there. Yet, should you ever come to our city again, I wish you would advise me in advance.... I have heard no opera since I went with you. I have never heard Parepa, Nilsson nor even Ristori. I did go to hear Charlotte Cushman last week but as I went alone I had a rather lonely evening. I must hear Nilsson, but when?

And so good-night, my friend, whom I claim not more for myself than for the two daughters who shall survive me.

My Friend: November 14, 1871

I wish it were possible for me to find rest this side of the grave, but it seems not to be. Work crowds me from every side. I do not seek it but it comes. If I could be voted out of the editorship of "The Tribune," I could limit the rest of my work, but duty seems to draw after it incessant application to do more on every side and there is no escape. Shall we never find time to talk matters of higher and enduring moments?

I have been chopping at Chappaqua every Saturday of late, and I have a lot of red cedar cut up into firewood and well-seasoned. You know how pleasant is the odor of burning cedar. Well, I reserve this to warm and light my hearth when I can—at some future day with my family about me, go up and spend three or four consecutive evenings—long, bright evenings—reading choice poetry and discussing higher things than those which engross such dreary letters as this from me.

My Friend: December 28, 1871

My sixtieth Christmas is going soberly and with abundance of work. I am no richer unless in friends for my last ten or twelve years of hard work, and I begin to long for quiet and rest. I have hardly known what home meant for years and am too busy to enjoy anything. I most regret the lack of time to read books. I hope I shall not die so ignorant as I now am.

I called on Mr. Barnum yesterday and walked to church with him. And so, with fervent Christmas wishes for your happiness, I am.

Yours,

Horace Greeley

What to do about Grant's renomination, what to do about the *Tribune's* future should he bolt the ticket, were vexing problems. If in his long career Greeley ever sought an opinion from any other person as to the course to pursue there is no record, but from Mrs. Allen he did. It is strange that in the most important decision of his career he turned for counsel to one having no interest in politics or in newspapers—just a friend remote from the world's activities. "Now give heed to a matter on which I do not wish anyone's good opinion but your own," he wrote to her on November 26, 1871. "But here I am at the head of a newspaper which is a great property and which others mainly own. If it were all mine I might not mind the risk, but it belongs to others and it must be seriously damaged by the course I am inclined to take. Moreover, if I take that course, I shall be widely believed to have thus sacrificed others' property to my own personal resentment—perhaps to my own ambition. Such is my perplexity—such the complex problems which active life is constantly proposing. Take a week to think of this and write me your conclusions."

Evidently Mrs. Allen warned him against bolting Grant. She seems to have said that she did not believe he dared to do it, for he replied on December 4: "My Friend: If I do not dare, please do not forget my reasons. And yet it is possible that I may dare.... And so good-night, for it is very late and my leader on the message yet to be proof-read."

There must have been at least one more restless letter to Mrs. Allen, for on January 9, 1872, he wrote her: "My Friend: I have no excuse for inflicting my tediousness upon you and will say nothing more of my perplexities [about bolting Grant]. 'Nothing is so cowardly as half a million dollars except a full million,' and it is a solemn truth. 'How hardly shall they who have riches enter the Kingdom of God,' is an awful truth. It does not appall me because it strikes so far away, but I know many whom it hits."

Though during that year of 1871 Greeley was discussed as a possible candidate against Grant, there is not one letter or conversation or alliance attributed to him that indicates that his dissatisfaction with Grant reflected ambition on his own part. On June 12, after his return from Texas, at a meeting in his honor at the Lincoln Republican Club, Greeley declared: "I can fully and heartily say that I desire no office, that I need no office and that I certainly shall seek no office whatever; the more quiet and peaceful my remaining days may be the better I shall be pleased. I am weary of fighting over issues that ought to be dead—that, legally, were dead years ago. I trust that the day is not distant wherein, putting aside all things that concern the past, we shall remember that grand old injunction of the Bible, 'Speak to the children of Israel that they go forward'!"

Again he put aside such an ambition when the Lexington, Missouri, *Caucasian* urged him for President. "You err as to the proper candidate," he wrote in reply October 18. "I am not the man you need. I am a ferocious protectionist. I have no doubt that I might be nominated and elected by your help but it would put all of us in a false position. If I, who am adversely interested, can see this, I am sure that your good sense will realize it. You must take some man like Gratz-Brown or Lyman Trumbull and thus help to pacify and unite our country anew."

Still the talk of Greeley persisted. When, in December, it reached an assertion that he was in Washington conferring on his presidential possibilities he took occasion to publish in the *Tribune*: "To the best of our knowledge, Mr. Greeley has been quietly attending to his own business at and in his own home and is happy to confirm the statement by others that he is too erratic, too crotchety and too unreliable to be a party to any back-door intrigue for the Presidency."

To his go-west-young-man friend Grinnell, now congressman from Iowa, Greeley wrote late in January: "Leave my name out of the question as a candidate. We ought to unite upon Supreme Court Justice Davis." And on February 12, to Mrs. Whipple at Westhaven, he said, "I don't want to support Grant for another term if I can help it. I may be constrained to support him but I shall hate to do it." To Beman Brockway: "I have had as much of Grant as I can endure. 'The Tribune' will probably suffer in this fight; if I owned it I would not mind that. I may yet have to support Grant, but I would rather quit editing forever. I shall favor the Cincinnati nomination unless that would require me to oppose protection to home industries. That I cannot do even if it should make me President." To Meeker, out in Greeley, Colorado, he declared on March 28: "Grant's nomination may drive me out of politics and newspapers. I wish I were out of politics and out of journalism forever and able to work moderately for an humble livelihood. Too much care is wearing me out. I should like to be free to spend at least a month with you in Colorado next year."

And then to his old friend William L. Stone, editor of the New York *Commercial Advertiser*, he wrote wearily: "I am tired of notoriety and wish I could shed it as a snake sheds its skin."

On his sixty-first birthday—February 3—there was but one big question torturing Greeley's mind: that question was not whether he would be nominated for President by the Liberal convention; it was what would happen to the *Tribune* if that newspaper should lead a bolt from Grant. Greater love for a newspaper no man ever had than he had for the newspaper he created and which was still recognized everywhere as his, to do with as he pleased. Was the hazard to its prosperity too great for the possible benefits? In 1844 he had arraigned the Abolitionists for nominating a third party ticket that defeated Clay. Four years later he had reluctantly supported Taylor when his heart was really with the Free Soil revolters, and in 1856 he had denounced the Know-Nothings for nominating Millard Fillmore and thus ruining Frémont's chances. Could he now consistently join a movement to bolt Grant?

Finally, to Mrs. Allen, he writes not of his own possible nomination but of his purpose to fight Grant:

March 13, 1872

My Friend:

You see that I am drifting into a fight with Grant. I hate it. I know how many friends I shall alienate by it and how it will injure "The Tribune," of which so little is my own property that I dread to wreck it. Yet, I would despise myself if I pretended to acquiesce in his re-election. I may yet have to support him, but I would rather quit editing papers forever.

The day before the convention met in Cincinnati, Greeley was out for national unity and forecast the appeal he was later to make as a candidate: "The biggest thing before the people is the question of honest men against thieves. What the country needs and imperatively demands is a reform in the administration of government. That is not to be attained by combinations of worn-out political hacks."

As the convention began its sessions he gave to Mrs. Allen this outline of his purpose:

New York, May 1, 1872

My Friend:

I am kept at the office this week by the absence of my lieutenant Reid, who has gone to the Cincinnati convention. I am fighting a battle at this distance with the free traders who want to impose a platform on the convention which will probably defeat its candidate. I am in their way and do not intend to get out of it. They may make the candidate as they please, but not the platform if I can help it.

CHAPTER XXIX

"A Lost Cause but Not a Lost People"

In the Republican national convention of 1860 a single editor, Horace Greeley, because of the confidence that delegates had in his judgment, turned a majority of them away from Senator William H. Seward, of New York, thus forcing the nomination of Lincoln; but in the National Liberal convention of 1872 four editors—Carl Schurz of the St. Louis *Westliche Post*, Samuel Bowles of the Springfield *Republican*, Horace White of the Chicago *Tribune*, and Murat Halstead of the Cincinnati *Commercial*—were unable to prevent the one result which they firmly insisted should not and must not happen there: the nomination of Horace Greeley as their candidate for President.

"Anybody to beat Grant" was the platform and the sole purpose of the "Quadrilaterals," as those four editors were popularly called by the delegates, but in the privacy of their own conclaves "anybody" was not meant to include their fellow journalist Greeley.

To this day no other convention of any party or of any faction has ever had so many editors on its roster, and certainly no equal number ever vacated their editorial chair unitedly to play the role of convention strategists. Led by Schurz, they had determined to give a cultural and intellectual tone to politics. Those in attendance at Cincinnati represented almost every phase of opposition to Grant, from free-trade theorists David A. Wells and Edward Atkinson to political purifier Schurz. Their attitude toward Greeley also had wide range—extending from editor White's outspoken antagonism to the declaration of Alexander K. McClure, then editor of the Philadelphia *Times*, that "there is no man in the country for whom I cherish greater affection"—though on each of the six ballots McClure voted for Supreme Court associate justice David Davis of Illinois.

No political boss ever planned control of a convention with greater zeal than did these leaders of the independent press of the country, nor ever planned so futilely. For after two days and nights of discussion and before declaring the convention adjourned sine die, presiding officer Schurz announced with unconcealed reluctance not only the adoption of a Greeley-prepared plank referring the tariff issue to the Congress districts but, worst of all to Schurz, the nomination of Greeley as the candidate for President. The impossible had become possible! The free traders had lost to Greeley their hold on the platform, and the "Quads" had lost to Greeley their presumed power to dictate the nomination.

No men were ever more confident of their control of a convention than were the Quads. On the eve of the meeting they apportioned chairmanships and committees while dining at the St. Nicholas Hotel, famous for its terrapin, its canvasbacks and its vintage wines. The Quads—Schurz, Bowles, White and Halstead—were the center of the editorial talent in attendance; but there were other editors eager to unite with them in naming a President pledged to rid Washington of politicians. Present were Joseph Pulitzer, then editing Carl Schurz's St. Louis *Westliche Post*, who was made one of the secretaries of the convention; William Cullen Bryant of the New York *Evening Post*, Henry Watterson of the Louisville *Courier-Journal*, Joseph B. McCullagh of the (later) *Globe-Democrat*, William Penn Nixon of the Chicago *Inter-Ocean*, A. K. McClure of the Philadelphia *Times*, John McLean of the Cincinnati *Enquirer*, Oswald Ottendorfer of the *New Yorker Staats-Zeitung*, and Manton Marble of the New York *World*.

Before the convention the Quads invited several of their important newspaper brethren to join them at dinner, but the first evening they did not include Whitelaw Reid, managing editor of the *Tribune* as well as personal representative of Greeley. If present, Reid surely would talk Greeley, and Greeley talk was taboo. "Greeley was this, that and the other in the plain language of the dinner party," declared Watterson, "but I told them that we shall need 'The New York Tribune'. If we invite Reid we cinch it. We all agree that Greeley has no chance of nomination, and so by taking Reid in we eat our cake and have it, too." This tempting analysis secured Reid an invitation; he accepted on condition that the Quads would agree to be his guests at dinner in the event of Greeley's nomination. Certain that Reid would never be their host, all accepted promptly.

For two days and nights the Quads acted as though they had the world in a sling. They united in attacking Justice Davis in all their newspapers on the morning of the convention because there was "too much politics" in his candidacy; for the same reason they also excluded Governor Benjamin Gratz-Brown of Missouri. The selection of a nominee was thus limited by the Quads' dinner party to Charles Francis Adams, Senator Lyman Trumbull and Horace Greeley. The last-named was included solely because they dared not rule him out. Editor McClure had declared himself for a ticket of Justice David Davis and Greeley, and during the dinner that evening he was not careful in his use of words denouncing the Quads syndicated newspaper attacks on the Illinois jurist.

"McClure, what the hell do you want anyhow?" asked Watterson impatiently.

"Want?" shouted McClure. "Want?—from these cranks? Nothing! Not a damn thing!"

There were seven candidates for nomination: Charles Francis Adams of Massachusetts, Justice David Davis of Illinois, Senator Lyman Trumbull of Illinois, Horace Greeley of New York, Benjamin Gratz-Brown of Missouri, Chief Justice Salmon P. Chase of Ohio, Governor Andrew G. Curtin of Pennsylvania. The appeal for them could not prevail against the sound contention that Greeley was the only one who would not have to be introduced to most voters in the thirty-seven states. He and his *Try-bune* had been neighborhood talk across the continent for thirty years. That fact made him the nominee. Charles Francis Adams, our able minister to England during the Civil War years, who led in the voting on five of the six ballots, was too closely patterned in the fashion of his grandfather and father, both of whom had been good Presidents but poor candidates, for both were defeated for re-election.

Two evenings later, as Reid's guests, the Quads offered chilly toasts to the one man they had not wanted as a candidate. "Frostier conviviality I have never sat down to," wrote Watterson. "Horace White looked more than ever like an iceberg, Sam Bowles was diplomatic but ineffusive, Schurz was as a death's-head at the board; Murat Halstead and I through sheer bravado tried to enliven the feast. We separated early and sadly—reformers hoist by their own petard."

A more austere Brahman type of nominee would have appealed strongly to the cultured editorial Quads, but the delegates realized that if they nominated Adams they would have to give him the same advice as, in 1888, General John C. New gave to Benjamin Harrison when the latter was a candidate for President. Harrison was on his way to his first speech-making meeting of the campaign.

"Now, Ben," urged New, "be a little human! Mix in with the boys!"

Harrison replied that he would try. Next day he reported, "I tried it, John, but I failed. I must be myself."

Harrison, too, was defeated for re-election.

Shortly after noon of May 3, as Greeley sat at his desk absorbed in writing an editorial, he was handed a one-word telegram: "Nominated. W.R." He had not expected a result in the balloting at Cincinnati so soon; he really believed also that Senator Trumbull of Illinois would be named. As he read the one-word message his face instantly lighted up with a glow of pleasure. Genuinely astounded and as though seeking confirmation, he looked inquiringly into the faces of men from every department gathering enthusiastically around him; the telegram dropped from his hand to the floor. A crowd thronging the triangle in front of the *Tribune* building was shouting for "Uncle Horace." Plainly overcome by a realization that he had been nominated for the highest office in his government, he at last walked to his office window and for fifteen minutes acknowledged tumultuous greetings.

With Governor Gratz-Brown for vice-president, the Liberal ticket was made up of two editors, both of whom during the campaign were to feel the merciless sting of their own colleagues. The unusual honor paid the profession was rewarded with attacks of unusual coarseness and brutality, especially in Tom Nast cartoons. "It is a crime in journalism," declared the Springfield *Republican* in disgust.

Yet this bitterly assailed leader was a man who had taken the long stride from a tree-chopper's farm to become a national figure as editor of a great newspaper. At a moment that for him should have been one of triumph completing a notable career, he was to realize, as he sat by the bedside of his dying wife, that in the passion of partisan conflict how fleeting is the memory of things done, how unlasting is the acclaim of an earlier day.

Unfortunately, this Greeley of 1872, with his urgent plea for a new day, was not the Greeley of the *Log Cabin* or the early *Tribune*. It was not the weight of years that now bowed his stout frame, or made his nights sleepless. Thus far in life he had known only work and search for knowledge. He knew nothing of play, nothing of companionships, nothing of the lighter side of life.

It was of this man of intense endeavor that editor Henry Watterson reported in his Louisville *Courier-Journal*: "The old man seized his flag and set out on his own account on a tour of the country, and right well this brave apostle of freedom carried himself."

"Swinging around the circle," as President Johnson in 1866 sought to give popular title to his own tour, was not then considered the thing for a presidential aspirant to do. Think of the trains carrying rival presidential candidates, of the radio broadcasts and the monster mass meetings that now make up a national canvass, and then recall that for a brief speaking tour through Ohio, Indiana, and Illinois, Greeley was assailed and cartooned as a "mendicant for votes," a "beggar for office." His determination to talk directly to the people was high in the list of "vagaries" charged against him.

Henry Clay was the only candidate ever to indulge in campaign speeches before Greeley undertook it. In 1832 Clay was silent, but in the 1844 campaign he spoke twice and wrote one letter about the annexation of Texas—all so much to the ballot-box gain of Polk, his silent opponent, that in 1847 Clay wrote to Greeley, "If nominated in 1848 I mean to write no letters, make no speeches—and be mum."

Lincoln was constantly urged during his campaign to elaborate his opinions in a speech. He never did. Following his return from his Cooper Union tour in February 1860 until his inaugural address as President he remained silent except to endorse the Chicago platform in an acceptance letter of four hundred words. "Look over my speeches carefully," he wrote in reply to a request for a new interpretation of the opinions he had expressed in the Douglas Senatorial contest, "and conclude that I meant everything that I said and did not mean anything I did not say and you will have my meaning then and now."

For the first two months of the campaign all the enthusiasm was with Greeley. "Borrow no trouble about the Presidency," the candidate wrote buoyantly to his friend Meeker out in Greeley, Colorado. "If it be for the best that our side comes uppermost, so be it; if not I shall have the more leisure to stop a week with you next year. How are my trees?"

In June the Democratic national convention, held in Baltimore, indorsed the Cincinnati ticket and platform, and Greeley later made an interesting contribution to political history in this letter to Mrs. Allen:

July 16, 1872

I have yours of the 14th and answer it at once because I have hidden where the throng do not find me, and have leisure that may not be mine another day. I was not much interested in the Baltimore Convention.

It did not seem to me possible that I should be nominated at Cincinnati, but I never doubted that Baltimore would accept the candidate of Cincinnati. There would have been no question of this if Cincinnati had nominated Davis, or Adams or Trumbull. It was harder for the Democrats to take me, but there was really no alternative but the utter defeat and probable dissolution of their party. The medicine was nauseous, but the patient was very sick, and could not afford to gratify his palate at the cost of his life.

The really astounding feature of the business is the adoption at Baltimore of the Cincinnati platform. Considering what you and I have known of Democratic hostility to negroes, negro suffrage, etc., it seems scarcely possible to realize that this is the same party that barely ten years ago so execrated the Emancipation policy, and so howled at me when I addressed to Mr. Lincoln my "Prayer of Twenty Millions." It is hard to realize that this was barely ten years ago—I grow dizzy when I think of it. And I can imagine no reason for the adoption of our platform unless the Democrats—I mean the controlling majority—mean to stay on it. For they might have endorsed the ticket and spurned the platform. I have done so myself. Whatever the result of the contest, the Liberal movement is a step in human progress. I do not believe it can ever be retraced.

In accepting the Democratic nomination Greeley made it clear that he receded not at all from his firm Republicanism, but he took his stand on the fundamental ground of maintaining our democratic institutions:

I have a profound regard for the people of that New-England wherein I was born, in whose common schools I was taught. I rank no other people above them in intelligence, capacity and moral worth. But while they do many things well, and some admirably, there is one thing which I am sure they cannot wisely or safely undertake, and that is the selection, for States remote from and unlike their own, of the persons by whom those States shall be represented in Congress. If they *could* do this to good purpose, then republican institutions were unfit, and aristocracy the only true political system.

"No other candidate could have put into his words a greater warmth, a purer sincerity, or a more unselfish devotion to peace than did Greeley," wrote Paul H. Buck in his book *The Road to Reunion.* "From the time Greeley was nominated until a month after the Democratic national convention," wrote editor McClure of Philadelphia, "everything pointed to Greeley's election and a tidal wave that would sweep Greeley into the Presidency seemed certain, but in August the great business interests of the country became alarmed and Greeley's popularity ebbed to a humiliating defeat."

"Greeley has been growing into the affections of his countrymen," said the Democratic New York *World;* "few men will question the honesty and nobility of his character. . . . He may be beaten, but it will not be an easy job."

"Greeley's speeches were marvels of impromptu oratory," wrote Kentucky's Watterson, "mostly homely appeals to the better sense of the people, convincing in their simplicity if the North were in any mood to listen and to reason."

"Grant commenced his administration by saying, 'Let us have peace'," said a *Sun* editorial. "But for more than three years he has kept the country in a turmoil. Now, taking up the disregarded and violated pledge of Grant, Greeley proposes to give the entire nation a generous peace. 'Let us go forward, ignoring the past,' says Greeley. 'No,' responds Grant, 'let us keep our own animosities alive and fight it out on that line.' Will not the people prefer Greeley's pacific program to Grant's belligerent slogan?"

Senator Daniel W. Voorhees, the "Tall Sycamore of the Wabash," and long Democratic leader of the Senate, said, "For elevation of thought, propriety of sentiment and for Christian statesmanship the speeches of Greeley have no parallel in American history."

It was from the New York *Times* that the most bitter arraignment of Greeley came: "If anyone could send a great nation to the dogs, the man is Greeley."

"A false Horace Greeley is being held up to scare the people," wrote editor Bowles in August. "The campaign is a shower of mud," commented the New York *Sun.* "We have watched eight campaigns," declared the New York *Observer,* "but for lying

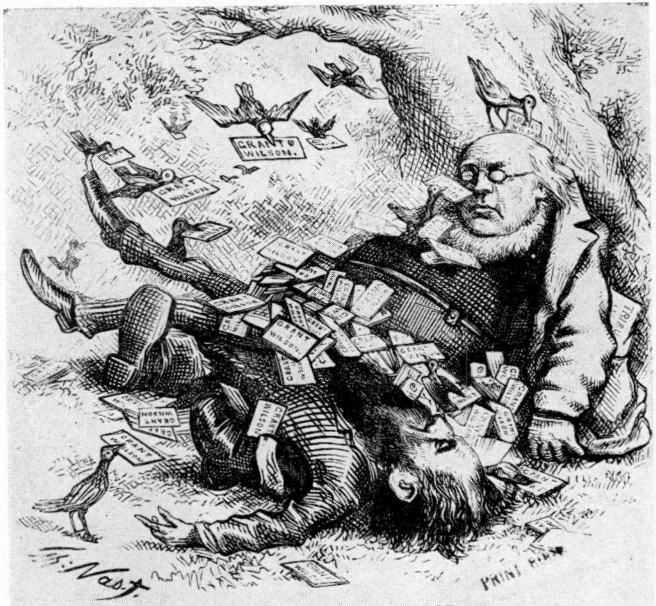

THE BABES OF THE WOOD.

Lost on the Way to the White House.

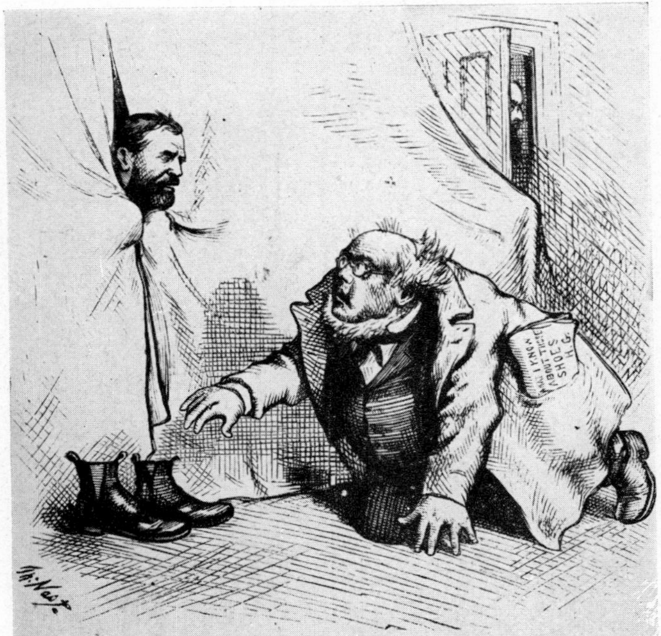

"DROP 'EM."

Nast Cartoons from the 1872 Campaign

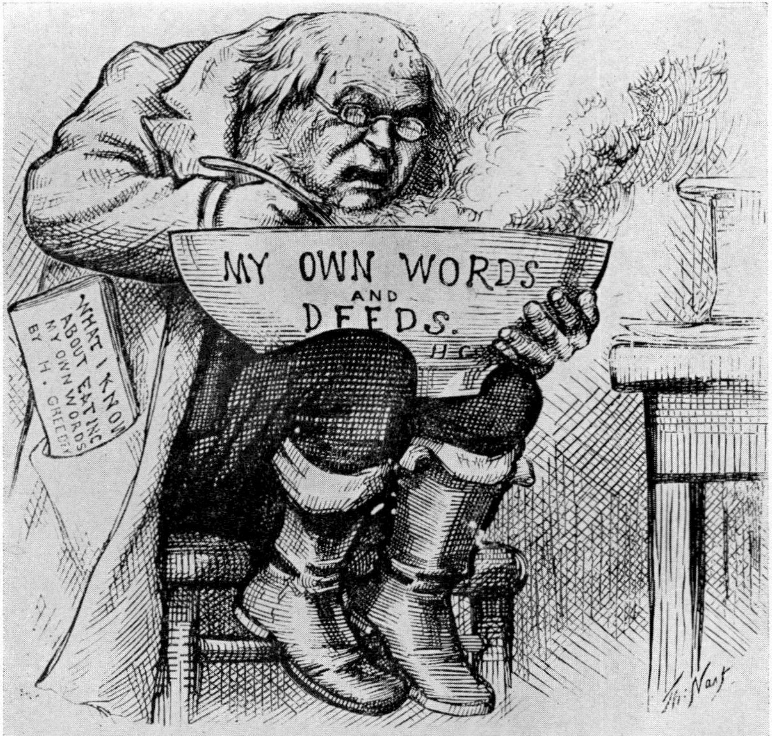

"RED HOT!"

Nast Cartoons from the 1872 Campaign

this one beats them all." Despite this outburst of vilification, several of Lincoln's cabinet members—Gideon Welles, Chief Justice Chase and Montgomery Blair—were early supporters as also was Justice David Davis.

Even Seward's last words to the public before his death in September, when asked his attitude toward the Greeley candidacy, were: "I have never stood in Mr. Greeley's way in anything he desired and certainly will not begin now."

Greeley's chief appeal was to put the peace of the nation above the resentments of a war that was over. Not once did he assail Grant. At the close of his canvass not one word had been uttered by him in anger, not one word of abuse of his opponent, not a single statement to regret or retract. He had made but one appeal to the people—"Unite! Patriotism, not politics, is the duty of the hour."

Greeley's platform was no new thought uttered for campaign purposes; it was "Magnanimity in Triumph" revived. As an example, take just a few lines from his Pittsburgh plea of September 19:

> They talk about Rebels and traitors. Fellow-citizens, are we never to be done with this? We demanded of our adversaries in the great civil war that they surrender their arms and go to their homes. They surrendered them. We demanded that they abandon Slavery, and they abandoned Slavery. We demanded that they enfranchise the Blacks, and the Blacks were enfranchised. None but White men now stand disfranchised on the soil of our country. We demanded that they stipulate that the emancipated slaves shall not be paid for, and that the Rebel debt shall never be paid, whether by the Union, or by the States, and they assented to that. So far as I can see, every single demand made on the part of the loyal States and the loyal people has been fully complied with on the part of those lately in rebellion. Every thing has been done that we asked; everything has been conceded; and still they tell us, "Why, we want them to repent." Have they not brought forth works meet for repentance? Theirs is a lost cause but they are not a lost people. ... We want peace, not vengeance.

In further speeches he called for the withdrawal of federal troops from the ballot boxes of the South:

The most unwelcome sight to a thoughtful American should be a soldier standing guard before the polls of any state. We want the time to come when elections shall be conducted without bloodshed. Better have wrong triumph for a time rather than have right triumph by force.... It is not for the sake of the proscribed alone that I speak; every community has the right to the best services of all its citizens. Men say to me, "Why, you don't want to elect Toombs, or Wise, or somebody else, do you?" No, I don't want to elect any of those men; but suppose other people do? Who are you, or who am I, to say whether they shall or not? It is not a question for me, but whether American citizens, who, you say, have the same right to vote and hold office as you, shall be at liberty to vote for the men they prefer, or shall be compelled to vote for the men you prefer. These questions reach not several hundreds but several millions of our people. "Well," they say, "what do the people care about this? The banks are making money, the people are prospering, the manufacturers are thrifty. Who cares that a few hundred or thousand men are disfranchised?" *I* care. I say a war which ended nearly eight years ago ought to have had nearly all its bloody traces wiped out before this time.

In July, Mrs. Greeley had returned from abroad a hopeless invalid. Tortured by her sinking condition, astounded by the virulence of the attacks upon him, wearied by anxieties for the *Tribune* and his own personal affairs, the last two months of the campaign were a race for the grave by both wife and husband far more than a race for the presidency by one of them.

Greeley is probably the only presidential candidate who ever made up his mind in early September that he could not win. He wrote Mrs. Allen: "I am not sanguine, for the money and office-holding buffers are against me; but we ought to win, so I guess we shall. If we do not, let us believe that all is wisely ordered for the best. When Clay was beaten by Polk I felt as though the universe were bankrupt, which is just where I was mistaken. My friend, let us do our duty according to our best light and for the rest trust God."

Again, on September 10, he reminded her: "I only wish to say that I trust you will not care what the result of our contest may be. Just now the skies are dark; a month hence they may be brighter. In any case I shall be what I am, and shall have less care out of than in office. While there are doubts as to my fitness for President, nobody seems to deny that I would make a capital defeated candidate."

To Mrs. Whipple he wrote on October 18: "I am glad that the election will soon be over. My home troubles are enough to make me forget it. Remind all my friends of my existence in fair health but poor spirits. You must not take our reversals too seriously. I may soon have to shed tears for my wife, but shall not shed one for any possible result of the canvass."

On November 4—two days before election—his letter to Mrs. Allen was marked "Very Private" and "Show This to No One But Destroy." It read: "I am not dead but I wish I were. My house is desolate, my future dark, my heart is a stone. I could not shed tears; they would not come; they would bring relief. Shed tears for me, but do not write again till a brighter day which, I fear, may never come."

To another friend next day he wrote: "I have been so bitterly assailed that I hardly know whether I am running for the Presidency or the penitentiary. In the darkest hour my long-suffering wife left me—not too soon for she suffered deep and long. I laid her to the grave with hard, dry eyes. Well, I am wound up—I have slept little for weeks and my eyes are still half closed but will open again."

Greeley, of course, was defeated. That is true. Assailed, as he said, as though a candidate for a penitentiary instead of the presidency; called home from the canvass to a dying wife—two months later he, too, was dead. That also is true. But neither fact is a sterner truth than that if ever a man broke the fetters of a lifetime of partisanship and, in patriotic hope for a united people, appealed to his fellow citizens to do likewise, Greeley did so. "Peace to the nation, power to the people, purity to the government" was his proclaimed platform. "If elected, I shall be the President of the whole people and not of any party. I accept your nomination in the confident trust that the masses of the people, North and South, are eager to clasp hands across the bloody chasm which has too long divided them, forgetting that they have been enemies in the joyous consciousness that they now are and henceforth must remain brethren."

Greeley polled 2,834,070 votes against 3,597,000 for Grant—a fraction over 43 per cent of the total. Because of his death his electoral vote was divided among others. Had he lived he would have had 63 votes from six of the thirty-seven states. Arkansas (6 votes) and Louisiana (8 votes) also really voted for him, but the return from those two states was rejected by Congress because of factional quarreling, such as occurred again in the Hayes-Tilden election. Without organized support, with a national administration in control of the South, and with "business" consolidated against him, Greeley's showing was remarkable. He made as good a run as did Clay in 1832 when the latter carried six states with 49 electoral votes against Jackson, or in 1836 when Harrison carried only seven states and 73 electoral votes against Van Buren; in 1840, when the same Van Buren carried only seven states with 60 electoral votes; in 1852, when Scott carried only four states with 42 electoral votes against Pierce. Taking into consideration all the presidential contests to date, the results of the Greeley candidacy are far from the opinion so frequently expressed.

In many ways the 1872 campaign was unusual. Greeley, who had never voted a Democratic ticket, was the nominee of that party. In 1856 Grant had voted for Democratic candidate James Buchanan. He did not vote at all in 1860 or 1864. Even in 1868, or in 1872, though then the Republican candidate for President, he did not vote.

Recall Grant's generous attitude toward Lee and toward Lee's soldiers at Appomattox; recall his "Let us have peace" when first named for President. With that background Grant, of all men, was in a position to inspire the country with a longing for unity by declaring that if elected he would be the President of the whole people and not of any party.

But that was left for Greeley to say.

CHAPTER XXX

The Last Days

BACK AT HIS desk in the *Tribune* office before noon of the day following his defeat was Greeley, eager in spirit but not equal to effort. There could be no doubt of the imperative need for rest. In the *Tribune* of November 8 he published "A Card" signed "Horace Greeley." These were the last words from his pen ever to appear in its columns. Thirty-one years and seven months earlier he had published "A Card" in the *Log Cabin*, announcing the coming of the *Tribune*. What a record he could look back upon!

His 1872 card read:

The undersigned resumes the editorship of The Tribune, which he relinquished on embarking on another line of business six months ago. Henceforth it shall be his endeavor to make this a thoroughly independent journal, treating all parties and political movements with judicial fairness and candor, but courting the favor and deprecating the wrath of no one. If he can hereafter say anything that will tend to heartily unite the whole American people on the broad platform of Universal Amnesty and Impartial Suffrage, he will gladly do so. For the present, however, he can best command that consummation by silence and forbearance. The victors in our late struggle can hardly fail to take the whole subject of southern rights and wrongs into early and earnest consideration, and to them, for the present, he remits it.

Since he will never again be a candidate for any office, and is not now in full accord with either of the great parties which have hitherto divided the country, he will be able and will endeavor to give wider and steadier regard to the progress of science, industry and the Useful Arts, than a partisan journal can do; and he will not be provoked to indulgence in those bitter personalities which are the recognized bane of journalism. Sustained by a generous public, he will do his best to make The Tribune a power in the broader field it now contemplates as, when Human Freedom was imperilled, it was in the arena of politics.

When Greeley left his office that afternoon not one of his associates expected to see him back again until after a long period of calm. Nevertheless he was there next morning, but in great distress because of an editorial entitled "Crumbs of Comfort," unfortunately published in the *Tribune* the first day of Greeley's announced resumption of editorial duties. John R. G. Hassard, an old associate, was the writer of the offending article, which read in part: "The man with two wooden legs congratulated himself that he would never be afflicted with cold feet. It is a source of satisfaction to us that the office will be free from blatherskites and red-nosed politicans. . . . At last we shall be let alone to attend to our own affairs . . . without being called aside to help lazy people who don't deserve assistance."

Ordinarily Hassard's clever writing and Greeley's response, if published, would not have excited serious attention, but chaos and rivalries in the office had everyone on edge. Greeley was especially incensed. He who for years had been the victim of so many office-seekers now came gamely to their defense. He insisted upon publishing the following:

By some unaccountable fatality, an article entitled "Crumbs of Comfort" crept into our last unseen by the editor, which does him the grossest wrong. It is true that office-seekers used to pester him for recommendations when his friends controlled the custom house, though the red-nosed variety was seldom found among them; it is not true that he ever obeyed a summons to Washington in order that he might there oppose this or that private scheme. In short, the article is a monstrous fable based on some other experience than that of any editor of this paper.

Here was an issue that seriously involved the future of the *Tribune*. To publish Greeley's editorial would have been resented

The Famous "Pirate Ship" Cartoon of 1872

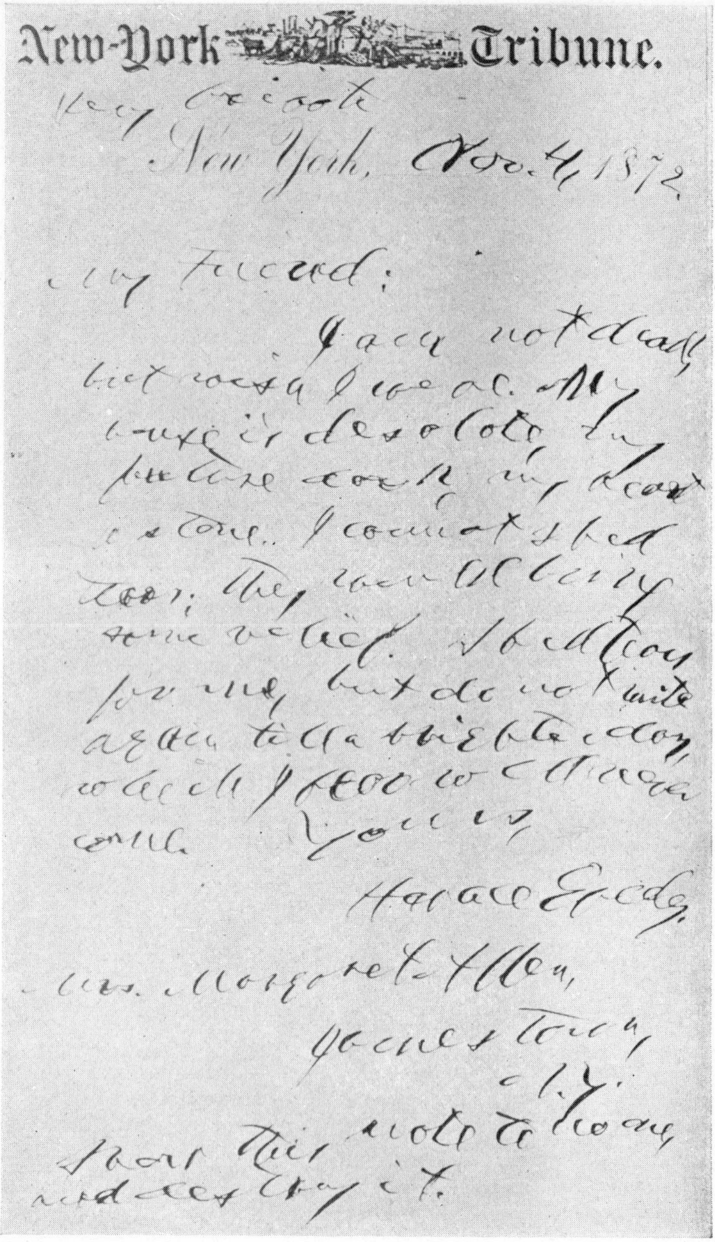

New-York Tribune.

Very private.

New York, Nov. 4 1872.

My Friend:

I am not dead, but wish I were. My house is desolate, my future dark, my heart a stone. I cannot shed tears; they would bring some relief. Shed them for me, but do not write again till a brighter day, which I fear will never come.

Yours,

Horace Greeley.

Mrs. Margaret Allen,
Youngstown,
N.Y.

[illegible] this note to-day, and destroy it.

One of Greeley's Last Letters to Mrs. Allen

by the entire staff; to refuse to publish it would be a blow at Greeley. Decision rested with Reid. He stood by the staff and undertook to pacify Greeley. They were the last lines Greeley ever wrote for the *Tribune*. Their rejection closed his career on the newspaper he had founded.

Greeley was still a guest in the home of his friend publisher Alvin Johnson on West Fifty-seventh Street. It was there that Mrs. Greeley had died only a few weeks before, and Johnson had invited Greeley and his two daughters to remain until election news had quieted down. On November 8 he wrote Mrs. Allen:

My Friend:

I write this because I wish to relieve myself of some bitterness but do not expect—in fact, I scarcely desire—that you should write me again these many, many days. I am indeed most wretched. As to my wife's death I do not lament. Her sufferings since she returned to me were so terrible that I rather felt relieved when she peacefully slept the long last sleep. I did not shed a tear. In fact I am beyond tears.

Nor do I care for defeat, however crushing. I dread only the malignity with which I am hounded, and the possibility that it may ruin "The Tribune." My enemies mean to kill that; if they would kill me instead I would thank them lovingly. And so many of my old friends hate me for what I have done that life seems too hard to bear. Enough of this. Speak of it to no one, not even Mrs. R., but return to cheerfulness and life's daily duties, forgetting as soon as may be

Yours,
Horace Greeley

And again on November 13, with only two weeks of life left, he sent her this pathetic note from Dr. Choate's sanitarium:

November 13, 1872
Out of the Depths

Dear Friend:

Utterly ruined beyond hope I desire before the night closes on me forever to say that though my running for President has placed me where I am it is not the cause of my ruin.

To Mrs. Whipple, his school-days friend at Westhaven, he wrote on the same day:

> I stand naked before my God the most utterly, hopelessly wretched and undone of all who ever lived. I have done more harm and wrong than any man who ever saw the light of day. Yet I take God to witness that I have never intended to wrong or harm anyone.

Greeley's mental condition had become so serious that he was persuaded finally to go to Dr. Choate's hospital at Pleasantville, not far from his Chappaqua farm. There his trouble was diagnosed as not a form of lunacy; Dr. Choate made a public statement denying the lunacy rumors. It was an exhausted brain that could return to normalcy—and would respond within two weeks or not at all. Unfortunately, it did not, for on November 29, after a day of fitful consciousness, he murmured: "It is done! I have fought the good fight. I Know that My Redeemer Liveth."

By his bedside were his daughters, Ida and Gabrielle, who only a month before had gone through the same ordeal with their mother. With them were three men who had been with Greeley since the first issue of the *Tribune*: business manager Samuel Sinclair, pressroom foreman Patrick O'Rourke, composing-room foreman Thomas N. Rooker.

Who today could put into revealing words the sorrow instant and everywhere that November day that Horace Greeley—plain, untitled Horace Greeley—was no more? Who, today, three-quarters of a century later, can accurately sense the regret in so many homes that "Uncle Horace's" counsel in his "Weekly Trybune" would be read there no more, that a familiar face and voice would be missing from county fairs, lecture platforms and public meetings, that now of the past was that unresting, eager spirit?

The tributes to the dead Greeley would have been to a living Greeley a rich harvest of his life's efforts; no Midas ever guarded his wealth more zealously than Greeley would have prized such appreciation.

While to the people Greeley's career was a notable example of devotion to country, loyalty to ideals and deep sympathy with struggle, it was to journalism that he gave lasting inspiration of independence and integrity. The first issue of Greeley's *Tribune* must forever be regarded as the birth of a journalism of conscious responsibility to the reader for truth in news and of courage to have its own opinions. In the history of newspaper-making in our country, replete as it is with so many examples of brilliant achievement, no other equals that of this wilderness-born, self-taught printer—friendless, penniless, jobless—tramping alone at twenty years of age to the place he called "the Commercial Emporium" of the nation and there creating by his own labor and his own resources the *New Yorker*, the *Jeffersonian*, the *Log Cabin* and the *Tribune*.

The heritage Greeley left to his profession as a solid foundation for newspaper power and prosperity is his never-to-be-forgotten defiance of Thurlow Weed: "I owe what little chance of usefulness I may have to the impression that I do no man's bidding but speak my own thoughts."

On December 4 the Church of the Divine Paternity on Fifth Avenue at Forty-fourth Street, New York City, held the most representative assembly of the national and state governments ever to attend funeral services for any citizen. They included President Grant, Chief Justice Chase, Vice-President Colfax, most of the cabinet members, the two Senators and the Governor of New York as well as the governors of many neighboring states. Rev. Dr. E. H. Chapin, who was Greeley's intimate friend, conducted the services, and Rev. Henry Ward Beecher and Rev. Thomas Armitage united with him in a last tribute. As the funeral cortege passed down Fifth Avenue and then down Broadway, both thoroughfares were crowded, business ceased and the bells of St. Paul's and Trinity tolled for this restless worker who had labored so many years in their shadow.

At the grave in Greenwood Cemetery, Brooklyn, more than a thousand friends gathered to listen to the final words of all from still another of Greeley's friends in the ministry—Rev. James M. Pullman.

But perhaps the tribute he would prize most highly came almost a year after Greeley's death from a Vermont farmer who, on hearing the *Tribune* mentioned by Joseph Bishop, remarked: "Does it still print? I thought Greeley was dead!"

CHAPTER XXXI

"The Young Editor of the Tall Tower"

WITH GREELEY gone the newspaper world wondered who was to be the new master of the *Tribune*. The total capitalization of the company was still the original one hundred shares, but they had been sold and resold in small lots so frequently that there was no certainty where a majority vote rested. So far as the future of the newspaper was concerned, however, the imperative problem was not who could secure stock control but who could bring the newspaper back to prosperity —in a word, who could rebuild the *Tribune* on new foundations. It could not survive solely on Greeley traditions. A different *Tribune* must arise out of the past. There was but one man on the staff who qualified for such a task. That man was Whitelaw Reid. He had youth, ability, experience and friendships—qualities which promptly commanded a confidence that secured for him voting control of the company.

On December 17 Reid made formal announcement that "a large majority of the stock is now concentrated in the hands of Mr. Greeley's chosen editorial associates, men whom he trained for this particular duty, whom he honored with his thoughts and his wishes, and whose purpose it now is to continue his work." Financially it was a hazardous undertaking. Thereafter success must rest wholly on the daily *Tribune,* which of itself had seldom paid its way. The "Weekly Try-bune" always had been a heavy money-maker, but with Greeley gone and changing times a weekly would soon be as far out of its period of popularity as was Greeley's *Log Cabin* of the Harrison campaign. Reid realized both the difficulties and the opportunity ahead of him. He acted with decision and confidence. His first resolve was to erect a building fitted for a modern newspaper; by 1876 he had moved the plant into the structure still standing at Nassau and Spruce Streets. At that time it was the highest building on Manhattan Island. Dana, looking up to him from the diminutive four-story *Sun* building next door, hailed Reid in popular phrase as "the Young Editor of the Tall Tower," and for many years he was greeted everywhere as such.

My printer days on the *Tribune*, detailed in the Preface, began less than five years after the death of Greeley. Many of the men who had served under him still continued in active employment and so, of course, stories of the departed chief were constantly going the office rounds—kindly anecdotes, all of them treasured and related in loyal memory. If there were any stories of different character I cannot recall ever having heard them. In one way or another some of the talk finally seeped down to my alley—so much of it that it seemed strange to me that J. Q. A. Ward's bronze figure of Greeley, then placed outside the new Tribune Building south of the entrance, could actually be the same man of whom I was hearing stories so frequently inside the building as though he still were a living presence there.

I had in mind, too, the Greeley whom as a child I had once seen in a Broadway stage, as already related—the kindly face, the big spectacles, the absorption in his newspaper. Ward's statue recalled that Greeley to me with lifelike fidelity. It was not unusual to hear of men stepping out of the passing sidewalk throng to look thoughtfully at it and to say to each other, "I once heard the old fellow lecture back home," or "My Dad read Greeley's paper as he did his Bible." Of the many statues then in New York City none attracted so much attention. Save that of Lincoln, it was the only one that did not have to be identified for most people.

Young as I was then, I realized from it all that there must have been something lasting about Greeley in the minds of those associated with him, for years after he had passed away the day's work frequently brought reminiscences of the way that the old chief would have reacted to various issues. It was plain to me that those who knew him best esteemed him most. That belief was strengthened when I read Bayard Taylor's tribute to Greeley at the unveiling of the statue at his grave in Greenwood Cemetery:

"Only those who stood nearest to Greeley can truly know how his life was glorified by self-denial and self-sacrifice, by labor that never complained and by patience that never uttered itself in words. A life like his cannot be lost; something of him has been absorbed in other lives."

What epitaph could say more?

Bibliography

Adams, Charles Francis: *Autobiography*, Boston, 1916

Adams, Henry: *Education of Henry Adams*, Boston, 1918

Anthony, Katherine S.: *Margaret Fuller*, New York, 1920

Baehr, Harry W.: *The New York Tribune Since the Civil War*, New York, 1936

Baker, George E.: *Life of William H. Seward*, New York, 1855

Bates, Edward: *Diary of Edward Bates*, U.S. Government Printing Office, Washington, D.C., 1933

Beale, Howard K.: *The Critical Years: A Study of Andrew Johnson and Reconstruction*, New York, 1930

Bell, Margaret: *Margaret Fuller*, New York, 1930

Bengston, Caroline: *The Founding of Union Colony*, Colorado, 1910

Benton, Joel: *Persons and Places*, New York, 1905

Bigelow, John: *Retrospections of an Active Life*, New York, 1909

Bishop, Joseph Bucklin: *Anecdotes of Many Years*, New York, 1925

Blaine, James G.: *Twenty Years in Congress*, Norwich, Conn., 1886

Bleyer, Willard G.: *Main Currents in Journalism*, Boston, 1927

Bowers, Claude E.: *The Tragic Era*, Cambridge, 1929

Bradford, George P.: "Reminiscences of Brook Farm," from *Century Magazine*, November, 1892

Brisbane, Albert: *Social Destiny of Man: Association*, New York, 1840

Brockway, Beman: *Fifty Years in Journalism*, Watertown, 1891

Brown, William G.: *Stephen Arnold Douglas*, Boston, 1902

Chambers, Julius: *News Hunting on Three Continents*, New York, 1921

Clarke, Grace G.: *George W. Julian*, Indiana Historical Collection, 1923

Codman, J. F.: *Brook Farm: Historic and Personal Memoirs*, Boston, 1894
Commager, Henry Steele: *Growth of the American Republic*, New York, 1937
Congdon, Charles T.: *Reminiscences of a Journalist*, Boston, 1880
Conway, Moncure D.: *Autobiography*, New York, 1904
Cornell, William M.: *Public Career of Horace Greeley*, New York, 1872
Cortissoz, Royal: *Life of Whitelaw Reid*, New York, 1921
Cummings, Amos J.: *Greeley Campaign Songster*, New York, 1872
Davis, Elmer: *History of New York Times*, New York, 1921
Dennett, Tyler: *John Hay*, New York, 1913
Derby, J. C.: *Fifty Years Among Authors*, New York, 1884
Fessenden, William Pitt: *Impeachment of Andrew Johnson*, Boston, 1868
Flint, Henry M.: *Life of Stephen Arnold Douglas*, Chicago, 1860
Frémont, Jessie Benton: *Memoirs of My Life*, New York, 1867
Fuess, Claude M.: *Carl Schurz, Reformer*, New York, 1932
Godkin, Edwin L.: *Reflections and Comments*, New York, 1895
Godwin, Parke: *Views of the Doctrine of Fourier*, New York, 1844
Greeley, Horace: *Autobiography*, New York, 1872
——— *Recollections of a Busy Life*, New York, 1868
——— *The American Conflict*, Hartford, Conn., 1867
Halstead, Murat: *Caucuses of 1860*, Columbus, Ohio, 1860
Harlow, Ralph V.: *Gerrit Smith, Reformer*, New York, 1939
Hart, Albert Bushnell: *Salmon Portland Chase*, Boston, 1899
Hassard, J. R. G.: *The Wonders of the Press*, New York, 1878
Hazeltine, Mayo W.: *Charles Anderson Dana*, New York, 1907
Higginson, Thomas Wentworth: *Wendell Phillips*, Boston, 1884
Howland, Louis: *Stephen A. Douglas*, New York, 1920
Ingersoll, Lurton D.: *Life of Horace Greeley*, Philadelphia, 1873
Jennings, L. J.: *Henry J. Raymond and Journalism*, New York, 1870
Julian, George W.: *Political Recollections*, New York, 1884
Knox, Thomas W.: *Republican Party and Its Leaders*, New York, 1892
Lawson, Elizabeth: *Thaddeus Stevens*, New York, 1942
Lee, James Melvin: *History of American Journalism*, Boston, 1928
Linn, William A.: *Horace Greeley*, New York, 1903
Lothrop, Thornton K.: *William Henry Seward*, Boston, 1896

McClure, A. K.: *Presidents and How We Make Them*, Philadelphia, 1901
McCullagh, Francis: *The Gordon Bennetts*, New York, 1929
McElrath, Thomas: *Horace Greeley*, New York, 1853
Martyn, Carlos: *American Reformers*, New York, 1890
Maverick, Augustus: *Henry J. Raymond and the New York Press*, Hartford, Conn., 1870
Meeker, Nathan C.: *Letters of Horace Greeley*, New York, 1874
Merriam, George S.: *Life of Samuel Bowles*, New York, 1885
Miller, Alphonse B.: *Thaddeus Stevens*, New York, 1939
Milton, George F.: *The Age of Hate—Andrew Johnson*, New York, 1930
Mitchell, Edward Page: *Memoirs of an Editor*, New York, 1924
Mott, Frank Luther: *American Journalism*, Boston, 1942
Nevins, Allan: *Frémont, Pathfinder of the West*, 2 vols., New York, 1939
O'Brien, Frank M.: *The Story of "The Sun,"* New York, 1918
Ogden, Rollo: *Life of Edwin L. Godkin*, New York, 1907
Parrington, V. L.: *Main Currents of American Thought*, New York, 1937
Parton, James: *Life of Horace Greeley*, New York, 1855
Payne, George Henry: *History of Journalism*, New York, 1925
Pike, James S.: *First Blows of the Civil War*, New York, 1879
——— *Horace Greeley in 1872*, New York, 1873
Pollak, Gustav: *Fifty Years of American Idealism*, Boston, 1915
Pringle, Henry F.: *Great American Editors*, New York, 1934
Redding, Leo L.: *Bennett of The Herald*, New York, 1914
Reid, Whitelaw: *Horace Greeley*, New York, 1879
Rhodes, James Ford: *History of the United States*, New York, 1919
Rourke, Constance: *Trumpets of Jubilee*, London, 1927
Salisbury, Annie M.: *Brook Farm*, Boston, 1898
Schuckers, John G.: *Life of Salmon Portland Chase*, New York, 1873
Schurz, Carl: *Henry Clay*, New York, 1899
——— *Reminiscences*, New York, 1907
Seitz, Don: *Horace Greeley*, New York, 1926
——— *The James Gordon Bennetts*, New York, 1928
Seward, Frederick: *Life of William H. Seward*, New York, 1877
Shanks, William F. G.: *Personal Recollections*, New York, 1896
Smith, Gerrit: *Speeches and Letters*, Boston, 1864

Sotheran, Charles: *Pioneers of American Socialism*, New York, 1892
Stedman, Edmund C.: *Margaret Fuller*, Boston, 1916
Stevens, Frank E.: *Life of Stephen Arnold Douglas*, Springfield, 1924
Stryker, Lloyd P.: *Andrew Johnson*, New York, 1936
Sumner, Charles: *The Crime Against Kansas*, Boston, 1856
Swift, Lindsay: *Brook Farm*, New York, 1904
Truman, Benjamin: *Letters from Andrew Johnson in 1868*, New York, 1913
Vallandigham, Clement L.: *The Great Civil War*, Chicago, 1863
Villard, Henry: *Memoirs*, New York, 1904
Washburn, Elihu B.: *Recollections*, New York, 1887
Watterson, Henry: "*Marse Henry*," New York, 1919
Weed, Thurlow: *Autobiography*, Boston, 1884
Welles, Gideon: *Diary of Gideon Welles*, Boston, 1911
Whipple, Edwin P.: *Recollections of Eminent Men*, New York, 1900
Willis, Henry Parker: *Stephen A. Douglas*, Philadelphia, 1910
Wilson, James H.: *Life of Charles A. Dana*, New York, 1907
Winter, William: *Old Friends of Other Days*, New York, 1909
Woodley, Thomas F.: *Thaddeus Stevens*, Harrisburg, 1934
Young, John Russell: *Men and Memories*, New York, 1901
Zabriskie, Frances N.: *Horace Greeley, Editor*, New York, 1890

Index